KiNG
of the ROAD

The Beginner's Guide to RV Travel

Everything You Need to Know to Plan, Take & Enjoy an RV Trip

Ted Pollard

King of the Road
The Beginner's Guide to RV Travel
Copyright © 1993 by Ted Pollard
First printing, July 1993

Remington Press, Ltd.
Box 8327
Radnor, PA 19087
(215) 293-0202

While every precaution has been taken to ensure the accuracy of the information contained herein, the publisher and author cannot accept any responsiblity for errors which may have inadvertently occured or changes made after publication.

Brand and product names are the trademarks or registered trademarks of their respective owners.

Library of Congress Catalog Card Number 93-84844

ISBN 0-9637125-0-0

Cover design by Mike Guntick
Cover photo courtesy of the Recreational Vehicle Industry Association
Typeset by Jeffrey Gorham in Linotype Melior and Adobe Stone Sans

Printed in the United States of America

Dedication

To my parents, who unexpectedly became martyrs when they were cruise directors for my first camping trip many years ago...

To my wife, Carol, her children Robin and Brit Martin, and Robin's friend Chris Randolph, and my son, Nick Pollard, who survived a month-long RV adventure on my first try at being cruise director...

To Zorro, my sweet parakeet, who spent the better part of eight months sitting on my shoulder or the computer while I was writing *King of the Road*. Her timely chirps and well chosen words inspired me to keep going through thick and thin. Her only fault was her typing—every time she landed on the keyboard, I had to correct her spelling!

To the memory of my mother, Mary Ellsberg Pollard, and my grandparents, Lucy and Edward Ellsberg.

Acknowledgements

I would like to express my feelings of gratitude to all of the people who helped make *King of the Road* a reality. To: my wife, Carol, who critiqued many of the chapters and created most of the lists and travel and cooking tips; Shelia M. Davis, Public Relations Manager of Winnebago Industries, for supplying photographs; Zock Clahan, for his support, enthusiasm, and sharing of marketing ideas; Kevin Smith of Media Camping Center, Media, PA, for giving me a "refresher" course on some RVing technicalities; Skip Deegans of Anderson's Campground Directory for reading the manuscript and sharing his RVing and camping insights; Bill Baker, Media Relations Manager of the Recreational Vehicle Industry Association, for supplying photographs, especially the lovely cover one; National Campers and Hikers Association for permission to use their Traveling Medical Consent Form; Barbara Rickards, my editor, for her probing questions, thoughtful ideas, and polishing up the manuscript; Bernd Hess of Global Motorhome Travel, for his support and enthusiasm for the project, supplying photographs, reading the manuscript, and making suggestions for the foreign travel section; Jeff Gorham for his typography and book design; Mike Guntick, for his beautiful cover design; and Ed Krimmel, my friend of many years, who shared his expertise as an author and publisher, and kept me on a steady course toward the finish line.

About the Author

Ted Pollard lives in St. Davids, PA with his wife, three children, ranging from twenty to twenty-three, two cats, and a parakeet, Zorro. When he is not enjoying an RV adventure, Ted does historic restorations of buildings, sits on two school boards, the local historical society board, is chairman of a national non-profit organization seeking reform of bank trust department practices, and is a township commissioner. In his spare time he enjoys tennis and sailing in Maine.

Contents

Forward

In 1986 when my wife suggested that we take a trip out West with our three kids before they "flew the coop," I had flashbacks to a similar journey I had taken with my parents in the late fifties. My subconscious kept telling me "Oh no, not again!" We lived outside Philadelphia at the time, and my parents, who were not campers by nature, did not know what was in store for them. My sister and I, ages eight and thirteen, respectively, and all the gear for a month long trip got packed into the family station wagon, and off we went.

I am sure you can envision the chaos that ensued during a five thousand mile round trip to Colorado in the middle of a very hot summer: the fights between my sister and me over who would sit in the sun and for how long (we learned to tell time very well!), and the cries of "I need to take a pee" or "I'm hungry" must have driven my parents nuts.

We tented the whole way, with only a few nights spent in motels (there weren't many at the time) so that we could have a hot shower and a dry bed. Campgrounds then were also few and far between and not nearly as well equipped as today's, so even the basic needs, such as showers and toilets, were pretty rustic. Strategic planning was essential. Every night was an adventure in the fine art of tent making. The tent had to go up, regardless of wind, rain or darkness. I quickly learned the importance of a ship having just one captain. There we were, two adults and two children putting up poles, pulling ropes and yelling at each other for half an hour! Once the tent was securely up we unpacked the car, lit the lantern and Coleman stove, and made a two-pot dinner. If the ice hadn't melted in the cooler, we had a cool drink. Next day, the process was reversed and off we went. Unpack. Put up tent. Take down tent. Pack. Every day!! This was really roughing it, but I did not fully appreciate the job my parents did until nearly thirty years later when I was cruise director for a month. My parents were heroes, although at thirteen I didn't realize it.

As we drove along on our first RV journey, two novice adult campers and four mid-teenagers, I reflected back to that early Western trip and wondered how my parents managed to survive all the fights and the hectic camping routine. Modern day camping in an RV was no comparison! There were no problems with putting up a tent (we didn't need one), with getting a meal (everything was just like at home), or having to find a bathroom (we carried our own). I must admit there was a little sibling squabbling, but nothing we couldn't control with ease.

Our 1986 version of the same trip with a beautiful 27' RV (recreation vehicle) and the availability of a great number of fully modernized campgrounds was really a dream come true. Because of it and the fun and excitement of our subsequent RV outings, I want to share what we learned with you so that your camping adventure will be just as rewarding as ours have been.

In 1988 we took our second Western trip, which was even better. As a result of our enthusiasm, many friends asked us about RV vacations. They wanted to know: "Was the driving easy?" "Was it hard to find a campground?" "How expensive was it?" and just simply "How can I do it?" These people were genuinely interested in taking an RV trip, but didn't know how to begin the process. We hadn't known what to do either, and learned by trial and error. Their interest, and the fact that we could not find any how-to book on the subject of RV travel, inspired me to share our experiences with those of you who yearn for the open road and desire to discover a new way to see the world. This book will tell you everything you need to know to plan, take and enjoy an exciting RV adventure. Happy Trails!

Chapter 1

What Is RVing?

Have you ever wanted to take a vacation where you could explore at your own pace with no schedules to meet, no worries about restaurants, motels or finding a restroom, no phones, escape the drudgery of packing and unpacking every day, enjoy family togetherness, **and** have all the comforts of home? Sound like a dream come true? It is when you take a trip in an RV and learn to enjoy the exciting RV lifestyle I am about to share with you.

What is this miracle vacation chariot called an RV, you ask? RV is a nickname for a group of recreation vehicles with totally self-contained living quarters. Nearly all models have heat and air conditioning, a bathroom with shower, a fully equipped kitchen, ample closet and storage space, and spacious sleeping areas. Many have microwaves and/or convection ovens, TVs and VCRs, stereo systems, and some even have washers and dryers. They range from basic pop-up trailers to luxurious bus-like mobile hotels, and everything in between. There are models for touring, full-time living, or seasonal use at a semi-permanent site. Chapter 2 contains details about the various types and styles of RVs.

There are over 60 million campers in the United States, including 25 million RVers roaming the country in 8.5 million RVs. What these people have discovered is the secret of enjoying a camping vacation or full-time lifestyle on the road at thousands of modern, full-service campgrounds or resorts surrounded by all the comforts of home. Never again will they have to pitch a tent in the rain, pack and unpack the car every day, or huddle around a smokey campfire roasting hot dogs for dinner! RVers have the same feeling of self-sufficiency that the pioneers must have felt in the original RV, the covered wagon, and have discovered that RVing is more fun, comfortable, economical and educational than other forms of travel. In ever growing numbers they are touring America, Europe and other faraway places, enjoying the convenience, freedom and flexibility RV travel provides.

RVing is for Everybody!

No matter what your age, sex, budget, physical condition, or the type of vacation you want, travel by RV can accommodate you. Campers from young marrieds to retirees have chosen RVing as a way to experience instant adventure, be close to the environment, and enjoy family and friends. More and more singles of both sexes are RVers these days, too. RVing is also a great way to escape the frantic pace of everyday life. There are no neckties, uniforms, job titles or roles to play. People are more casual and relaxed while they are camping. Camping invites friendliness, and you will return from your vacation relaxed and with a new outlook on life.

RVs allow the traveler to experience America's spectacular scenery firsthand, see history come alive with visits to noteworthy sites, and take an educational or adventure tour that you and your family will never forget. You can feel like a pioneer traveling cross country, or you can be like Huck Finn and take a barge trip down the Mississippi. You can travel to many parts of the world, or live like a nomad. Whatever you choose, the RV gives you the freedom to do it.

There are RVs that fit all budgets, from basic eating/sleeping units to very fancy luxury models costing hundreds of thousands of dollars, and there are models that fit all recreational and lifestyle needs. Whether you are a sports enthusiast, want to be close to nature, or just want to live your dream of adventure, you will enjoy RVing, even if you are physically challenged. It's fun, easy, and a very economical way to travel.

Besides taking a vacation, there are many ways to enjoy an RV. Visiting friends or relatives is so much easier because you won't have to impose on them; or, if your children or grandchildren visit you, they can stay in your RV. The "welcome" sign will always be out. Visits to kids in college, antiquing expeditions, and taking in sporting events are all fun in an RV.

The Sports Enthusiast

Several models of RV are popular with the sports enthusiast because they allow easy access to out-of-the-way places. They are ideal for fishing in the summer, hunting in the winter, boating any time, and along with the larger models, are great all year round for tailgating at sporting events, races, parades and festivals. They are the ultimate transportation, entertainment and lodging center for the traveling sports fan.

The Physically Challenged

While not everyone can backpack or tent-camp due to age or physical restrictions, **anyone** can enjoy outdoor living and traveling in an RV.

For the physically challenged traveler, and those with medical problems, an RV is the preferred mode of travel. Any type of meal can be prepared when needed, a bed is always available, and an RV can be customized fairly easily to meet special needs. With spacious living quarters for family, friends and medical assistants, no other mode of transportation offers as comfortable travel for the physically challenged. There is an excellent specialty magazine, *Disabled Outdoors*, that targets those with physical disabilities, and shows how to enjoy many outdoor activities and travel very comfortably in an RV.

Travelers with Medical Problems

For those with medical problems, such as diabetes, special diets or the need for frequent periods of rest, an RV allows the traveler to take care of any medical requirement and still be able to enjoy the outdoors. I recently read about a man with Lou Gehrig's disease who had taken a six week jaunt in his RV. He and his wife take frequent trips and travel with an aide who assists with the medical care. Many people with medical problems would be unable to travel at all if they had to rely on cars, planes or trains. Even those with chronic health problems don't have to be limited in travel, as long as they have a thorough medical exam and consultation with a doctor knowledgeable in travel medicine prior to leaving. While on the road, medical attention can be obtained at a hospital emergency room or at a free-standing medical clinic. The clinics are nice because they are open after normal business hours and there isn't the long wait that is often the case in the emergency rooms.

Retirees

Many people decide to pull up stakes when they retire and join the "snowbird" flight to a warmer climate, or travel full-time. This is their chance to break loose from society and the years spent putting down roots. It is an escape from the drudgery of doing the "same old thing." Instead of having a second home and being tied down to living in one location, own an RV!

An RV can qualify as a second home if it has basic sleeping, toilet and cooking facilities, thereby making the interest deductible on any loan used to purchase it. You can now enjoy the best of both worlds if you move to a smaller house, and either travel full-time or have a pad for your RV at a vacation house or an RV resort. Real estate developments in many destination locations are now being designed with concrete pads and utilities set up for RVs, in order to accommodate the rapidly growing number of people who have discovered this way of life. You can settle down for a season, and enjoy palms in the winter and pines in the summer!

Although there is no accurate count of how many people live full-time in their RVs, best guesstimates run into the hundreds of thousands. With modern telecommunications and special services for these nomads, such as mail forwarding, living on the road for long periods of time is really not that difficult. Camping areas, ranging from desert rendezvous on public lands with no services to luxury RV resorts, are springing up to meet the surge in the number of people enjoying this way of life. RVs can tow a car and many of these full-timers do, so that they can sightsee or go shopping without having to carry their "house" with them. This is the ultimate in life-on-the-road flexibility! When you eliminate today's high housing costs, living on the road is very inexpensive and makes an excellent alternative to the traditional lifestyle.

RVing offers additional advantages to senior citizens, too. Many are on fixed or greatly reduced incomes, so traveling by RV allows them to avoid the high cost of staying in motels and eating in restaurants. Senior travelers can also benefit from the many social activities RV camping provides, such as those offered by RV clubs at their rallies, campouts and conventions. Pot luck suppers, square dances, sing-alongs, and arts and crafts activities give RVers a chance to meet new people and make new friends. Through these activities and others offered by the clubs, it is easy to develop a very active social network on the road. Campgrounds may also have a variety of activities geared toward retirees. Senior RVers can also enjoy more quality family time when they take their children or grandchildren on a trip or visit them in their mobile "spare bedroom." The flexibility, freedom, comfort and economics associated with RVing make this form of travel ideal for retirees. Millions of them are traveling the highways and byways of America, creating their own version of Jack Kerouac's "On the Road."

Families

An RV trip will give the family a chance to spend quality time together, and develop a special relationship from shared experiences. Campground living, meals, sightseeing, recreational activities, and time on the road will create a unique opportunity to enjoy special moments as a family. Even sleeping and chores become an adventure! You will enjoy an economical, educational vacation at a relaxed pace, with all the comforts of home—what could be better? As parents or grandparents you will be able to introduce the younger generation to the outdoor life and share in the excitement of their discoveries. These are memories that will last a lifetime! From the vacation planning process to the trip itself, camping promotes family unity.

Singles

For singles who want to take an RV trip but don't want to do it alone, joining an RV club may be a way to find a travel mate. Some clubs are for singles and have "travel matching" services or advertisements. In addition, a unique company, Travel Companion Exchange, Inc., was founded several years ago to fulfill the needs of single, widowed and divorced travelers by acting as a clearinghouse for information and travel tips. They have a travel companion listing service and an informative newsletter.

Working on the Road

There is a rapidly growing segment of the population that has not only discovered the freedom and affordability of living on the road, but also has been able to combine that with having a job. With faxes, mobile phones, and computers, many have found that RVing is the ideal way to enjoy both living and working.

For those of you who want seasonal work and to camp in one place, many state and national parks, resorts and campgrounds will trade campsites, amenities, discounts, and perhaps a salary for work. One RV-related publication, *Workamper News*, details many of these opportunities, as well as full-time positions in recreation-related industries. Jobs on the road include park management, maintenance, food service, gardening, concessions, tour guides, office work, and RV sales and service. You can basically live for free in a lovely setting, meeting friendly people and enjoying the great outdoors! The Good Sam Club has a campground host program for facilities run by the National Park Service, US Forest Service, Bureau of Land Management, and the US Army Corps of Engineers. They developed this program in the mid-1970s to help keep these public campgrounds open, and it has been very successful.

Caravan Tours

If you don't want to travel on your own, you can join one of the many caravan tours that go to Europe, Mexico, Central America, Alaska, Canada, and other faraway places and on specialized tours or rallies, such as fall foliage, festivals, parades, the Rose Bowl, barge trips or just general sightseeing. These trips can last from a few days to more than a month. They are organized and escorted by experienced RVers who have selected the routes, made all the necessary reservations at campgrounds and sightseeing events, and can help in case of a breakdown or emergency. On some caravans, you are allowed to travel at your own speed, meeting up at night or at a predetermined time for an event, while on others, you travel like a wagon train.

On these caravans you will learn how to travel, use and live in an RV, enjoy the camaraderie of your fellow campers, have all the travel details taken care of, and experience an adventure tour to faraway places you might not visit by yourself. With expert guides and backup help if trouble strikes, you have the security in knowing that you are not alone. Ask the caravan tour operator what their refund policy is in case you have to cancel, and what insurance is needed if you go to a foreign country. For a list of companies specializing in caravan tours, see Appendix 13, the RVer's Resource Guide.

Publications

To learn more about RV camping, call the Go Camping America Committee at (800)-47-SUNNY and ask for their detailed camping vacation planner. This is an up-to-the-minute source for information on every aspect of an RV vacation. The Committee is an educational partnership of camping and RV industry associations.

If you want to read more about RVing and the RV lifestyle, there is an extensive list of publications in Appendix 13. In addition, both *Workamper News* and Cottage Publications, publisher of the *RV Traveletter* and the *Guide to Free Campgrounds*, offer a wide variety of books on travel and RVing. Contact them for copies of their travel library catalog. These publications are dedicated to outdoor recreation, and offer travel tips, vehicle reviews, RV rally and show information, and an inside look at what the RV lifestyle has to offer.

Whether you want to travel for a day, a weekend, or longer, RVing offers unsurpassed convenience, flexibility, affordability and the freedom to travel on your own terms, surrounded by all the comforts of home. Having your living quarters with you allows you to travel at your own pace and roam where you please, free from the hassles of schedules, reservations, crowds and jam-packed highways. You eat what you want, when you want, sleep in your own bed and don't have to live out of a suitcase. You can go on a quick tour or get away from it all and create your own "free-as-a-bird" lifestyle. Traveling in an RV is a great revitalizer for tired spirits, because being outdoors is calming, provides opportunities for family togetherness, and allows time for quiet personal reflections. The variety of vacation possibilities is limited only by your imagination. RVing is for adventure lovers of all ages!

Chapter 2

Learning About RVs

Now that you have decided to investigate the possibility of taking an RV trip, the first thing to do is research the various types of RVs to find out more about them. Before rushing out to the nearest dealer, however, you should have some understanding of what an RV is and the wide variety of choices available.

RV is a nickname for a whole family of over-the-road camping and recreation vehicles that provide living quarters while you travel, camp and enjoy the outdoors. They are easy to drive, as they have power steering and brakes, cruise control and automatic transmissions. There are styles to fit every recreational need and pocketbook, from the camper who wants the simple, back-to-nature model to the sophisticated traveler who wants all the luxuries of home while on the road. Prices range from under $2,000 to hundreds of thousands of dollars. Even if you are contemplating buying an RV, it is a good idea to look at all the options and rent one or two styles before you make a choice, since there are pros and cons for each type.

What Kinds of RVs Are Available?

While the scope of this book is to inform the reader about the joys of camping in larger RVs, it is important to know about the wide array of camping vehicle options, as well as terminology so as not to be confused by what's available. They fall into two main categories: towable and motorized RVs.

Towable RVs

Towables are self-contained camping units designed to be towed by a motorized vehicle. They come in four main styles: folding camping trailers, truck campers, travel trailers, and park trailers. These are generally owner-operated and used for frequent camping trips or full-time living. Often they are cleaned and restocked after a trip so as to be ready when the desire to take off strikes again. For this reason they provide great flexibility, but unless you have a friend who has one you can borrow, they are difficult to come by for the infrequent camper. Only a few agencies have them for rent, so you will probably have to settle for a motorized unit.

Folding Camping Trailer. This style of RV, commonly known as a "pop-up," is basically a tent on wheels with a few added amenities and is reminiscent of the covered wagon of pioneer days. It is an inexpensive, light-weight unit with collapsible sides that fold down for traveling and are easily set up for

Figure 1, Folding Camping Trailer

camping. Its main advantages are that it is compact, can be pulled behind most cars or vans, and has spacious sleeping and dining facilities for up to eight people. Some models even have toilets and showers (see Figure 1).

Truck Camper. This type of RV has a remov-able camping unit that is mounted on the bed or chassis of a pickup truck. It is popular with sports enthusiasts because of its compact size and versatility, and four-wheel drive models can be used in rough terrain. These RVs are often used to pull other recreation equip-

Figure 2, Truck Camper

ment, such as snowmobiles, off-road vehicles, and boats. The truck camper can have most of the amenities of larger RVs, including kitchen and bathroom facilities and sleeping for up to six people (see Figure 2).

Travel Trailer. These RVs come in two styles: ones that can be pulled behind a car, van, or light truck, and fifth-wheel models that are coupled to the bed of a pickup truck. Part of the fifth-wheel model extends over the truck bed, thereby creating private bi-level sleeping quarters and shortening the overall length of the towed trailer. Travel trail-ers are very popular with full-time travelers, as they have all the amenities necessary for luxuri-ous living, yet can be unhooked

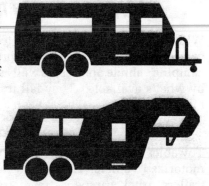

Figure 3, Travel Trailer & Fifth Wheel Model

and the trailer left at the campground while sightseeing or doing errands. Because so many of these RVs are used by full-timers, several models have a "slide-out" section that widens or lengthens the living area by several feet when camping. They sleep 4-8 people comfortably and range from 10'-40' in length (see Figure 3).

Park Trailer. These are transportable units designed primarily for seasonal or temporary living, and are usually connected to utilities on a permanent or semi-permanent basis. Some models have a "slide-out" section, too, thereby

Figure 4, Park Trailer

making them more like cottages. This is a very convenient feature that makes this type of RV popular with "snowbirds" who move their home with the changing seasons. They sleep up to eight people (see Figure 4).

Motorized RVs

Motorized RVs come in two styles: motorhomes or van conversions, and are self-propelled camping vehicles that provide at least four of the following permanently installed living systems: cooking, refrigeration, self-contained toilet, heating or air conditioning, portable water system, including water tank, faucet and sink, separate 110/120-volt electrical system, LP-gas supply, and sleeping facilities. Motorhomes are divided into three sub-styles: conventional or Class"A" and "C," van campers or Class "B" and micro-minis. Technically, van conversions are not motorhomes, as they don't have all the facilities mentioned above, but are used for many non-camping recreational and travel purposes.

Van Conversion. This type of RV is a conventional van that has been modified for comfortable daily or recreational use and may have a sink and sleeping quarters for two people, but is not fully equipped for camping. It is often used as a tow vehicle for other recreation equipment (see Figure 5).

Figure 5, Van Conversion

Van Camper. The van camper is also a conventional van that has been modified for recreational use and will usually have a raised roof, as well as kitchen, fresh water storage, 110-volt hookup, sleeping, and sometimes, bathroom facilities. Van campers are also called Class "B" RVs.

Figure 6, Van Camper

Van campers sleep from 2-4 people, but are intended for weekend or short vacation outings, not extended travel. (see Figure 6)

Micro-mini Motorhome. The micro-mini motorhome is a scaled down version of the conventional motorhome, with the same amenities. While it looks like a small Class "C" RV, it technically is not one. The main difference between the two is that the micro-mini is built on a modified mini-truck chassis, while the

Figure 7, Micro-mini Motorhome

larger versions are built on either a special modified van or truck chassis. As in the larger motorhome, there is access to the living quarters from the cockpit. However, the driver's area in the micro-mini is closer to the ground, similar to a car's, whereas in the larger motorhomes the whole driving and living space is considerably higher off the ground. Micro-minis feature a "cabover" bed arrangement and make compact, comfortable campers for 2 adults and 1-2 small children. (see Figure 7)

Motorhome. This type of RV has two distinct styles, the Class "C" and the Class "A" models. They are both recreation camping and travel vehicles that are totally self-contained and have roomy living quarters and complete bathroom, kitchen and dining facilities—just like home! One of the main differences of this type of RV versus the others is that the driver and co-pilot can easily access the inside of the vehicle from the cockpit. The Class "C" is built on a special modified van cutaway chassis, while the Class "A" is built on a truck chassis. These motorhomes can be powered by either gas or diesel, and most have their own source of heat, electricity and air conditioning, and have large holding tanks for waste and fresh water, making them ideal all-around vehicles for family travel.

Motorhomes range from 18'-40' (or longer!) in length and from $30-400,000, or more, depending on the customization and amenities, and sleep from 4-10 people. Units that are 33' or longer are generally used by full-time RVers, as they have room for more storage and creature comforts such as bath tubs, ice makers, trash compactors, dishwashers, and washers and dryers. The latest development in motorhomes is the "slide-out" that has been common for years in trailer models. This adds a great deal of room and a new dimension to motorhome traveling! Some RVers tow a car or pickup so they can shop and sightsee easily. Many people use these "land yachts" for extended vacations or for full-time living, so taking a car along becomes necessary for added freedom and convenience.

Class "A" and Class "C" motorhomes are the most prevalent styles of RVs in rental fleets and are the types of vehicle featured in this book. For those who want to camp and have all the luxuries of home, these RVs are certainly the way to go.

Figure 8, Class-A Motorhome

Many people I have talked to would not be good candidates for the owner-operated styles, since most want to put the key in the ignition, take off, and still have all the comforts of home. The best solutions for this type of traveler are the RVs shown in either Figure 8 or 9, better known as Class "C" and Class "A" recreation vehicles.

The Class "A" RV, which we have used on all of our trips, is our favorite, whether traveling with kids or by ourselves. Besides being bigger in all dimensions, the bus-like wrap-around windows provide magnificent panoramas for everyone inside.

The Class "C" RV, on the other hand, has many of the same advantages as the Class "A" as far as roominess, but the main disadvantage is that it is a "cabover." As you can see from Figure 8, part of the cab hangs over the windshield, which then has to be smaller in height than in the Class "A," thereby

Figure 9, Class-C Motorhome

blocking some of the wonderful scenery. In areas where the view is not directly in front of you, the driver and passengers have to bend forward quite a bit to look at the mountainous scenery; this can be quite bothersome. However, if you plan to look mostly straight ahead, not up, a Class "C" will be very enjoyable, indeed. In other respects, the Class "A" and Class "C" RVs are basically the same.

Additionally, your perception of clearances, both to the side and above, is quite a bit different in the Class "A" as opposed to the Class "C." In the Class "A" you are seated higher and have good forward visibility, whereas in the Class "C" you are seated closer to the ground and the cabover blocks your upward view. In the Class "C" the sides extend a few inches farther out on both sides of the cab, unlike the Class "A," so you must be more careful when parking or passing another vehicle.

Smaller children like to ride in the berth over the cab in the Class "C," as they can look out of the small window that faces the front. Bigger children and teenagers wouldn't be comfortable doing this, so choosing the right RV for your family is partly defined by the ages and sizes of the passengers. However, from a safety standpoint, I **strongly** urge that no children be allowed to ride in the berth, and all passengers have seatbelts on while you are underway.

Another advantage of the Class "A" over the Class "C" is that you and everybody else sit about a foot higher off the ground and you don't feel as if you are in a car with a big box behind you. The seating in the Class "C" is about a foot higher off the ground than in the micro-mini, which is like your car, and is similar to being in a large Ryder or U-Haul delivery truck. Being higher off the ground gives you a different perspective of your surroundings, wonderful views of the countryside, and helps you spot changing traffic conditions. Remember, getting a good view is a major reason for the trip!

Depending on the time of year and the location of the rental company, Class "C" RVs are easier to come by than Class "A," and often considerably cheaper. These are two important factors affecting your rental decision. Class "C"s are also much easier to drive in Europe or other continents, where the road conditions and congestion around cities and towns make driving more difficult than in the US.

Visit a Dealer

Now that you have learned about the basic types of vehicles, take a Saturday and visit one or two local RV sales or rental companies. Look in your local telephone yellow pages under "recreational vehicles." Pretend you are interested in buying one so the salesperson will be sure to give you a complete rundown on all the models and their features. Make sure you get sales literature from the dealer so you can familiarize yourself with the terminology, the different features, and especially important for a trip, the various layouts offered. While you are at the dealer, pick up a copy of an RV-oriented publication so you can start to learn more about the RV way of life. Many well-stocked newsstands will have magazines on RVing, too. The more you know, the more you'll sound like a pro!

There are many manufacturers of RVs and all of them have several models, so it is easy to get confused with the myriad of details and options on each one. The basic types I will be discussing in this book alone—Class "A" and Class "C"—have many options! You will really be impressed with the feeling of hominess in today's RV. With spacious beds, modern kitchens and bathrooms, comfortable dining and living areas, heat, air conditioning, running water and electricity, traveling in an RV will make you feel right at home! No more roughing it and worrying about putting up the tent, starting a fire, or taking a hot shower! To add to your traveling pleasure, many RVs are equipped with state-of-the-art stereo and TV sets, VCRs, microwaves and/or convection ovens.

Take plenty of time to inspect the inside of several RV styles. You will see the variety of layouts, the well-planned kitchen facilities, how much storage there is, the various sleeping arrangements and the array of amenities. Look carefully at the closet and storage space for clothes, food and cooking utensils, so you will have a good idea of what is available when you pack or shop. Be sure to sit in the front seats to get a feel of the size of the RV and the differences in forward visibility

An RV's Galley (photo courtesy of Winnebago Industries)

The Interior of an RV (photo courtesy of Winnebago Industries)

between the Class "A" and the Class "C" models. There are also large side windows that will give all passengers good views of the vistas of the open road. Note the curtains and blinds that give privacy at night and relief from the sun, and the strategically placed lighting for work, reading and dining. For typical floorplans, see Figure 10.

Ask the sales agent plenty of questions so you can begin to familiarize yourself with the RV and how it operates. Find out how the dinette and couch make into beds and have him show you some of the mechanical systems, such as the heat, propane, air conditioning, toilet, and waste tanks, and how the dumping procedure works. You don't need to go into great detail about these things, but get a general overview so you learn how easy it is to live aboard an RV. If you have children, take them along, too, as part of the preparation process for their great adventure. Start to picture you and your family traveling over the open road in a portable home! You will soon be King of the Road!

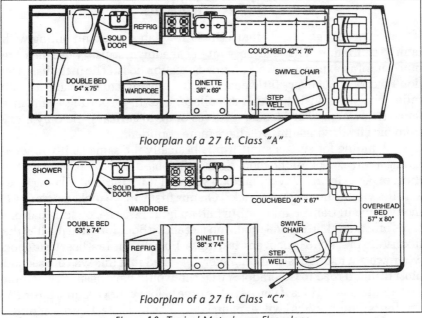

Floorplan of a 27 ft. Class "A"

Floorplan of a 27 ft. Class "C"

Figure 10, Typical Motorhome Floorplans

After you have checked out the various styles and become more familiar with layouts and equipment, see if you can take an RV for a test drive. My wife proudly informed me that our first motorhome was going to be hardly bigger than my Lincoln Town Car. That took some of the jitters away. Within a few miles you will learn to your delight that driving an RV is really quite simple and that your fear of having to drive a "truck" has vanished. With automatic transmission, power steering, power brakes, dual side mirrors and very large side windows, maneuvering an RV along a street or driving on a highway is really pretty simple. Driving tips are explained in detail later in Chapter 12.

Go to an RV Show

Many metropolitan areas have RV/camping shows throughout the year. If there is one near you, plan to go. You will be rewarded with several hours of being able to examine a wide variety of RVs, from pop-ups to ones the size of a bus. Try not to fall in love with a particular model and expect the rental agency to have it, but go to the show to learn more about RVs in general. A list of RV shows can be obtained by writing the Recreation Vehicle Industry Association (RVIA) (see the RV Industry Association section in Appendix 13).

Take a Trial Run

If you have enough time before THE TRIP, plan a weekend outing with family or friends. This can be your shakedown cruise, but since the outcome of an expensive, well-planned vacation doesn't lie in the balance, don't worry about every little detail—have fun! Plan to drive at least 100 miles one way—visit the kids at college, take in a sporting event in a faraway town, or visit friends, relatives or an historical park. Stay away from big city driving until you have more confidence.

Planning for such a short trip is basically the same as if you were taking a car, except for the food. Your main objective is to experience the thrill of being in an RV. Very quickly you will learn the joys of being "like a turtle with its house on its back." On our first trip we picked up our 27' motorhome in Denver, and within half an hour I was negotiating hairpin turns on a mountain several thousand feet above Boulder. I had not had the luxury of a practice trip or even a test drive! Boy, did the first beer taste good when we got to our destination! Later, I learned that this was the second most difficult road in Colorado! A trial run would have been very helpful to me and is a good idea if you have the time before your vacation. Basic RV driving is quite easy, as I will explain later, but a little practice never hurts.

As you will soon find out, there are no problems getting a beverage or a snack, going to the bathroom (be sure to draw the blinds!) or fixing a meal—just pretend you are at home. You can stop any time, anywhere and be very comfortable. With one of the popular campground guides available from the rental agency or your local bookstore, finding a nice, full-service, modern campground will be a breeze. If you have any questions about the operation of your RV, or how to do the hookups, just ask the campground personnel or a fellow RVer at the adjoining campsite. I have found RVers to be very friendly and willing to lend a hand. Don't forget—they were all first-timers once.

You will find, as we did, that an RV is truly the ultimate family travel and camping vehicle for all seasons, any type of trip, and for all pocketbooks. It also has universal appeal for all ages and types of people, and can be the preferred mode of travel for those with various types of medical or physical disabilities.

With your shakedown cruise successfully over, you are ready to plan for THE TRIP. Read the following chapters carefully, make notes, and ask lots of questions of the rental agent or other RVers; they will be glad to help. The more informed you are the less nervous and uncomfortable you will be and your trip will be much more enjoyable.

This book is meant to be a guide. Follow it carefully and you will be certain to have an exciting and memorable trip.

Chapter 3

Planning Your Trip

Gathering Information

There is a saying that location, location, location is what creates real estate value. In traveling, it is planning, planning, planning that makes a vacation successful. You must do your homework—lots of it. It sounds like work, but it isn't. It is fun, exciting, and easy, once you know how to do it, and you will be rewarded by having your travel dreams come true. Just think of the trip planning as the beginning of the vacation—the excitement builds each time you get new information!

To start the planning process, ask yourself these few questions:

> *"Where do we want to go?"*
> *"What do we want to see?"*
> *"How long will it take to see everything?"*
> *"How much will it cost?"*

When you have all these questions answered, you will be ready to start arranging your trip. If you ***don't*** plan, your trip probably won't be as rewarding as it could have been, and may actually be very stressful and frustrating. That certainly is no fun! What you will learn in this chapter is how to plan a successful trip.

Make the planning process a family project and your vacation will become a shared experience with memories that will last a lifetime. No matter what age your children, let them have some say in what you are going to see and they will feel as if they have made a major contribution. This will be ***their*** adventure, and they won't feel as if they are being dragged along on ***your*** trip. Show them the brochures and read them some of the stories about the pictures. This will get their imagination going and they will be excited about the vacation and want to help make it a success. A trip should be a great learning experience, and with everyone in the family participating in the planning, you will have better cooperation and more enjoyment. And each day, you can keep reinforcing the learning experience by reading about what you are going to see and show the kids maps with your route marked. They will continue to take a great interest in the journey and this will give them something to do between sightseeing stops.

Where Do We Want to Go?

The first question you need to ask yourself is "Where do we want to go?" Have you had the desire to travel to some far-off part of the country, or to Europe or some other corner of the globe? Wanderlust has been around since the time of Marco Polo. All of us have dreamed at one time or another of exploring faraway places. Is there a sporting event, festival, architecture or history tour, fall foliage, the romance of the wild west or some other lure that beckons you? How about visiting relatives, kids at college, former neighbors, childhood friends, or the old family homestead? Or, how about taking off for parts unknown? On each of our trips we have been able to combine several of these activities into a very rewarding vacation. Just dream a bit and you will come up with many exciting ideas.

What Is There to See?

Sources of Travel Information

Once you have picked the general direction you want to go, it is time to start researching the answer to the second question, "What do we want to see?" The first step is to request travel information from the states, provinces or foreign countries you intend to visit. Use the phone numbers in Appendix 9, Travel Information Centers, to request travel packets. Allow three to four weeks to receive this information. These travel packets will include a guide highlighting the state's or country's nicest tourist sights, a list of festivals and events of interest, a tourist-oriented map, and perhaps a campground directory. Tell the tourist information center that you will be camping, otherwise, they may not send you the directory. The beautiful pictures will give a great boost to your imagination. Study the maps carefully as they may indicate the scenic routes and you can plan to integrate them into the rest of your trip.

Another source of travel information is your local bookstore. See if they have a travel guide of the area you want to visit. There are also numerous specialized guidebooks for various activities, such as bicycling, hiking, birding, sailing, studying geology, etc., that will give you very detailed information on what you want to do. If you can't find guidebooks for the area that interests you, don't panic, just stop at a major bookstore when you get to your destination. Thumb through these guides carefully to make sure they have the sort of information you need.

Travel information can also be found at local tourist information centers or the Chamber of Commerce. Welcome centers are often found on major highways at state lines. Some states that are vacation destinations, such as Maine and the Western states, are much better at providing this data than others. The tourist information centers or Chamber of Commerce will have brochures of local attractions, festivals and events, and detailed maps of the area showing points of interest. Much of this material is not published in guidebooks or the state travel brochures, so look at it carefully before you move on. There may be plenty of things to do locally, and this can save you a lot of driving. You will find the most valuable resources of travel information are at the local level, but unfortunately, you can't get it until you are on the road. Your overall itinerary needs to be flexible enough to allow for lots of local sightseeing. What you need to plan initially is your general route, allowing plenty of time for impromptu side trips.

The material provided by the tourist information centers will give you the highlights of what to see, so you can start to organize your trip around some of the major sites. From there, sightseeing ideas in local guidebooks will fill in the gaps and provide more places to see, and finally, local tourist information will give you an up-to-the-minute calendar of events and sites that might not have made it to the guidebooks. By using this three-step planning process, you will have everything necessary to plan the sightseeing you want to do.

There are other resources that may be useful, as well. If you are a member of the American Automobile Association (AAA), you have access to an excellent series of TourBooks listing all their recommended accommodations. Since you will be in an RV, you probably won't need the lodging information, but there are detailed listings of sites and points of interest under each city, town or country. Each listing describes what you can see at the site, hours of operation, cost (if any), directions to the site, and a phone number to call for more information. We found this material very important in supplementing what we found elsewhere. Some of the local guidebooks were too general or not well organized. With the AAA guides, information on a specific town is easily obtainable. In addition to the guides, AAA can also help you get an international driver's license, and even rent an RV. If you are not a member of AAA, joining is inexpensive, and their maps, TourBooks, and other travel help are more than worth the cost to join.

As tour director, I planned the daily route the night before and at lunch time or during breaks, but if we changed our route or I hadn't gone into enough detail, my co-pilot could easily get information on towns and sites ahead of us from the AAA guides. Probably you will have never heard of most of the places you will be passing by, and there may well be lots to see. A great part of the fun of traveling is to explore "parts unknown," so by reading all available material, you will learn what there is to see and do. With kids in tow, you will constantly be on the lookout for things that will interest them, so don't plan for just what you want to see or think the children ought to see. It is very important to a successful and meaningful trip to have plenty of activities for the kids to do. You will enjoy the vacation more when they are happy!

Visiting National Parks

If you are planning to visit a National Park, the Sierra Club publishes a detailed series of handbooks for the parks which are well worth getting. When you get to the park, stop at the headquarters before you travel through the park and purchase one of their picture/story guides in their National Parkways series. These are very informative and will give you a complete description of what there is to see. Some parks have two guides, but one has mostly pictures and doesn't tell you much about the park itself. Be careful which one you buy.

The National Park Service offers tourists several types of passes, called Passports, which can be used at any of the national parks, monuments, historic sites, recreation areas and national wildlife refuges that charge entrance fees. The passes cover the holder and passengers in a private vehicle for park entrance fees only, not user fees, except as noted. If you are planning to visit two or more parks, the pass will pay for itself, as single-visit entrance fees range from $1-4 per person or $3-10 per carload.

The Golden Eagle Passport is for people age 17-61, and permits unlimited entry to all the parks. It costs $25 and is good for a calendar year. It may be purchased in person or by mail from all National Park Service and US Forest Service headquarters or regional offices (see Appendix 13, RVer's Resource Guide, for addresses), at all Fish & Wildlife Service regional offices, and at any National Park or national wildlife refuge where entrance fees are charged.

The Golden Age Passport is a free, lifetime entrance pass to all the parks for those 62 or older, and it also provides a 50% discount on user fees for such services as camping, boat launching, parking, etc. It must be applied for in person, with proof of age, and may be obtained at most federally operated recreation areas where it can be used.

Another pass, the Golden Access Passport, is a free lifetime entrance pass to all the parks for people who are blind or permanently disabled. It also allows a 50% discount on user fees. You must apply in person and may obtain the passport at most of the federally operated recreation and refuge areas.

Lastly, there is an annual Park Pass, which permits unlimited entrance to a specific park for the holder and any accompanying passengers. The cost is $10 or $15, depending on the location, and it may be purchased by mail or in person at the specific park.

Travel and Recreation Guides

In 1982, Reader's Digest published an exceptionally good travel book called *America From the Road*, a state-by-state guide to interesting and often missed sites or points of interest. Maps indicating these sites and a proposed tour route are included. Of all the travel books I have seen, this is by far the best and easiest to use. The text is brief yet detailed enough to give the information needed for each place of interest. The pictures are excellent and will inspire you to visit the sites! Many of these are scenic areas that might be overlooked by guidebooks, and the directions to the best view are explicit. Majestic landscapes, crystal lakes, geologic formations, caves, gardens, architecture, as well as famous landmarks are covered in depth. If your time is limited and you want to see a variety of interesting places, this is the guidebook for you.

Realizing how successful *America From the Road* had been, Reader's Digest published *Off the Beaten Path* in 1987. It's subtitle, *A Guide to More Than 1,000 Scenic & Interesting Places Still Uncrowded and Inviting*, gives you a good indication of its contents. This book is very similar to the earlier one; however, there are fewer, scattered sites per state, which means you cannot plan convenient tours.

One of the major joys of traveling by RV is to see some of the country's majestic scenery, free from the crush of crowds, and both these books give the traveler a good idea of what to choose from. But, I made the mistake of taking *America From the Road* with us on the first trip, not realizing that I would accumulate a lot more travel information along the way—and have to carry it all!! On subsequent trips I simply photocopied the pages I needed from the book and took just those along.

A recently published guide, *The U.S. Outdoor Atlas & Recreation Guide*, by John Oliver Jones, is a comprehensive state-by-state guide to more than 5,000 wildlife and outdoor recreation areas, including national parks and forests, state parks, and hundreds of other public and private sites. Full-page maps and charts give detailed information about the sites in over 50 categories. It is an indispensable planner for every outdoor activity, including camping, hiking, touring, hunting, bird watching, fishing, biking, boating, skiing, and many more. This book has absolutely everything you will need to know about these outdoor recreation areas.

Another recently published book, *Parks Directory of the United States,* has detailed information on over 3,700 national and state parks, forests, battlefields and other recreation areas. It describes the facilities, activities and special features for each site. It is an expensive book, however, so see if your library has it.

From the information you have now gathered, you can answer the first two planning questions: "Where do we want to go?" and "What do we want to see?" Look over all the guidebooks and brochures, consult with family members, and come up with a general route incorporating some of the major, well-known sites, and many of the lesser-known and scenic sites. This is about all the research you can do from home; the rest will be done on the road using local guidebooks and information gathered from Chambers of Commerce or tourist information centers.

How Long Will It Take?

The third planning question, "How long will it take to see everything?" is more difficult to answer, yet very critical to the overall tour plan. First, you will not be used to the slower pace driving an RV requires, so don't plan your route as you would in your car. Second, you will be doing a lot of "off the beaten path" detours and sightseeing, as this is where the interesting sites are. These side roads will be much slower than the major highways. Third is a more individual problem: how well organized is your family and do you like to poke around? If you like to take your time seeing things, you can't visit as many sites. In other words, don't plan so many things to visit that you will have to rush to see them all. Your vacation will be ruined. Also, can you get the troops up and going in the morning? You will lose valuable travel time if you can't. On a two-week trip you will lose a whole day of sightseeing if you waste half an hour a day! However, if you are able to organize your trip well, you will still be able to see quite a lot and have a relaxing and successful vacation.

While I am talking about "breaking camp" and the time it takes, just think about having to take a journey by car, packing and unpacking every day, or searching for a restaurant and waiting to be served. This really kills a lot of time, let alone the expense, and will make you appreciate RV travel all the more.

On our travels out West we averaged between 150-300 miles a day. Don't forget that the West isn't called the "wide open spaces" for nothing! I planned the trip so that we would usually have at least two sightseeing stops in the morning and the same in the afternoon. Whether the stop was at an historic ranch, a museum, park, or geologic spot, we broke up the trip and still covered a lot of ground. Not only was this important for me as the driver, but it also gave the kids something to look forward to. The co-pilot would read to us about what we were going to see so everybody had an idea of what to expect. After the stop we discussed what we had seen, why we liked it, and what we learned. By the time that conversation was over it was almost time to see the next one, and I hadn't heard one "Are we almost there yet?"

In Europe, on the other hand, with much shorter distances between points of interest, you will probably average 100-200 miles a day. Driving time will be longer than in the United States, however, because the roads are narrower and quite congested, and you will have to pass through more towns.

Depending on the pace of your trip, your daily travel will be at one end of the mileage range or the other. National Parks will take a lot of time, even a day or more, so, if you go to them, allow plenty of time to see what is there. A quick drive-through will not be enough to enjoy the picturesque vistas. If you are planning to take long hikes, raft trips, visits to large museums, or other time-consuming events, plan your daily travel accordingly.

One basic travel caveat: don't plan your trip around such a tight schedule that there is no time for the many "scenic detours" or just poking around. The unexpected makes traveling fun! Part of the enjoyment of an RV trip is your ability to explore the highways and byways, and you never can tell what special places you will find. There are so many unexpected surprises even the best guidebooks overlook!

Don't worry about keeping to your initial tour route, but make it tentative and keep readjusting it as you travel. On our first trip to Colorado we rolled into Gunnison in the late afternoon expecting to leave early in the morning. I had read very little about the area, so I stopped at the Chamber of Commerce to get some local information, and discovered at least two days' worth of sites to explore. That was at the very beginning of the trip, so I quickly learned to allow for more flexibility and make adjustments to my travel planning. That worked wonders for the month-long trip and made it much more relaxing! We finally got to see the sites we missed on a subsequent trip—what a wonderful excuse for another RV adventure!

Flexibility is the name of the game!! If what you are seeing is fun take the time to enjoy it and unwind! Being able to change plans at will, stop where and when you want, eat wherever and whenever it strikes your fancy, and not having to worry about motels is the real essence of RV travel.

As tour director, if you find this "poking along" is getting you off schedule and you need to make readjustments to the itinerary, tell your fellow travelers if you plan to cut out any major sites. They could be very disappointed to miss them. However, if you want to keep to a tighter schedule you will have two choices: speed things up by cracking the whip and getting the family going faster, or cut out some of the side trips. For me, the slower pace was preferable. We certainly were able to see a lot and made many adjustments to the plan, but there were few disappointments.

As the trip nears its end, make sure you pay close attention to the distance back to your rental agency. You should be able to judge travel speed by then, but allow extra time for unexpected problems such as traffic jams, flat tires, rain, getting lost, finding the dump and propane stations, unpacking and returning the RV, and getting to the airport.

How Much Will It Cost?

One of the first questions you will have when you contemplate taking an RV trip is the cost. In the back of your mind you think it is expensive because an RV is so big and has all the luxuries of home. As I mentioned earlier, the cost of buying an RV can run up into the hundreds of thousands for a luxury motor coach. However, the RVs in the rental fleets will be economy models by comparison, although by no means skimpy in their accommodations. The purchase prices of RVs in the rental fleets run roughly between $30-75,000, depending on size and amenities.

Compare Alternative Vacation Costs

Compare the cost of an RV vacation to the traditional one using a car or airplane, staying in hotels/motels, and eating all meals in restaurants. The surprising factor is that a traditional vacation is considerably more expensive than one in an RV. Food and lodging costs are much cheaper using an RV, and transportation is not much more than if you flew to your destination and rented a car. The convenience, quality family time, and the overall flexibility of traveling by RV will show you why over 25 million Americans enjoy the RV way of life.

Drive/Fly? Time vs. Money

After you have decided where you plan to vacation, the next question is how to get there. If you have decided to follow your rainbow to some faraway place, the decision will be whether to drive there and back, or fly and pick up the RV at the destination.

One major consideration to think about is the time involved in getting there. If we had driven to Colorado from Philadelphia, we would have spent at least three long days on the road before the vacation actually began; then the same number on the way home. We would have lost a week of our month's vacation. It made sense, therefore, for us to fly to Denver and pick up the RV there. With a shorter vacation time, this factor is even more important.

Some friends of ours who own an RV have solved the travel/time problem by driving one way, arranging with friends to meet them at their destination and make the trip in reverse, then flying home. By doing it this way, they extend their actual sightseeing time. This is really a good idea if your ultimate destination is far away.

However, if you can't decide whether to drive or fly, do some basic cost comparisons between the two methods of transportation. Compare the cost of the flight versus the daily rental expense, and the cost of gas, food, tolls and campground fees. Add to this the time saved and what that will do for your sightseeing plans, then make your decision. Your main goal, don't forget, is to have an enjoyable and memorable vacation, and not spend endless hours driving. Even if it costs a bit more, it may be preferable to fly in order to have more time sightseeing. This is especially true if you have kids in tow, as long drives with nothing to do can be deadly and quickly ruin the vacation for everyone!

If you go to Europe, try to get a nonstop flight, so you will be more rested when you arrive. Having less jet lag will save precious time, too, and you will be able to get your RV trip off to a good start! Frankfurt is an ideal beginning point for an RV trip, since it is in the center of Europe and you can reach most countries in one day's drive.

Estimating the Cost of an RV Vacation

At this stage in the planning process you have made your decision to drive or fly to your departure point. The last important detail is to research the various rental agencies serving your destination to find out the cost of renting an RV. This process is explained in detail in Chapter 4. With this information in hand, you can start to pencil in the rest of your expenses. Use the Cost Estimator in Appendix 1 to make these calculations. To help you estimate, use the following guidelines for budgeting, and you will be able to come up with a pretty good idea of the vacation's total cost:

1. Daily/weekly/monthly RV rental and mileage and insurance charges.

2. Cost of airline tickets and parking, or transportation to the airport.

3. Campground fees of about $12.50 per night for 2 people. Look at one of the campground guides mentioned in Chapter 6 for the costs in your travel area; add $1-1.50 per person over 2; family resort campgrounds with many amenities and planned activities may run $18-23 per night.

4. Fuel cost—estimated travel distance, divided by 10 mpg, times the cost of fuel, say $1.15 per gallon, will give you a pretty good budget figure. This cost may vary quite a bit, depending on the part of the country and time of year. Check with the RV dealer to get fairly accurate figures. You may also get better gas mileage, but this will depend on the type of driving you do and the size and weight of the RV.

   In Europe, the RVs have diesel engines which get approximately 20 mpg, and with shorter driving distances, plan on $75-100 per week for fuel costs. Fuel is much more expensive than in the US.

5. Food—calculate how much food will cost per person, per day. This could vary greatly depending on whether you cook in the RV all or most of the time, or if you eat out a lot.

6. Sightseeing/activity fees—this category covers entrance fees to parks, museums, rafting, old time train rides and other sightseeing adventures. Unless you plan on doing several expensive activities on your trip, you can expect to spend $10-15 per day, per person. This figure allows for an occasional expensive activity. Most entrance fees, however, will be in the $2-5 range, and in many places are free.

7. Souvenirs—part of the fun of your vacation will be to collect things(!!) to remind you of the trip. We have managed to collect quite a variety of items, ranging from lots of guidebooks to a geologist's hammer, a nice collection of interesting polished rocks and fossils, antique bottles from some of the towns we visited, western hats, belts and antique spurs, Indian jewelry, rug beaters, branding irons and barbed wire. Whatever you collect, the memories of your trip will live on! Before you buy that cute four foot fuzzy dinosaur, however, think how you will get it home!

Making Reservations

If your RV dream vacation is within your budget, you are now ready to make the next move—choosing an agency and making reservations to rent the RV. Details of this process are explained in detail in Chapter 4. If you plan to fly to your departure point, make airline reservations at the same time.

Now that you have your RV and travel reservations, you are ready for the next stage of the trip—organizing what needs to be done before you go away. There's lots to do in order to get ready, so allow at least one month to pull everything together. Some people are more organized than others or have more time and can get things pulled together in a week or two, but I have found, as organized as I am, that I am still harried right up until the time we leave. There never seems to be enough time! So, as the saying goes, plan ahead. Hopefully, this guide will help you streamline this phase of the trip. Photocopy the checklists in the Appendix so you can carry them with you as you make your preparations. Chapter 5 will give you some of the items I feel are necessary on an RV trip, so use these as a base and tailor the lists for your own particular needs.

Traveling with Pets

I don't recommend traveling with your pets unless you are "full-timing" or going to stay in one spot for several weeks. Most readers of this book, however, will be on a short vacation and on the go all the time, so having a pet around can be a lot of extra trouble for you and dangerous for it. Most RV rental agencies don't allow pets, either, because of the possibility of pet stains, damage from claws, and the extra time and expense needed to clean and fumigate the unit. Many state and national parks, wilderness areas and other public lands don't allow pets, because of the danger of introducing non-native species of animals into the wild and the possible transmission of diseases. If you want to take your pet along, check with the park. Another good reason to leave Bowser at home is that you will be in very close quarters in the campgrounds, and pets can be very annoying to your new neighbors. Cats can bother some people, too, but if your dog is the type that barks at everybody walking by, leave it home! However, if you take a pet with you, keep it on a leash at all times when it is out of the RV and clean up any mess it makes.

If you do take your pet along, be prepared in the event it gets away from you. First, have a special collar tag made with the phone number of a friend or relative who will be home while you are away, or the place you are staying if you will be there your whole vacation. Pets usually can find their way home if the territory is familiar to them, but won't be able to when you are on the road. Second, take along a good photograph of your pet that can be photocopied and posted or given to the local police, ASPCA, veterinarians and the newspaper. This may be a big help in having your pet returned.

Pets have special requirements when they travel, too, so don't forget their toys, shampoo, flea powder, food and dish, medication, and collar and leash. Put your vet's name in Appendix 5 in case you need it in an emergency.

There aren't any restrictions on traveling with a pet in the continental United States, but be sure to take along any vaccination information from your vet. There are restrictions in Hawaii and Alaska, so check with your vet or local ASPCA for information. Pets traveling to Mexico will need an International Health Certificate for Dogs and Cats (Form 77-043), which must be certified by a veterinarian no more than 72 hours before departure from the United States. You will also have to provide evidence of your pet's inoculation against rabies and distemper within the six-month period preceding the certification. If your pet is out of the United States for more than 30 days, the certification process must be repeated before it can re-enter the country.

Dogs and cats over three months old entering Canada from the United States must be accompanied by a certificate signed by a veterinarian stating that the pet has been vaccinated against rabies during the preceding 36 months. The certificate must adequately describe the pet.

Planning on the Road

Somebody in your party will have to be cruise director, that all-important function which entails gathering the information, planning the day's route, keeping everybody moving, and choosing a campground. Just how the cruise director and pilot/co-pilot roles divide is up to you, and you may want to switch them from time to time. Some people prefer to drive, while others would just as soon be passenger/navigator and/or cruise director. I was pilot and cruise director, so as soon as I had completed the basic travel research, I discussed what seemed interesting with the co-pilot. The co-pilot did more research during the day as we drove along, so it was important to communicate.

Trip planning doesn't end when you leave home—the job has only just begun! It is a continuing process. As the vacation progresses you will have to make daily adjustments to the overall tour route, due to weather conditions, the length of time it has taken you to sightsee, all those "scenic detours" and unexpected places you discovered and the shops you just couldn't resist. You will have to make adjustments during the day, too, so don't plan to push for a destination that is too far away. If you do, your trip will be one big rush and you will have missed the whole point of the trip—to relax and enjoy what you are doing.

Each night, after you have settled into the campground, plan to spend an hour or so reviewing where you have been that day and where you are going to go next. Take a colored felt tip marker and highlight information for the next day's sightseeing. This will make it much easier for the co-pilot to follow the tour and be able to read about the sites ahead to the rest of the passengers. After a few days you will get a pretty good feel of how long it takes to drive and look at various sites, but, as each site and road conditions will vary widely, allow plenty of extra time.

Study the maps and the distance covered carefully to see how the mileage fits into the overall distance for the whole trip. You don't want to be stuck far from your RV rental center on the last day.

Before you leave the campsite each morning, write out your general course on a 5"x7" tablet and give it to your co-pilot. Put down towns you will pass through or near, route numbers, what sites you want to see, including some basic directions, and your probable destination. Briefly review the map together, too. That will avoid having to quickly look at the map as you approach an intersection and try to figure out which way to go. Review route numbers periodically throughout the day so they become familiar to both pilot and co-pilot and keep the map handy and folded so you can quickly find where you are and what to look for. Show the co-pilot what campgrounds are available at the proposed destination, and discuss the options during the day. Pick at least one alternate destination, too, in case the course of the trip changes, which can happen frequently. Plan to arrive at the campground in daylight, as making camp is much easier. We found this technique worked well, saved a lot of anxiety, and made things move more smoothly.

In addition to going over the planned route, discuss the day's itinerary with the co-pilot and other passengers so that everybody knows what to expect. Have any brochures or guidebooks handy and well marked so the co-pilot can easily find the necessary information. The co-pilot can read about the up-coming points of interest to the others in your party, and this will make the trip more informative and enjoyable to all. Having a well informed co-pilot will make the driving and tour directing jobs much easier!

Do some planning at lunch time or during travel breaks, too. Some areas may interest you more than others, but you won't know until you are there. Have your co-pilot read up on the towns ahead of you as you drive along, so you know what to expect. I found that even though I had thoroughly studied the travel information the night before, there was so much that I needed help keeping track of the flow of sites. During the breaks you can review what the co-pilot read, study brochures or travel information and make adjustments to your schedule. By early afternoon, if you need to make reservations, you will know how far you will get that day and can call a campground.

During these planning sessions, take a colored felt tip marker and go over the route you have traveled. This will be part of your trip archives that you can show friends and also have as a handy reminder if you need to fill in gaps in your diary or identify an unknown photo.

Discuss what you have read with family members and see if they are interested. Don't force activities on the children, but try to provide a variety of things to do. Plan to visit something for everyone. My co-pilot and I like to antique, but can you imagine dragging four teenage kids through antique shops all day? The trip would be ruined for everybody!

Foreign Travel & Restricted Areas

After you have been bitten by the "RV bug" and want to do more extensive traveling, you may decide to go to a foreign country. Motorhoming is quite popular in Europe, Australia, New Zealand, Canada and Mexico. See "Foreign RV Rental Agencies" in the RVer's Resource Guide, Appendix 13, for more information on agencies that rent RVs abroad. There is usually no problem taking an RV you rent in the United States to many parts of Canada, but most agencies restrict travel to Mexico, Northern Baja, Alaska and parts of Canada without special permission, insurance and extra fees. American rental agencies usually forbid travel to Newfoundland, the Yukon, and the Northwest Territories in Canada due to the long distances, difficult terrain in many areas, and extreme temperatures. Check with them well in advance of your trip to see what their requirements are. Insurance for Mexico may be obtained from Sanborn's Insurance Service, McAllen, TX (512) 686-0711 and other gateway cities, or from Allen W. Lloyd, S.C., Mariano Otero, Guadalajara, Jal., Mexico. This insurance must include property damage and public liability. For other helpful travel information, consult the campground directories that have extensive sections covering travel into Mexico and Canada, as well as tips on customs restrictions, currency exchange, gas, traffic laws, and RV parks. For a free guide, *Driving to Mexico*, contact a Mexican tourism office or call (800) 446-8266.

In addition to insurance, RVers will need valid driver's licenses and an original and a copy of the vehicle's registration or title. Rented RVs must have a letter from the rental agency giving permission to travel into Mexico. Also, you must have an international credit card in the driver's name in order to get a 180 day travel permit, which is issued at the border for $10. If you don't have a credit card, they won't accept cash for the permit, so you will have to post a bond for the blue-book value of the vehicle or make a refundable deposit for the value of the vehicle at a Mexican bank.

Divorced parents traveling with children must obtain permission from the other parent giving them authority to travel to Mexico.

If you go to Mexico you will want to buy a travel guide to find out about travel conditions and sites, but you and your passengers will each need a Mexican Tourist Card. These can be obtained at the border, by mail from a Mexican Consulate, a Mexican Government Tourism office (see

Appendix 9), or from Sanborn's Insurance Service. You will also need proof of citizenship in the form of a birth certificate, voter registration card, declaration of citizenship sworn before a US Immigration official, or a passport. To save time at the border, obtain the card in advance.

Traveling to Canada is quite easy, as citizens or permanent residents of the US do not need passports or visas, and US and international driver's licenses are valid. Canadian tourism officials suggest, however, that native-born citizens carry some identification papers, such as birth, baptismal or voter's certificate. Naturalized citizens should carry a naturalization certificate or some evidence of citizenship. Permanent residents should carry their Alien Registration Receipt Card. This should help expedite border crossing both ways. Visitors from other countries should have a valid passport. For more information, check with the nearest Canadian Tourism Office.

To enter Canada with an RV, your rental agreement must have an endorsement stating that the vehicle is permitted into Canada. Also, check with your rental agency regarding necessary RV insurance. You will need a Canadian Non-Resident Inter-Provincial Motor Vehicle Liability Insurance Card as proof of financial responsibility. It is available only in the US through US insurance companies. If you have any questions, call the Insurance Bureau of Canada at (416) 362-2031.

RV Travel Abroad

Taking an RV trip to Europe, Australia or New Zealand or other foreign country will take the same kind of planning as trips to Canada or Mexico. Call the tourist boards and airlines for information, including a map of campsites, and obtain travel guides from bookstores to aid you in the planning process. RV touring is called "caravanning" in Europe, in case you are wondering what they are talking about! See Appendix 9, Travel Information Centers, for contacts.

Since any kind of travel in Europe is different than in the United States, it is a good idea to read as much about it as possible. RVing is no exception. David Shore and Patty Campbell have written an excellent how-to guide, *Europe By Van and Motorhome,* that really covers "all the bases" of RV travel in Europe. For ten years they have traveled extensively in campers in Europe, and explain everything you need to know. To order, write to them at Shore/Campbell, 1842 Santa Margarita Dr., Fallbrook, CA 92028, or call (619) 723-6184 or (800) 659-5222. The price is $13.95 ppd.

European RVs tend to be smaller and lighter than their American counterparts. This is due to the high cost of fuel and because most European roads are much narrower and more serpentine than ours, so maneuvering a big rig would be quite difficult. When you are gathering information on RV models, pay close attention to the sleeping configurations, as they are quite a bit different than ours. European RVs are quite compact and are not as lavishly equipped as ours. Air conditioned units are not as common, and many RVs have portable chemical toilets that can be dumped into a conventional toilet. US-style dump stations are almost nonexistent, and the electricity supplied at many campgrounds is minimal by our standards. The rest of the camping experience is pretty much the same.

Typical European Motorhomes
(photos courtesy of GMT)

Bookings

Many travel agents will be able to help you book an RV. They, in turn, will make the reservations through a broker. The other booking option is to contact American and European RV rental agencies that will be able to assist you in the planning process, as well as provide the RV. Compare their vehicles, prices, services, and what they will provide in the way of bedding and kitchen supplies, as there are substantial differences. Currencies can take wide swings, so make sure to find out how the rental agency is going to calculate the rental fee. Will it be in dollars or foreign currency? If the dollar is strong, for instance, it might pay to rent in the local currency.

A valid US or Canadian driver's license and a passport are all that are required to rent an RV in Europe. Insurance and other necessary documentation will be taken care of by the rental agency. As camping is very popular in Europe and the rental agencies may book up early, make your reservations as far in advance as possible. Six months ahead is really not too soon! Contacts can be found in the North American and Foreign RV Rental Agencies sections of Appendix 13 or from your travel agency. If you want to island hop around the British Isles or go from there to the continent, contact Scots-American Travel Advisors, agents for several ferry lines at 201-768-1187. There are several European campground directories which are discussed in Chapter 6.

International Camping Carnet

If you are planning to tour Europe, contact the National Campers and Hikers Association (NCHA). Through its affiliation with the FICC, the Federation International of Camping and Caravanning, NCHA offers its members the International Camping Carnet (pronounced "car-NAY"). The carnet is a kind of RVer's passport for camping in Europe. Many of the campgrounds in Europe are operated as private clubs for members only, but with the carnet, NCHA members automatically become members of hundreds of FICC affiliated campgrounds and clubs across Europe. It makes locating camping facilities and reserving campsites abroad almost as easy as at home. At most campgrounds you must either leave a passport or the carnet for identification. The carnet is valid for one year and is only sold to members of issuing organizations. For information on NCHA, see the RV/ Camping Clubs section in Appendix 13.

The carnet can also be obtained through the American Automobile Association (AAA) or from various European automobile clubs. The cost is only a few dollars and is well worth the price, as many campgrounds give discounts to holders of the carnet.

Insurance.

Your US or Canadian auto insurance is not valid in Europe, so you must have an International Green Insurance Card, commonly known as a green card, as proof of liability coverage. If you rent an RV, you will be supplied with a green card along with your other documents. If you have more questions about insurance, contact one of the leasing companies, AAA, the Canadian Automobile Club, or the American International Underwriters (AIU) in Wilmington, DE at (800) 343-5761.

Fuel and the Metric System

In many parts of the world, fuel is sold in liters, so you will need to know how to translate liters into gallons. The following table should help:

> 4.54 liters = 1 Canadian/Imperial gallon
> 3.78 liters = 1 American gallon

For expanded conversion tables, see Appendix 12, Metric Conversion Tables.

Restricted Areas

Deserts

Certain desert areas of the United States, most notably Death Valley, are restricted for traveling during certain times of the year by the rental agencies because of the greatly increased potential for breakdowns and danger. Death Valley, for instance, is generally off limits from May 1st through September 30th, and in Arizona, travel on the Apache Trail east of Tortilla Flat to Roosevelt Dam may be forbidden at any time. If the route you plan to take passes through these areas, check with the agency to see if it is all right.

Bridges and Tunnels

Because RVs have propane tanks, they are restricted from passing through certain underwater or underground tunnels and over a few bridges. These are mostly located around the larger metropolitan areas. Check your route ahead of time if you are going to be near one of these areas so both you and the co-pilot can be on the lookout for the alternate route. There should be signs on the approaches to warn you, but, as a car driver, I never paid any attention to this prohibition, and really hadn't thought of it until I read the RV manuals. Although I don't advise it, many campers choose to ignore the tunnel restrictions, and just turn off the propane system before entering a tunnel. The warning signs are there for a good reason! Some of the campground directories mentioned in this book have information on these restrictions.

Winter RV Adventures

During the winter months, many mountain passes are closed to RVs as well as cars, so check with the rental agency regarding your proposed route. However, some mountainous areas have campgrounds catering to winter activities such as skiing, snowmobiling, ice skating, etc., so the local authorities try to keep the roads passable. There are some really fantastic ski-oriented campgrounds in the Alps, as well as in certain parts of Canada and the United States. This is just one small example of the many year-round activities that you can participate in with an RV that makes this mode of travel so exciting!

A well-planned trip will assure you and your family of a relaxing and rewarding adventure on the road—and a lifetime of wonderful memories!

Chapter 4

Making Arrangements

Finding a Rental Agency

From the planning process you followed in Chapter 3, you already know where you want to begin your trip and how you are going to get there. Unless there are a lot of things you want to see between home and your destination point, it is preferable to fly out and pick up your RV. This is also true if getting there would take more than a day. There is no sense wasting valuable vacation time on the road! If you fly, your only rental opportunities will be from one of the national agencies or a local rental company. Using a national RV rental company is usually the best solution if you are going on a long trip, as they are well set up to help the touring RVer and have locations at many destination cities. They also have a nationwide network of repair and service facilities which may come in handy if you have a problem. In some cases they will let you drop off the vehicle at another city, which you can't do with a local rental company. The place to start looking for an RV is in the listings of national or foreign RV rental companies in Appendix 13, the RVer's Resource Guide.

If a national company doesn't have RVs in your proposed destination city, or if they are booked up, you can find local RV rental companies in other states by going to the library and checking the RV rental listings for your destination city in the yellow pages. Look under "recreational vehicles," "motor homes," or "campers." Some of these listings may be just dealers, but others may offer rentals. If nobody advertises rentals, call a dealer and ask who handles rentals in that area. Tell them what kind of trip you are planning. Another very good source of rental information is a directory published by the Recreation Vehicle Rental Association (RVRA), *Who's Who in RV Rentals*, which lists over 250 RV rental dealers in the US, Canada and Europe. For ordering information look under RV Industry Associations in Appendix 13.

If you can't arrange a rental in your destination city, pick a nearby city and try again. For instance, if Denver is booked up, try Salt Lake City or Phoenix. At least you will be close to where you want to end up. Your itinerary will change somewhat, but that will give you new opportunities, and is certainly better than being disappointed. In high travel seasons or popular tourist areas rentals from the national companies may be hard to get, so searching for a local rental company may be the only alternative.

Since many areas of the country aren't serviced by national rental companies or don't have local rental companies, you may have to rent an RV near your home or drive quite a distance by car to a national or local rental company closer to your destination. This is why investigating rental opportunities is such a vital part of your vacation planning. The major destination cities, however, will have either a national or local company to serve you. If you have to drive to the rental depot, check to make sure they have on-site car parking available.

Some travel agencies, such as AAA's travel department, can make bookings with RV rental companies, sometimes at a discount, so this can be another alternative source to check.

What Are the Expenses?

Once you have found either a local or national rental agency, work closely with them in planning this aspect of your vacation. They will be providing you with planning advice, an RV that is ready to go, and services during the trip. When you first contact them, ask for a list of all the expenses, starting with the daily, weekly and monthly rates. The weekly rate should be considerably less than the daily rate, but the rates are often quoted on a daily rate basis. For instance, should you need the RV for only four days, the rate might be $130 per day. The weekly rate, however, might be only $110 per day or $770 per week. Discounts may be offered for trips of three weeks or longer.

Have the rental agency send you its rate schedule and other information provided prospective renters. This should cover types of vehicles in their fleet, floorplans, insurance, "convenience kits," and other services. In addition to the convenience kits, which include kitchen equipment, towels and bedding, they may also be able to rent you lawn chairs, a TV, and bikes, if you need them. You will need to start learning the terminology, and comparison shopping never hurt. If there are several rental agencies in your destination city, ask all of them for this information. Rates vary considerably depending on the RV model and size, the location, and the season, so if you can schedule your trip for an off-peak time, you will not only save a lot of money but miss the crowds, too. Families with kids tend to travel from June to August, which is usually the high season, making rentals harder to come by and more expensive. If you want to travel during this time, make reservations several months in advance.

What Questions Should I Ask?

One of the items you might not think of asking about is the kind of insurance coverage required to rent an RV. This can be quite tricky and expensive, and the way it is handled may vary from company to company. The cost of special insurance can be quite a lot, but not having it can add to your potential liability and up front security deposit. Read about the insurance options in detail in Chapter 7, Picking Up the RV, before you talk to a rental agency so you will know the terminology and what questions to ask.

It is also important to ask about the model RV and the sleeping layouts offered. The number and ages of people in your party, the type of scenery on your trip, and your budget will dictate whether you want a Class "A" or Class "C" RV. Perhaps either will be OK. Be careful of smaller units that claim to sleep 5/6, as some of the sleeping areas will only accommodate small children. Look at the measurements in their floorplans and compare them to your beds at home. Usually the dinette and couch will make into a bed accommodating one adult or two children, and if you have a Class "C," the cabover makes sleeping quarters for a teenager or two small children. There will be other regular-sized beds for two adults in most rental RVs.

The rental company cannot guarantee you a specific vehicle, but should be able to tell you which class RV you will get and the type of sleeping arrangements that particular model has. Tell them how many will be in your party and how big your kids are, and have them send you brochures showing the layouts with bed sizes. Children don't mind roughing it a bit the way adults might, but you don't want to be too cramped, either.

Ask the rental agency about the mileage charge. Often you will get "x" number of free miles per day, perhaps 100, and then be charged for any miles over that figure—averaged out, of course, over the length of the trip. The mileage charge will vary by the model RV you are renting. If you are going on a relatively short trip, this figure may be immaterial, but if you are going to travel several thousand miles it may add up to a tidy sum.

Another important question to ask yourself at this time is whether you will be returning to the point of departure with the RV or will travel to another city and return home from there. If you want to travel one way, some of the national companies will allow you to do this, but will charge an extra fee which can be quite substantial. The local companies can't do this, of course. We have flown from Philadelphia to Denver, rented the RV and driven around the West, then flown home from Denver. Our trip planning would have been completely different if we had driven out and back or driven out and flown back. You may not be able to rent from certain agencies if you don't plan to return home from the same city.

Several other reasons for using a national company are important in the decision-making process. As with big car rental companies, they will be more likely to have a backup in their system should something happen to the RV they rented to you. Also, although we don't like to think about it, breakdowns and accidents do occur, and the nationwide agencies have the ability to get repairs done at local service facilities and have the charges billed to them. When you are questioning your local rental agency, if you go this route, be sure to ask how repairs and breakdowns are handled and what their service network is like in your travel area. Another concern when trying to choose between a local or national company is the type and age of vehicles rented by the local agencies. Often they will rent privately owned RVs that owners use a few weeks a year, and these units may be older and have higher mileage than those of the national companies, and therefore be more likely to need service. Some of the larger local rental companies, however, have strict policies about vehicle age and mileage and maintain very modern fleets.

While you are interviewing the rental agencies, be sure to ask what they can supply in the way of camping necessities. By renting equipment from them you can travel light with just your personal items and not have to worry about "packing everything but the kitchen sink!" This is ideal for a short trip of a week or so, but on longer trips you may prefer to take your own supplies.

Most agencies have basic "convenience kits" that will contain the necessary cooking equipment, dishes, utensils, linens, towels, pillows and bedding needed for the trip. Charges for the kits usually run between $35-50 per person. Ask for a detailed list of what they provide and fill in other items from lists found elsewhere in this book. Necessary cooking supplies and bedding are covered in a later chapter. Depending on the number of people in your party, the length of your vacation, and the travel logistics involved, using the agency's kits may make a great deal of sense. You really can keep an RV trip simple! Providing your own supplies may be cheaper if you have the time to organize them and the cost of getting them to the rental agency is not too great. Shipping out a trunk of supplies to a friend or relative certainly makes sense, however, as you will know exactly what you have and won't have to lug things with you. Some agencies may store a trunk if you want to send it out ahead, so check with them when you make your reservation.

Make Reservations Early!

Call the RV rental agencies near where you want to start your vacation to see if they have RVs available. The number of RVs in rental fleets is a lot smaller than in the car fleets in relation to those who want to rent them, so the supply can be quite tight. The closer you get to your departure date, the more difficult it will be to rent the model and size you want.

Like renting a car for a trip, the RV rental agency may not be able to give you one with the exact options or the exact sleeping configuration you want, as usually only availability of a model is guaranteed, and that is really the important thing anyway. However, check with the smaller rental agency if you are going to rent from them, as they may be able to specify an exact vehicle. The larger, nationwide ones cannot.

Ask the agency if they will guarantee the class RV you want, too. This is very important and has fouled us up twice when we were given a Class "C" instead of a Class "A." As I have mentioned before, if you are going to parts of the country with big panoramas or high mountains, driving a Class "A" RV is extremely important. Having a Class "A" is also advantageous if there are more than two travelers, because anybody sitting behind the front seats can see out the front much better than in a Class "C." The cockpit area of a Class "C" is a step down from the living area, which inhibits forward visibility for anyone not seated in the cockpit. In addition, the cabover section in a Class "C" cuts down the height of the windshield by 6"-8" and sometimes even the driver may have to crane his or her neck to see a panorama—the line of sight is so dramatically reduced.

Try to make your reservations several months in advance, especially in the peak travel season. Football games, parents' weekends, fall foliage tours, and other specialized activities also make supply tight during certain times of the year. One of Philadelphia's major RV rental agents sells out a year in advance for Penn State football games! If there are no agencies or vehicles available where you want to begin your trip, try another city close by. This will mean having to adjust your route, but it will beat having to drive long distances in order to begin your vacation.

Much of what you will be doing with the agencies will be new to you, so don't be afraid to ask questions. Use the handy checklist in Appendix 6, Questions to Ask When Renting an RV, to make sure you have covered everything with the rental agencies.

After you have found a rental agency that suits you, make your reservation and get them to send you a confirmation, as well as information on their company, and what else they may require of you. When you get the material, look it over to see if you understand everything and have any questions. The reservation cost is generally $200-300, but some companies charge 25% of the basic rental figure, with a minimum of $250. This cost is applied toward your overall rental charge at the time you check in. Also, find out what the dealer's cancellation policy is, as this can be quite costly.

One consideration that should not be overlooked when you are making your travel plans is that most rental agencies are closed on Sundays and holidays. You will need to coordinate your pick-up and drop-off around this schedule. People are so used to being able to rent a car anytime, that this point can be easily overlooked.

After comparing the basic rental details, excess mileage charges, insurance coverage, and the availability of renting the convenience kits (if needed) with several companies, you will make your reservation and be ready for the next step—Organizing the Trip!

Chapter 5

Organizing The Trip

Before You Go & While You Are Away

We have tried to teach our children that "learning through experience" is part of the educational process and a necessary evil needed for adulthood. In preparing for an RV trip, however, I suggest you skip this tidbit of wisdom and learn from other people's ideas or mistakes. Finding yourself thousands of miles from home with a crisis on your hands that could have been avoided can easily ruin your vacation. Here are some tips that can help avert a crisis or just make traveling easier.

Money. Let's start with a very important item. Cash. Divide actual currency between the adults in your party so that in the event one wallet or pocketbook is lost or stolen, the other adult can come to the rescue, at least temporarily. Also, when sightseeing or shopping, the adults may split up and either one might need money. If any of the teenagers is financially responsible, give him or her a small amount of money to be used by you in case of emergency. An extra $10 or $20 could come in very handy if you need food or some other necessity. After you have picked up the RV, stop at a bank and buy a few rolls of quarters, which you will need for laundry, tolls, and vending machines. Keep enough cash on hand in case you break down and aren't able to use a credit card. Some repair facilities and shops do not accept credit cards, and in many rural areas, the telephone systems can't accommodate modems for credit card approval and automatic teller machines (ATMs). At the beginning of your trip, secrete emergency funds in your RV in case you need them. Just make sure everybody knows where the money is hidden!

Second, travelers' checks. Do the same as you did with the cash, but make sure each adult has checks made out in his or her name so that either one can get cash if need be. Just think of the situation if one adult got injured or very ill and was not able to sign checks and the another adult had no checks in his or her name. That could lead to a very trying situation during an emergency, so being properly prepared is vital.

American Express travelers' checks come in handy in these situations as they can be signed by two people and used by either.

Third, credit cards and money money access cards. It is very wise to have ample credit available on your credit cards. Most rental agencies, gas stations, restaurants, campgrounds, motels (should you need one during a layover for repairs) honor credit cards. They also provide an easy way to keep track of your expenses. Be sure to pay down (or off!) the balance on your credit cards at least ten days before you leave, so the checks have a chance to be processed and credited to your account before you need to use any one of them. Also, check to see if your credit cards will expire during your trip. On our last trip, one of our credit cards expired right after we left. That was slightly embarrassing when I tried to use it. Luckily, we had several others. Just imagine if it had been our only one and we were counting heavily on it to cover our trip expenses. Disaster! For safety, write down all your credit card numbers in Appendix 4, and the phone number of whom to call in case of loss. While you are checking things, check your driver's license expiration date, too. One last thing about credit cards—you can get cash advances on them, too. This, along with using ATMs to gain access to your bank accounts, is an easy way to manage your finances while on vacation.

With today's rapidly advancing technology, the use of automatic teller machines (ATM) has made getting access to your money at home much easier. There are several large networks, such as MAC, PLUS, CIRRUS, and others that allow you to get money from your bank account. Be forewarned, however, that the system you are hooked into may not be available in the area where you are going. Check with your bank before you leave, and if possible, get a booklet of the outlets in their system. The use of the ATMs will be very helpful if you are expecting dividends, paychecks or social security checks to arrive at home and somebody is able to deposit them for you. Make sure you leave a deposit slip with them!

Use the Cost Estimator in Appendix 1, and add at least 25% as a safety margin for the amount of cash and credit you have available. Souvenirs and "unforeseens" add up quickly, and as prices of food and gas can vary widely from your home town's prices, trying to pin down exact costs is nearly impossible.

Telephone Credit Card. In this day and age of hi-tech communications most people have a telephone credit card. If you don't, it is quite easy to get one from your telephone company. Make sure each adult has the number and is instructed on how to use it. Responsible teenagers should also be informed on its use, in case of emergency only. The card is especially useful when calling to check in at home, at the office, make reservations, or in an emergency.

Clean Out Wallet. There are certain credit cards and other items in your wallet or pocketbook that you won't need on vacation. Take these items out and store them in a safe place. You will be surprised at how much will be left home!

Accordion Carrying Case & Manila Folders. These handy items come in several sizes and styles and can be purchased at your local stationery store. I use the 8 1/2"x11" size case for storing documents and receipts, and the large 10"x15" size for travel and tourist information. For the latter, I like the carrying case with four or five dividers, one for each state. Make sure the case is durable, as you will be putting a lot of heavy material in it. For the 8 1/2"x11" size, I use manila folders for each subject, such as medical or RV rental information. This makes finding what you need a breeze and it won't get lost. Carrying cases with an elastic versus tie closure are easier to use.

Medical Consent Form. Today's lawsuit happy public has made the use of a medical consent form very important (See Appendix 3 for an example). This is especially critical if you are taking children who are not your own; this includes grandparents who have grandchildren traveling with them. Also, in some states, the divorced parent who does not have custody can have trouble getting medical treatment without approval from the custodial parent—which may be difficult for a lot of reasons. Some doctors and hospitals may be reluctant to treat a nonrelative without a consent form. It is also important to have that child's family physician's name and phone number, as well as a list of drugs that should not be administered. Take several copies in case one gets mislaid and put them in a manila folder in your accordion case for easy reference.

Medical Insurance. One area that can easily be overlooked is medical insurance. Make sure all adults carry medical insurance ID or Medicaid cards. Put copies of claim forms in a manila folder in the carrying case so they can be located easily. If you have non-family members with you, make sure they have put the medical insurance information on their medical consent form and given you copies of their claim forms.

Medical Records & Inoculations. If you have any special medical needs or problems and might need life saving medical attention while you are away, take copies of your medical records with you. Having complete medical records will expedite treatment. Keep this information with the rest of the medical documents. Make sure your shots, especially tetanus, are up to date. Several years ago I took my son, then about fifteen, to the doctor for boosters. I guess my son wanted to get back at me, because he asked the doctor to check my records. Sure enough—I needed a tetanus booster!

Prescriptions. There is nothing worse than becoming ill far from home and in many vacation spots, medical help may be hard to find. If you are on medication or might need it during your trip, be sure that your prescriptions won't expire while you are away. Get new ones filled out before you leave in case you run out or lose the medication, and put them with the other medical information. Carry this information with you in case your luggage gets lost. Write down in Appendix 4, Important Information, what medications you are taking and the prescription, just in case you lose those filled out by your physician. Also, find out the generic names of the drugs, as this may simplify filling the prescription, and save you money. Take along extra medication to last beyond the trip, as you don't want to run out if you get delayed somehow. Our daughter ran out of her thyroid medicine with a week to go on a recent cross-country bike trip and we had to Express Mail some to her. She had lost her backup supply. If you have the potential of having a life-threatening seizure or attack, be sure that the other adults in your party are aware of it and what medication to give—this could save your life!

Doctors. No matter how healthy you may be, it is wise to have your doctors' names and phone numbers written down for easy access. Use Appendix 5, In Case of Emergency, to record this information. It is very comforting to know you can reach your own doctor if the need arises. The doctor will have your complete medical history available at a moment's notice and can relay any pertinent information to the attending physician. Find out what blood type you are if you don't know it, and write it down in Appendix 4, Important Information.

Glasses and/or Contacts. I am "blind as a bat" so I am very aware of not going far from home without a second pair of glasses. In addition to a spare pair of regular glasses or contacts, take a pair of prescription sunglasses, too, if you wear them, as they will certainly come in handy, but don't use them as your backup. I had to use sunglasses as a backup on an extended European trip when my regular pair got bent, and it was awful. If I were to lose my only pair my trip would be ruined. As a precaution, put your glasses and/or contacts prescription in the back of this book in Important Information, Appendix 4. At least you could have a pair made in a few days. In fact, with today's technology, some opticians can make a pair in a few hours. People with contact lenses may be lucky if they can get replacements at a local optical store, or have a spare set sent by Express Mail as we did one time when our daughter went swimming with hers on! On her cross-country bike trip she used disposable ones with no problem. Don't forget the supplies for the contacts! Take a pair of Croakies (those wonderful glasses attachments that go around your neck) to hold your glasses on if you plan to do anything that could cause you to lose them, such as sailing or white water rafting.

In Case of Emergency... Although I always like to think positively, there may arise the need to call family or friends in case of an emergency. List in Appendix 5 the names, addresses and phone numbers of all parents, children, siblings, friends, veterinarian, lawyer, neighbors, and business associates who should be contacted if an emergency arises. Don't think you can rely on your memory, since your mind plays tricks with it when you are under stress.

Names and Addresses of Friends. Although this doesn't need much explanation, I want to stress the value of keeping in touch. People like to receive mail from traveling friends, so take their addresses along. A postcard and a few words will do. Share your enthusiasm and that may inspire them to take a trip. If you have a camcorder, tape a "letter" to your family or friends and show them some of the scenery your are enjoying. Use Appendix 2 to record this information.

Bills. I hate to mention the word, but bills are a fact of life. Nothing new. However, when planning your trip, especially one for a month or longer, make plans to pay them in advance or have someone pay them while you are away. Of special importance are your mortgage, credit card and other payments, that, if missed, can affect your credit rating. I still have to explain to potential creditors why I was late on a $20 payment three years ago (we had been away for a month and I missed a billing cycle by a few days.) Perhaps a friend or neighbor who is watching your house can be asked to pull out certain bills from your mail and pay them with checks you have pre-signed and made payable to your creditor.

Security at Home. As with any vacation, plan security for your house or apartment. Have your mail held at the post office, or have someone reliable pick it up every day; make arrangements to have plants watered and pets looked after or boarded; stop the newspapers. Set timers on several lights—turn on at dusk and off at various times during the evening. Empty the kitchen trash—you don't want to come home from a nice trip to the smell of weeks old rotting garbage!; remove any food from the refrigerator that may go bad. Turn down the thermostat, but if temperature is going to be below freezing, have a neighbor check the house daily. Have someone change shades and drapes periodically to give it that "lived in" appearance. Unplug electrical appliances, TVs, radios and computers; turn off the hot water heater; make sure all the doors and windows are locked and sliding glass doors are immobilized. Alert friends and neighbors that you will be away and leave a key with a trusted person so they can get in in case of emergency. Leave your itinerary, including phone numbers or contacts, with a friend or relative and check in periodically; leave family contact numbers with a neighbor. Notify the police or sheriff of the dates you will be away so they can check the house. If you have several cars, make arrangements with someone to move one around in the drive so that anyone casing the neighborhood will think somebody is home. Make sure arrangements are made for the lawn to get mowed (or snow shoveled). Put valuables in a safe-deposit box. A few precautions can save a lot of heartache. Many a vacation has been ruined by vandalism or theft, so taking precautions can at least set your mind at ease as you depart. Use the handy Before You Leave Home Checklist in Appendix 8 to make sure you have done everything.

Passports. If you are going to Canada, Mexico or other foreign countries, take your birth certificate or passport, and any proof of special immunizations that are required. Check all the passports to make sure they are current and won't expire while you are away. We had a near calamity over this issue just days before our son was to leave for a trip when we discovered that children's passports expire in five years instead of ten. After some rushing around and a few panic phone calls, we fortunately were able to get a passport, so it is wise to check passports many weeks before your planned departure. His trip was nearly ruined.

Insurance. While I have already mentioned medical insurance, check your life, auto, homeowner's, and any other type of policy you have to make sure that they are up to date and won't lapse while you are away. This may not be as critical if you are going to be gone a week or two, but may become a factor if you plan to be away longer. It would be a terrible tragedy to have a policy lapse and then need the coverage.

Send Trunk. After you have prepared your list of things to take with you, plan far enough ahead so that you can send a trunk of items, especially kitchen and other bulky or heavy articles. Send it to a relative or friend you will be seeing the first day or to the RV rental agency. Check with them first to make sure they can accommodate you. Also, check with UPS or another carrier to see how long it will take to get there—then add a week on top of that just to be safe. The cost of shipping a trunk should be about $15, and it is well worth it, as your alternative is to lug 60-70 pounds with you on the airplane. Put a set of labels in the trunk for the return shipment, too.

Things to Pack

As I have mentioned several times before, good organization is the key to a successful trip. So, after you have made your plans and reservations, the next step is to decide what you will need to pack. Most of the items should be taken with you, but some may be purchased when you are on the road. Unless taking items with you is a burden, it will make traveling more enjoyable if you don't have to spend vacation time hunting for that missing thingamabob in unfamiliar territory. Plan ahead!

Items below marked with an (*) will be explained in more detail at the end of the chapter. The phrase "necessity is the mother of invention" becomes very clear as the RVer seeks to solve problems on the road!

Trip Information

You will need to take all the information you gathered in the planning process. On our first trip I had several travel books that covered all fifty states. Along the way I purchased quite a few guidebooks that gave good local information, and altogether they became quite a lot to carry around. On the subsequent trips, I wised up and took only photocopies of the pages that pertained to the states we were going to visit, thus saving five or ten pounds of excess weight!

The following list summarizes the travel information you have gathered:

- ☐ campground directories
- ☐ maps
- ☐ RV rental information
- ☐ tourist information
- ☐ travel guidebooks—AAA, National Parks, Reader's Digest, etc.

Organize everything in the accordion carrying cases mentioned earlier. Have one pocket for general information, such as airline schedules and the RV rental documents, and one pocket for each state's travel information. Pack any books or directories separately, as they will be too bulky for the carrying case.

Clothing

Remember the cardinal rule of RVing—you are not in a fashion show!— so leave all the fancy duds at home and take practical clothing. It may be difficult to convince self-conscious teens of the fact that they won't feel naked without three changes of clothes per day, so sharpen up your sales skills. Limit the size luggage they can take and give them a plausible excuse, such as "there isn't much storage space in the RV," or "we can't carry that much on the airplane." Once you are on the road, they will quickly forget to worry about their clothes and how they look! Most campers are pretty laid back, so plan to dress accordingly. Space is limited, but most RVs have a sizeable closet for hanging clothes, and a number of compartments or drawers for folded ones. Just remember, keep it simple, and pack sparingly!

The type of clothing needed will vary with geographical area and the season, as well as special needs for any activity you may focus on, such as biking, hiking or fishing. Even if you expect the area to be hot, take some warm clothing, as many areas will have wide temperature swings between day and night. We have been at the Grand Canyon in August and had to wear warm clothes at night. Plan your wardrobe so that you can layer the clothes. This will give you much more flexibility and you won't have to take as many items. An extra pair of comfortable walking shoes is a **must** in case one gets wet. Take flip-flops, at least for the kids, to wear to the campground's showers.

Rain gear is also a must and we have found that ponchos are great. Not only do they pack well, but they can also be used as ground cloths if you or the kids want to sleep out under the stars in sleeping bags. The ground can be quite damp, so using a poncho/ground cloth will save having to dry out the sleeping bag in the morning. Anything that saves time and space will enhance your trip. Duck shoes are great for the rain, and will save you from having to dry sneakers.

Take clothes that are comfortable, easily washable, wrinkle free, won't show every spot, and can be worn, mix and match, with several outfits. This way you will get the best use from what you take. By packing wisely you will minimize what you have to carry with you—extra baggage or weight can be a real burden! I found that a pair of corduroy slacks and two pairs of shorts were all I needed for a month's trip. Jeans are great, too! I also had a pair of khakis that I wore on the plane, and used in case I needed another pair of long pants while the laundry was being done.

Each person in your party should have enough clothes to last them the same number of days as everyone else so that you can plan your wash schedule. Most campgrounds have laundry facilities, but you don't want to spend time doing laundry if you don't have to. Washing every five to six days worked out well for us, and if we ran short of something, we could wash it by hand in the RV. However, it is better to do laundry more often than to carry too many clothes!

Use the following checklist as a packing guide:

Clothes Packing Checklist

- ☐ Socks/stockings
- ☐ Underwear
- ☐ Pants/jeans/skirts/shorts
- ☐ Light shirts/blouses/tops
- ☐ Turtlenecks
- ☐ Belts
- ☐ Walking shoes/sneakers/sandals/duck shoes/hiking boots; (2 pairs per person!)
- ☐ Sweater/sweatshirts
- ☐ Wind breaker and heavy outer shirts/jacket
- ☐ Down vest (if it may get very cold)
- ☐ Ponchos/raincoats/umbrella
- ☐ Sleep wear
- ☐ Hats
- ☐ Bathing suits/masks/snorkels/goggles
- ☐ Flip-flops

Tool & First Aid Kits

We found that there are many useful items you normally wouldn't think of that can come in handy on your trip.

- [ ] first aid kit large enough for the number of people in your party*
- [ ] adjustable wrench*
- [ ] flashlight—preferably waterproof with a Halogen bulb for brightness
- [ ] fuses, assortment of 2,5,10,15,20,30,40 amp*
- [ ] pliers
- [ ] pocket knife or sheath knife
- [ ] two (2) medium sized screw drivers (1 Phillips)—a combination set with several heads is preferable
- [ ] converter*

Personal Items

- [ ] covered soap dish—one for each sex
- [ ] diary*
- [ ] spare glasses or contacts (and supplies) and sunglasses
- [ ] insect repellant & Bounce*
- [ ] jewelry (keep it simple!)
- [ ] passport and immunization records
- [ ] personal care items & medicines
- [ ] reading material—magazines, general reading, topical reading*
- [ ] shaving or makeup kits, including toothbrush, toothpaste, dental floss, etc.
- [ ] suntan lotion
- [ ] vitamins
- [ ] writing paper, envelopes, stamps (regular & post card) & pens
- [ ] names and addresses of friends (Appendix 2)

Kitchen Necessities

A complete list of items needed for the RV's galley can be found in Chapter 10, Food and Cooking, but the things listed here can be brought from home. If you choose to rent the "convenience kits" offered by the rental agencies you can fill in whatever else you may want to take from the lists in Chapter 10.

- ☐ medium or long wooden matches (store these in a jar) or a butane fire starter
- ☐ recipes and cookbook
- ☐ hibachi—unless you are leaving from home you can buy one on the road for $10-15. Some campsites have grills, but don't count on it. If you are really into barbecuing, plan to carry your own.
- ☐ good pair of all purpose scissors
- ☐ your favorite spices and herbs

Recreational Items

Unless the focus of your trip is on a recreational activity, such as biking, hiking, fishing, etc., take only the items listed below. Your recreational time will be limited to the evenings or short hikes to see scenery and these items will be a good way to keep the kids occupied.

- ☐ back or day pack*
- ☐ baseball & gloves, football, skis or other sporting equipment
- ☐ bikes—take these only if you are leaving from home and are going to do serious biking. They are not needed otherwise, and are much more trouble than they are worth!
- ☐ binoculars
- ☐ compass—if you are going to hike
- ☐ Croakies—to hold your glasses on
- ☐ Frisbee
- ☐ pedometer
- ☐ reference books—birds, geology, wildflowers, trees, critters, etc.
- ☐ specific items necessary for a particular activity you plan to do
- ☐ water bottle*

Bedding and Luggage

Unless you are going to be outfitted by the rental company, you will need to take blankets, sheets, pillows and pillowcases, towels and washcloths and sleeping bags with liners. When you reserve your vehicle, ask the agent what they can supply in the way of bedding and at what cost. If it is not too much trouble, taking your own is preferable as you will know what you are getting. Even if you do have the rental agent supply the bedding, take along a few extra towels, especially large ones that can be used for swimming. All towels that are taken should be the thin kind so they will dry faster. We packed bedding for five people into a large army duffel bag. The kids liked to use sleeping bags, so my wife made washable liners for them by sewing up sheets. Using sleeping bags makes breaking camp much easier and they can quickly be unrolled for day time naps.

Bedding Checklist

- ☐ pillow—1 each
- ☐ pillowcase—1 each
- ☐ blankets—2 each (light & heavy)
- ☐ sheets—1 sewn together or 2 each
- ☐ towels & washcloths—1 each
- ☐ sleeping bags—optional
- ☐ mattress pads—1 each if not using sleeping bags
- ☐ ground cloth—needed if you are going to sleep outdoors (poncho can double for this)

For our last trip, my wife made up a special multi-purpose bed-roll that was very functional:

She sewed together at the bottom:

1. mattress pad
2. heavy blanket
3. light blanket

They can be used in three different ways, depending on the temperature, with the sheet placed between the appropriate layers:

1. heavy on bottom, mattress pad in the middle, and light on top, or

2. light, mattress pad, heavy, or

3. pad, heavy, and light—if it is really hot, the light blanket can be pushed to the bottom & pulled up if needed

The sheet is made into a bag, with the bottom edge sewn, and both sides sewn part way. This makes for easy access.

Luggage

Although luggage is basically a utilitarian item, having the right kind on an RV trip is important. There are numerous storage compartments on the outside of the RV, and I strongly suggest that you take soft luggage which can easily be squeezed into them. You will find that hard luggage is very cumbersome. As I mentioned earlier, you can convince the kids not to take their whole bedroom if you tell them that space is limited and give them a duffel that is just the right size for them. You can make up a packing list of clothes and toys that will fit into that duffel. Practice while they are at school just to make sure!

As I have mentioned earlier, we have sent a trunk out so that we didn't have to carry as much with us. Check with the rental agency to see if they will store it for you while you are traveling.

Miscellaneous

- ☐ Airline/train tickets
- ☐ Calculator—good for mileage, expenses
- ☐ Camera, film & flash bulbs—wide angle disposable camera for panoramas (check the battery in your camera; there is nothing worse than trying to take a great shot and having the camera not work!).
- ☐ Chairs (lightweight outside folding ones)*
- ☐ Clothes hangers 2-3 per person
- ☐ Clothesline
- ☐ Clothespins (clip)—6 per person*
- ☐ Colored markers*
- ☐ Playing cards (and book of card games) and other small games
- ☐ Sewing kit including safety pins & scissors
- ☐ String
- ☐ Tablecloth (vinyl)
- ☐ Travel alarm clock (or watch with alarm)
- ☐ Whisk broom—for cleaning the floor of the RV
- ☐ Yellow tablet (5"x7")*
- ☐ List of what you have taken*

Helpful Hints

The need for some of the items mentioned above on a camping trip may seem odd to you, so I will explain further.

Adjustable wrench. On our first trip we had no tools at all, as I guess I expected them to be provided by the rental agency. With a little improvisation I was able to screw in the screws that came loose, but I could not adjust my side mirror that loosened up and flapped in the wind. This was critical to our safety, and I had to stop at gas stations and ask for help. You are probably thinking "You idiot, why didn't you go to a hardware store and buy a wrench?" That would be a logical question at home, but in the middle of nowhere that isn't a practical solution. Another time I did have a wrench and used it to adjust malfunctioning windshield wipers. An adjustable wrench will have many uses!

Back or day pack. If you are planning long hikes as part of your trip, you will need a backpack and other hiking gear. However, we found there were numerous opportunities to take extended walks where we might need water, snacks, suntan lotion, extra clothing, camera and the like, so it was easier to have a small day pack for this purpose. A fanny pack can also hold these items for at least one person, and is less cumbersome than a larger pack.

Clothespins (clip). You will find all kinds of uses for these handy little gadgets. They are really useful for drying towels (clip on to clothes hangers), drying clothes, or closing packages (chips, etc.), among other purposes.

Colored markers. These are not for the kids but for the adults! Take along two bright highlighters (I like yellow and pink) and one dark marking pen. You can mark the route you have traveled and special sites or towns visited. I used them every day in my trip planning to indicate towns, places of interest, and the proposed route, so that my map reader could be better informed. I also used them to highlight special points of interest in the guidebooks. Not only could the co-pilot follow my tour route, but she could find things quickly on the map. In addition, she could read about upcoming sites in the guidebooks and keep all of us informed. This made the trip much smoother and more enjoyable. By having the highlighted guidebooks handy, she was able to read about areas we were passing through, so we could learn about the geology, flora and fauna, or history of the area. The trip really came alive! Can you imagine saying to your fellow travelers after the fact, "remember that unusual rock formation we saw this morning? It was important because..." The impact of the moment has been lost and your trip will not be as exciting and informative.

Converter. If you are going to Europe or a country that uses 220-volt power, it will be necessary to take a converter so that you can uses 110-volt appliances.

Diary. Go to your local book store and buy a diary. You probably haven't kept one since you were a teenager, but this will be a wonderful memory jogger for years to come. On every trip I have taken I have always said to myself, "I will never forget what that was or where that photo was taken," but, lo and behold, I did—every time!—and without a diary for help, that special moment in time would have been forgotten shortly after I arrived home. Besides noting down the day's sightseeing, record sightings of birds, new wildflowers, critters, or other things that interest you. Having this information will be useful later for discussion or identifying photos.

For the children, get a drawing tablet so they can record their impressions for posterity. If they are old enough for creative writing, get a diary or spiral notebook, too, and get them to write about their daily experiences. What they write doesn't have to be long, but just the act of writing will not only reinforce the day's trip, it will also improve their writing skills. It will also be hilarious to read three decades later! In addition, writing will give them something to do to break up the day, which is especially important if it is rainy or you are driving a long distance. You will be amazed at the different impressions of the same thing each one has! If you can't find a suitable diary at the bookstore, photocopy the sample diary page in Appendix 10 or order the *King of the Road Diary and Trip Planner* by using the form at the back of this book. The diary and trip planner was custom-designed for the RV traveler and will make a nice permanent repository for all your memories. And it has handy pockets to organize all those little expense slips that always seem to get lost.

First aid kit. As the Boy Scouts say "be prepared." This is certainly true on a trip where you will probably be far from medical help and may need immediate attention. Having a well-stocked first aid kit with you will really come in handy if you need it. You can either buy a small kit at the pharmacy, order one from a company that makes them for outdoors people (see Appendix 13, RVer's Resource Guide), or make one up from your own supplies. The last is cheaper, and if you have some sort of carrying case, is preferable, as it will be more complete. Take along a small first aid book if you have one in your medicine cabinet. If you buy a kit, you can customize it by adding your personal medications and items from our list. Use the following checklist as a guide:

- ☐ a variety of bandaids
- ☐ gauze roll and pads
- ☐ adhesive tape
- ☐ antiseptic
- ☐ cotton balls or swabs
- ☐ antibiotic ointment
- ☐ anti-itch cream
- ☐ aspirin/acetaminophen (Tylenol)/ibuprofen
- ☐ antihistamines (Benadryl)
- ☐ decongestants
- ☐ bee sting kit
- ☐ tweezers, scissors, needle and safety pins
- ☐ thermometer
- ☐ personal medicines and healthcare products—anything you use regularly or might use in case of emergency: allergy, thyroid, high blood pressure, diarrhea, motion sickness, antacid tablets, laxatives, vitamins, sleeping pills, etc.
- ☐ sunblock(waterproof)—SPF of at least 15
- ☐ moisturizer—good for sunburns

You might be far from any pharmacy, so it is a good idea to be prepared for anything. See Chapter 14, for some first aid tips.

Fuses. Buy a small box of assorted 2, 5, 10, 15, 20, 30, 40 amp automotive fuses. This is an item very easily overlooked, but if you blow one on the road, it may well become the most important 3/4 inch item in the world! A fuse can blow from old age, an overload, or a short.

Insect repellant. Although it should be obvious to take insect repellant, we have found a remedy to get rid of yellow jackets that may come in handy: buy regular scent Bounce fabric softener and place a sheet or two around the picnic table or rub it on your clothes. My wife carries a sheet in her pocketbook, and it has come in handy many times. For some reason yellow jackets don't like the smell. Another consumer product that has unexpected uses is Avon's Skin-So-Soft bath oil. Many outdoors people claim it keeps bugs away when they apply it to their skin.

List of what you have taken. Just as important as having an inventory of your possessions at home is having a list of what you have taken on the trip. In addition to the need for an inventory in case of theft is the need to know what you have in case your suitcases or trunks don't make it to your place of departure. The lists are also useful when you are packing to return home.

On our second trip, we sent a trunk with all our kitchen equipment to my brother-in-law's in Boulder, Colorado. It was exactly the same trunk and contents we had used two years previously, and I had weighed it again at home. Unfortunately for us, the UPS driver could not find my brother-in-law's cabin (we learned that the trunk had actually made it to within 100 feet of the cabin!), so returned the trunk to his depot, where some overly officious worker decided to weigh it. Why now? It was overweight according to their scale, so they sent it back to Philadelphia. The carrier thoughtfully refunded the freight charge, but we were stuck without supplies needed for a ten day vaction! So, if you ship a trunk, watch the weight!

Luckily for us, we had made several lists and knew what was missing. Between items we picked up at the grocery store and those borrowed from my brother-in-law, we were completely outfitted by the time we were ready to start our trip. However, it did cost us money and would have been very expensive if we hadn't been able to borrow. Without the lists it would have been much more difficult to reconstruct what we needed, and they really saved us a lot of valuable time, too. Can you imagine preparing your first meal far from civilization and not having the veggie peeler? Horrors!

Outside chairs. We didn't need outside chairs because we were "on tour," i.e., driving and sightseeing during the day, and eating, travel planning and reading in the RV at night. Many of the campgrounds have picnic tables, so we used them to eat "out" to break up the routine. However, if your vacation is geared around socializing with neighbors, sunning, fishing, or just relaxing and "hanging out," then these are a good idea. Take them with you if you are leaving from close to home, or buy cheap ones at a hardware store on the road. Some rental companies will now provide them for an extra charge. They will get in the way, so be prepared to tie them onto the roof or put them in the storage compartments.

Reading & reference material. You will have time to read and relax, so take along some interesting books, preferably paperback, including reference books on your areas of interest, such as birds, wildflowers, geology, critters, etc. Having this reference material will greatly enhance your travel experience, as you will be able to learn firsthand about what you are reading. Seeing unusual animals, being able to identify them and finding out how they live is really fascinating.

When you are in an interesting place, see if there are local books that will give you more of the history of the area. On our trips out West we like to pick up books about the golden age of mining towns, desperados, wagon train stories, or women of the wild West. We started to relive the history of the area as we traveled through it, and our trip took on a completely different complexion. Several times we drove over high mountain passes knowing that a hundred years before a band of brave pioneers had done the same thing—without roads! At one place, called Hole-in-the-Rock, near Bluff, Utah, the pioneers had to lower their wagons one thousand feet over a cliff with ropes. We had picked up a copy of *Incredible Passage*, by Lee Reay, which recounted this story, and read it just as we were passing near Bluff. Seeing the area and reading the book really made us appreciate our life today!

Water bottle. This is a very handy thing to have along if you plan to take hikes or have kids who always need something to drink. On our trips out West we have often taken long hikes to see some scenic wonder, and found having water with us a necessity. Even if there are sparkling streams nearby, don't drink from them as they may be contaminated by a parasite called *Giardia* that is transmitted by animal and human waste. The result is a very unpleasant dysentery-like stomach ailment.

Yellow tablet. There are several important uses for this tablet. First, use it for your shopping lists. We found the 5"x7" a handy size, because it fit easily in the glove compartment or door pocket, and was readily accessible to the co-pilot. It is also useful for notes on what you have seen that will later be recorded in more detail in your diary. Lastly, and something we discovered after several trips, was its usefulness in plotting the day's course, including routes to be taken, towns, sightseeing places, and campground information.

Chapter 6

Campground & RV Club Information

There are literally thousands of campgrounds to choose from in every corner of North America and in Europe. They have a wide variety of sites and amenities to satisfy every camper, from the one who wants the rustic experience to the one who wants everything a fancy resort has to offer. To fully enjoy your vacation you will want to be able to find the campgrounds that meet your recreational needs. On our trips we didn't care very much about the amenities as we did all our activities on the road, but we wanted quiet sites with as much natural beauty as possible. However, if you are an angler, hiker, boater or are seeking fancy amenities, you will need to pay attention to what the campground has to offer. This chapter will describe the types of campgrounds and where to get information about them.

As you develop more interest in the RVing lifestyle, you will want to join one of the many RV clubs that offer social activities, trips, and information through their publications.

Types of Campgrounds

There are four different types of campgrounds, and you should become familiar with the differences.

Privately owned campgrounds and RV parks. These campgrounds are open to the public, but are classified as "privately owned" or "commercial" to differentiate them from "public campgrounds" that are on government land and run by a government agency. There are over 8,500 of this type across the country, and if you are touring in an RV, they are the most common and will be the ones to look for. Read the descriptive information in the campground directories, as these campgrounds can run the gamut from rustic to full-blown luxury resorts. Most of them will have a complete complement of facilities so you won't have to rough it, but can enjoy the outdoor life and the camping experience and still have the comforts of home. Typical facilities include playgrounds, game rooms, pools, laundries, showers, camp stores, picnic tables and BBQ grills, and other recreational opportunities such as boating, fishing, hiking, horseshoes, horseback riding and nature trails. Some of the larger ones will have planned activities for all ages, including hayrides, movies, theme weekends, arts and crafts, bingo, and pot luck suppers.

RV resort parks. These parks provide RVers the first class facilities and amenities that are traditionally associated with luxury hotels or resorts. With their extensive recreational facilities, they are geared for families and others who want longer stays, not the overnight touring camper. Often these resort parks are the vacation destination. There may be such additional amenities as golf, tennis, hot tubs, saunas, health club, restaurant, telephone and cable television hookups, indoor pavilion and a variety of planned activities—all at a fraction of the cost at a conventional luxury resort. Parks on the water may have a marina and boating related facilities. Some resort parks offer RV pads for sale as condominiums, which can be rented when their owners are not present. They also have sites that can be rented on a daily, weekly or monthly basis. Often these resort parks are near destination locations and have become favorite vacation spots for "snowbirds."

Membership and ownership camping resorts. As the name implies, these resorts cater to owners or members of various affiliated camping and RV resorts or associations and offer more luxury amenities and recreational facilities than most of the privately owned campgrounds. As this type is generally not available to nonmembers or owners, I will not discuss it in much more detail. However, as your interest in RVing grows, and as you start having more free time, they are a very nice alternative to owning a second home.

Generally, you become a member of the national network by buying a condo or a time share in a "home resort." Once you have become a member, you can stay at any affiliated resort for a very nominal charge. As a member, you can become a "snowbird" and change residences with the seasons, take mini-weekend vacations at a variety of resorts, or anything in between. Some resort chains limit the length of your stay to a week at a time, so check their policies before you buy. Information on the membership resort chains can be found in Appendix 13, the RVer's Resource Guide.

State, local and national parklands. Various governmental agencies own millions of acres of some of the most scenic land in the country, and it is available to the public for camping at little or no charge. These public lands are made up of National Parks, National Forests, wildlife refuges, recreation sites, state and local parks, and other government held land managed by a multitude of governmental agencies. People who don't live in the 12 western states which contain much of this land can't possibly realize the magnitude of the government's holdings. The Bureau of Land Management's (BLM) holdings, for instance, are about equal to one-eighth of the total land in the country!

There are over 8,000 campgrounds on this land, known as "public campgrounds," offering a more rugged camping experience than commercial ones. When it comes to outdoor recreation, public land can provide almost any activity you can imagine—and amid some of the most spectacular scenery in the country! Settings on public lands include desert, mountain ranges, alpine tundra, evergreen forests, miles of sagebrush, rivers, streams and red rock canyons, and offer a wide diversity of recreational opportunities.

Whether you want to go boating, hiking, backpacking, horseback riding, hunting, fishing, mountain biking, bird watching, rock climbing, white water rafting, spelunking, see historic or prehistoric cultural sites, or just observe nature and take photographs, check out the opportunities on public land. Some Federal and state recreation areas require special permits for backpacking and boating, so if you plan these activities, check with the individual park.

This public land is usually for the rustic camping experience and is generally more appropriate for tenting, 4WD vehicles and smaller RVs, as access roads may be impassable for larger vehicles. The National Parks we have been to, however, accommodated all size RVs. Before you go to a park, check with the ranger to see if it can accommodate your size RV and what hookups, if any, are available.

The Bureau of Land Management (BLM), created in 1946, is part of the Department of the Interior, and manages over 270 million acres, ranging from deserts to lush forests and wind swept tundra, and from ancient Indian ruins to historic ghost towns. Included in this land are 2,000 miles of the Wild and Scenic River System, 2,200 miles of National Trails, nearly 6,000 miles of general hiking trails, 85,000 miles of streams, 4 million acres of lakes and reservoirs, over 470 developed recreation and camping sites, and 150,000 cultural properties, including 350 listed in the National Register of Historic Places. Write for a copy of their "Recreation Guide to Public Lands:" BLM Public Affairs, 1849 C Street NW, Room 5600, Washington, DC 20240.

The Forest Service (USFS), which falls under the jurisdiction of the United States Department of Agriculture, has over 4,000 campgrounds in its 156 National Forests. The land is managed as a multiple-use resource for sustained yields of water, forage, wildlife, and wood, as well as for recreation. These forests total more than 191 million acres, which is about the size of California, Oregon and Washington put together, and have 100,000 miles of trails, 10,000 recreation sites, 83,000 miles of streams and rivers, 1.8 million acres of lakes and thousands of miles of scenic byways. So you can see, they are geared for your recreational enjoyment! For a list of the National Forests, including phone numbers for each forest, write to their national headquarters: USDA Forest Service, Office of Information, PO Box 96090, Washington, DC 20090, and ask for brochure FS-418.

The National Park Service (NPS) manages 71 million acres in 49 states, and many of their 368 locations have campgrounds and a wide variety of recreational opportunities. Contact their Office of Public Inquiries, PO Box 37127, Washington, DC 20013-7127, (202) 208-4747 for information on various parks. These campgrounds fill up early during vacation season, so it is wise to make reservations, or get to the park early and register, then go sightsee.

The Army Corps of Engineers, the nation's largest provider of water recreation, manages over 450 lakes and 11 million acres of land and water in 43 states and has over 53,000 campsites available. Their facilities offer camping, fishing, hunting, hiking, cross-country biking, bird watching, and many other outdoor activities. Most sites have marinas or boat launching facilities. They have recently published ten regional brochures with maps describing the recreational facilities at their sites. To request these brochures, write them: US Army Corps of Engineers, Regional Brochures, CEWES-IM-MV-N, 3909 Halls Ferry Road, Vicksburg, MS 39180-6199.

There are also many state and local parks that have camping and recreational facilities. You may not have to go far from home to enjoy the great outdoors! Contact your state travel information center for a list of these facilities, or look in one of the outdoor recreation directories mentioned earlier.

So, if you are into outdoor recreation or just exploring, by all means gather information on the availability of campsites on public lands. There are thousands of campgrounds available to accommodate you, but in the vacation season it may be necessary to make reservations, if they take them. You may only have to make them a day or so in advance, not for your whole trip. If you are in doubt, call the park. Facilities will be much more primitive than in private campgrounds, so you may well have to be self-contained. See Appendix 13, RVer's Resource Guide, for how to get more information on these campgrounds.

Campground Directories

To find a campground that suits your travel needs, one of the most valuable resources you can take on your trip is a good campground directory. It will provide you with comparative information on the thousands of campgrounds across the country or abroad. I suggest you get one before you leave home, become familiar with how to read the listings, and discover the variety of campgrounds where you are planning to travel. A successful first night spent on the road is important in getting the trip off to a good start, so before you leave home, you should try to have an idea of where you will be that night. You will already have planned the general direction of your tour, so look in the directory to see what campgrounds are available where you plan to spend the first night, and make a reservation. Ordering information for the directories listed below is in Appendix 13, the RVer's Resource Guide.

United States

There are three well-established national directories I have used that have done a thorough job of researching the more than 18,000 campgrounds and RV service centers in the United States, Canada and Mexico and list the ones that meet their quality standards. Woodall's *Campground Directory*, which has a national edition as well as Eastern and Western editions, Trailer Life's *Campground & RV Services Directory*, and Wheelers *RV Resort & Campground Guide* have thousands of campground and RV service center listings. They may be available at the library, purchased through your local bookstore, or directly from the company.

On a regional basis, *Anderson's Campground Directory* is excellent if you are planning to camp in the ten states it covers from Pennsylvania to Florida. The directory has maps for each state, with each campground located by a reference number. It also lists each campground's activities in detail, tells what there is to do nearby, and contains a brief comment describing the campground.

AAA has a series of CampBooks covering the continental United States, Canada and Europe which provide detailed listings of private campgrounds that meet their standards, as well as listings for many state operated parks and recreation areas. Go to your local AAA office for a copy.

KOA (Kampgrounds of America) puts out an excellent directory of its own campgrounds, including a state-by-state atlas showing their locations. This directory, called *KOA Directory, Road Atlas and Camping Guide*, is free at any KOA, or may be ordered directly from KOA headquarters.

There are two directories I have found that list thousands of free or nearly free campgrounds. Many of these free campgrounds are located in local, state or National Parks or other public lands, and often the settings are spectacular. Services and amenities may be more primitive, however. Information on Don Wright's *Guide to Free Campgrounds* and the *American P.C. Campground Directory* can be found in Appendix 13, the RVer's Resource Guide.

If you are traveling in just one state, write to the state tourism bureau for information on camping as well as their travel information kit. Many states have campground associations that will send you a directory for free or at a nominal charge, or it may be included in the travel kit. The Recreation Vehicle Industry Association (RVIA) will send you a list of state campground associations with their information packet. All European tourist offices will provide free camping information on their respective country, too. To contact the tourist bureaus, see Appendix 9, Tourist Information Centers.

Europe

For European travel, get a copy of the *Europa Camping + Caravaning International Guide*, known as ECC, which lists more than 5,500 campgrounds in Europe, the Near East and North Africa. Campground entries are in German, French and English, and give detailed information about the services and amenities offered. There is even a "help" phrase section in seven languages. I would suggest getting a copy well in advance of your trip so you can become more familiar with foreign travel, camping, VAT taxes, ferry schedules and driving regulations. For ordering information, see the Resource Guide.

The British Automobile Association puts out a directory called *AA Camping and Caravanning in Britain* that is available in the United States from the British Travel Bookstore in New York.

Probably the best European campground directory is the *Camping Fuhrer* put out by the German Automobile Club (ADAC). It is in German; however, the key information is represented by symbols and with a pocket dictionary, you should have no trouble figuring it out. You can buy a copy in a German bookstore or at ADAC offices.

Canada

Picking a campground directory for Canada is more difficult than for the United States. The *Camping Canada Campground Directory* lists over 4,000 campgrounds, which is by far the best coverage of any directory. However, it doesn't provide as much detailed information as the three major American directories do. The Woodall and Trailer Life directories provide more information about the campground, especially the hookups, size RV allowed, and recreation, but have far fewer listings than the Wheelers directory, which has most of the basic information needed. So, depending on how long a trip you will be taking in Canada, I would suggest getting the *Camping Canada Campground Directory* and one of the other three American ones. If the campground is listed in the Canadian directory, but not an American one, be sure to call ahead to see what facilities they have and if they can accommodate the size RV you have.

Understanding the Listings

These directories have all the information you will need about any given campground. To find a campground, turn to the state or province you are going to be in, then look up the town where you want to stay. If there is a campground there, the directory will give you a complete rundown on it. If there is no campground, look at your map and find another town close by. In addition to the campground listings for a particular town, the Woodall and Trailer Life directories have listings for nearby RV service centers and sightseeing and recreational opportunities.

The following is a sampling of the information provided about each campground in the directories:

- type of ownership, i.e., private (but open to the public), or public (run by a state, local or federal agency)
- description of the setting, e.g., grassy flatlands, wooded hills, near a town, etc.
- dates campground is open
- directions on how to get there
- description of sites: number of spaces, pull-thrus, maximum size RV, availability of hookups and types of electricity, maximum length of stay
- restrictions: pets, children, boats, etc.
- description of their facilities: restrooms & showers, BBQ grills, picnic tables, dump station, propane, groceries & RV supplies, ice, security, pay phone, laundry, cable TV, etc.
- description of recreational amenities on the premises: horseshoes, playground, swimming, fishing, boating, rec room, lake, planned activities, arranged tours, etc.
- cost and what credit cards are accepted
- phone number & if they take reservations
- town locator code so you can find it on their state map

The directories also have other sections that will be useful in your trip planning. Trailer Life's directory, for instance, has colorful individual state maps showing campgrounds and service centers, RV troubleshooting charts, turnpike and tollway information, bridge, tunnel and ferry regulations, rules of the road and towing laws, state-by-state calendar of events, list of state tourism agencies, a table showing each state's fishing fees, and a list of camping facilities catering to active and retired military personnel. This last feature is very nice, as there are a lot of military RVers. However, since there are special rules, regulations and other travel considerations when traveling to Mexico or Canada, the lack of a section covering these is a drawback.

Woodall's, on the other hand, has very informative sections for going to Mexico or Canada, as well as several pages of information on each state, including climate, travel information sources, fishing/hunting license fees, a description of some of the most popular attractions, and a listing of major annual events. Information on special driving laws and rules of the road, turnpike and tollway information, and bridge, ferry and tunnel regulations are also included.

The Wheelers directory doesn't list fees, the rationale being that the base fee structure and the charges for the number of people and hookups varies so much from campground to campground that it makes it difficult to pinpoint the total fee range. This directory is nice because its listings of campsites on public land and the type of RV park are easily identifiable with their coding system. Another unique feature of this directory is a central toll-free number for reservations at all of its advertisers.

The KOA directory has excellent state maps with numbered circles indicating their sites, a description of the facility with a small map showing you how to get there, and a detailed chart indicating the amenities at each campground, including a breakdown of the charges for hookups. By finding the numbered circle for the town you want on the state map, you can quickly locate the information under the campground listings. This is a very nice feature, although the directory has a major shortcoming by not describing the campground's setting, the number of sites, and the size RV it can accommodate.

The Woodall's, Trailer Life, Wheelers and ECC directories have various rating systems for each campground and whether it is affiliated with the KOA, Good Sam, Best Holiday Trav-L-Park, or Yogi Bear's Jellystone Park Camp-Resorts. These affiliations are important because some campgrounds give discounts to club members. Each of the major directories has extensive ads for campgrounds, service centers, and recreational areas that give additional information necessary to have a successful trip, but if you are going to be concentrating on either eastern or western states and flying to your RV rental agency, you might want to consider a Woodall's regional edition, as it is much, much lighter.

RV Clubs

Just like for any other activity, hobby or sport, there is an RV club for people with similar interests. There are brand name clubs for owners of specific types of RVs, clubs for women RVers, singles, campground chains, active or retired military, and clubs for all types of RVers. For contact information, see Appendix 13, the RVer's Resource Guide.

All of these clubs hold rallies and conventions on local, state, national, and in some cases, international levels, and they also have caravans and campouts. Social activities for all ages include supervised playtime for kids, teen activities, functions geared for retirees, potluck meals, square dancing, craft fairs and other forms of entertainment. Camping clubs are truly family oriented! They also offer travel services such as mail forwarding, and can provide general camping information through their newsletters and magazines. Club members can build a network of friends at campgrounds across the country when they display their club's emblem on their RV.

The Good Sam Club is probably the largest camping/RV club in the world, with over 850,000 members and a wide array of benefits. As mentioned earlier, campgrounds, service centers, and recreational facilities that are affiliated with (not owned by) the Good Sam Club give members a discount which can quickly pay for the nominal membership fee. Just present your membership card before making a transaction.

They also have numerous other services for members: a full service travel agency, trip routing service, emergency road service plan, life/health and vehicle insurance, RV/auto financing, and a mail forwarding and travel message center; in addition, they offer caravans and rallies, a comprehensive campground/RV services directory, *Trailer Life* and *MotorHome* RV magazines by subscription, *Highways*, a monthly magazine for members crammed with tips, ideas and a calendar of events, and many other services. The club, with more than 2,000 local chapters, is for full-timers as well as first-timers, so you can utilize whatever services you need.

For membership information, call: 800-234-3450, or you can sign up at any Good Sam affiliated campground or service center.

Campground Chains

There are several national nonmembership campground chains that provide a variety of services to campers. They have a reservation system and a directory of their affiliated parks, but one of the most important aspects of a chain is that you can depend on the quality of each park. One bad park will taint the chain's reputation, so they go through a rigorous yearly inspection. The parks are usually located near major attractions and have a wider array of amenities than some of the independent parks. Contact information on the chains can be found in Appendix 13, the RVer's Resource Guide.

Best Holiday Trav-L-Parks is a group of over 75 campgrounds run by an association. To be a member, a park has to be well rated by Trailer Life, Wheelers, and Woodall's, and they are generally located near a major city, beach, landmark or tourist attraction.

Founded in 1962, KOA (Kampgrounds of America) is an international system of franchised family campgrounds with over 600 locations throughout North America. Most locations have a wide array of amenities, some even have saunas, tennis, golf, hot tubs and restaurants. In addition to the regular tenting and RV sites, more than half of their facilities have Kamping Kabins for rent for those who don't have an RV or don't want to pitch a tent. By purchasing a KOA Value Kard at any of their locations you will receive a 10% discount on camping fees for two years. You may order the card in advance by sending your name and address and $6.00 to: KOA Value Kard, P.O. Box 31734, Dept. D, Billings, MT 59107-1734.

Yogi Bear's Jellystone Park Camp-Resorts is a network of approximately 70 franchised campgrounds located mainly east of the Mississippi, with a few locations in Ontario, Canada. Their amenities and recreational facilities are geared toward the whole family, and the company reports that visitors usually stay several days. Most of the resorts have pools, playgrounds, video theater, retail store, laundry, miniature golf, snack bar and game room.

Unless you are planning to go to one campground for a lengthy stay, you will find most campgrounds will meet your basic overnight needs. For a lengthy stay, especially with kids in tow, get brochures and do your research ahead of time, as you will want to make sure the campground has plenty of family activities and sightseeing opportunities nearby. When you are on a tour, however, you will be moving to a different campground every day or two, so if one campground doesn't meet your expectations, the next one probably will.

Chapter 7

Picking Up Your RV – Getting Started

What to Do When Picking Up the RV

If you are flying to a distant city or country to begin your RV trip, make arrangements with the rental company to pick you up at the airport. If they can't or won't meet you, make sure you have their address handy so that you can give it to the taxi driver. Sometimes they will pick up the taxi fare, so don't hesitate to ask.

Go Over the Rental Agreement

Renting an RV is hardly more complicated than renting a car. The rental agreement will have all the terms and conditions that are standard in vehicle renting, such as insurance, who is authorized to drive the RV, damage, use of the RV, limits of liability, theft, payment, etc. Just as in renting an auto, the rental company will fill in the present mileage, mileage rate, free miles, all the insurance and driver information, and the rental charges. Make sure your initial rental deposit is properly credited on this contract. Most rentals are based on calendar days, not 24 hour time periods, so make a note of the date and time of return called for in the agreement. I made the mistake of miscalculating the days on our last trip—I went from Saturday to Saturday and got charged for fifteen days instead of the two weeks (fourteen days) I had planned on. Other vacationers are depending on you to return the vehicle on time, so the return date/time is very important, and there is usually a penalty for each hour you are late. The rental company will have to spend considerable time getting the RV ready for the next renter; it is not just "gas and go."

On our trips, we were required to prepay the full amount of the rental, including estimated mileage charges, plus a $500 security deposit. A refundable security deposit will be charged if you decline

Personal Accident Insurance (PAI), Vacation Interruption Protection (VIP), or Collision/Comprehensive Damage Waiver (CDW) options, and may be charged even if you take these options. Make sure the options are explained to you in detail, as having them may cost you $10 or more per day. Not accepting them will increase your front end costs dramatically because of the security deposit, and may increase your liability, so plan ahead and make sure to figure this short-term expense into your budget. With VIP coverage and credit card payment, the rental company may reduce the amount of the security deposit substantially.

Insurance

The various forms of insurance need to be explained in more detail as they can be quite confusing, and costly, too! To summarize, you will need to know:

- what the basic insurance coverage is
- what the deductible limits are
- what options you can buy to reduce the deductible limits and your potential liability

Rental companies generally provide basic insurance covering bodily injury, property damage, uninsured motorist, no-fault, fire and theft, and medical payments. They will also have collision and comprehensive, usually with a deductible of $2/2,500. This deductible is your responsibility unless you purchase the Collision/Comprehensive Damage Waiver (CDW) from them, which then brings the deductible down to the $300 range. The larger rental companies are now including the CDW in their basic rental rate, but check to be safe.

Vacation Interruption Protection (VIP), which further reduces the renter's collision damage exposure and covers expenses in the event of a mechanical breakdown requiring the vehicle to be in repair for more than twelve hours, is offered at an additional fee. This coverage, which ranges from $6-8 per day, will also cover some food, lodging, transportation and medical expenses during the breakdown.

None of the above insurance options covers damage from unauthorized or off-road use, including campgrounds, damage to the wheels, tires, undercarriage, or damage caused by striking overhead objects, such as tree branches, tunnels, gas station canopies, etc. Have the agent explain the various coverages to you and make sure you fully understand your liability. The options can add a lot to the cost of your trip, but an accident would put quite a dent in your wallet—as well as the RV!

Before you leave home, check with your auto insurance agent to see if your policy covers rental RVs. In the past some policies did, but the insurance industry is constantly changing. If it does provide coverage, take a copy of the policy with you and your agent's name and phone number. If you plan to pick up the RV on a weekend, notify the rental agency ahead of time so they can get any endorsements needed from the insurance agent before you come.

Other Charges

If you need convenience kits, they may run $25-50 per person for the trip. The last cost you can expect is a prep fee that may run $50-100 for getting the unit ready, and also includes a full tank of propane and the necessary toilet chemicals. This fee may include picking you up at the airport.

Payment should be made with a credit card, traveler's checks, cash or a certified check made out to the rental company, since they probably will not take a personal check. Many of the rental companies will also require a major credit card for credit and identification verification purposes, along with a valid driver's license.

Inspect the RV

The rental agent will walk around the RV with you to examine it for any damage and will mark anything found on a chart. Keep your eye out for dents, scrapes, cracks or dings on the windshield and broken light lenses and make sure they are noted on the chart. Get a copy of this chart in case there is a dispute, as you will be responsible for anything on the vehicle that is not marked down.

Learn How the RV Operates

The next step is to have the agent go over the operation of the RV and its equipment with all the adults in your party, even if they are not planning to drive. Due to some unforeseen mishap, one of them may be called upon to drive, and it is always good to have several people know how to operate the equipment. You may think you are paying attention to everything, but later when you have a fourteen year old tell you how to light the pilot, you suddenly realize you weren't! There is a lot to learn and much of the equipment will be new to you, so don't be bashful about asking questions. Take notes if you have a bad memory, and if you have a video camera (and the RV has a VCR!), record what the agent is showing you. Some of the agencies will give you a brief road test, and I strongly suggest you do this if it isn't mandatory. You will quickly learn the basics of driving an RV. Allow about an hour for this RV orientation.

Some of the items the agent should cover are:

Exterior:

- how the propane system works
- how to light the propane hot water tank
- how to empty the holding tanks or porta-potty
- how to fill the water tanks—city & gravity
- how to use the electrical hookup
- what to look for under the hood
- where the spare tire and jack are and how to use them
- how to load and lock the storage compartments
- how the exterior step works

Interior:

- how to use the water pump
- how the batteries operate
- how to operate the toilet
- how to operate the A/C and generator
- how to operate the furnace
- how to operate the refrigerator
- how to use the various monitor panel gauges
- operation of smoke, LP-gas & CO alarms
- location of emergency exits and fire extinguisher
- location of fuses and circuit breakers

General Questions to Ask:

- what the fuel capacity is
- what type of gas to use & what mileage to expect
- what the GVWR (Gross Vehicle Weight Rating) is and what it means
- what the height & length are
- general driving tips for this particular rig
- what the cost of operating the generator is
- how repairs are to be handled

Operating all the RV's equipment is covered in more detail in Chapter 9, Know Your RV, but it is always wise to get a thorough lesson on your actual vehicle. Make sure you know what the fuel capacity is and find out from the agent approximately what gas mileage you might expect. You will learn this very quickly as you travel, but it is a good idea to know ahead of time. Ask the agent what the height is, and mark it down on a piece of paper and stick it on the dashboard or other convenient place. Both the pilot and co-pilot should know it, so repeat it to each other several times. Car drivers are never concerned with height, but RVers have to be. Also, find out from the agent what the safe maximum driving speed is.

There is a separate charge for using the generator, usually $1-2 per hour, or $5 a day for the whole trip. On our trips out West in the summer we didn't use the generator much at all, so I would recommend paying for the hours of metered usage.

Before You Leave, Ask the Agent...

Don't forget to ask the agent how to handle repairs, breakdowns and accidents. Usually you will receive discretion for repairs up to a set amount, say $50, and be requested to get authorization for larger amounts. Save all your receipts for reimbursement. Most rental companies are tied into a network of authorized RV service centers that will help you in case of a breakdown or accident. The national rental companies will probably have an 800 phone number that you can use to call them if trouble arises and they will help you find the nearest repair facility. Make sure their 800 number is written down in your leasing package. In addition, many of the travel guides described earlier have sections on RV service facilities in case the rental company doesn't have an affiliate close by.

Before you leave the rental agency, ask them in what condition they expect the RV to be returned. Of course, it should be clean, and they will want the propane and gas tanks filled and the waste tanks emptied. Usually you can empty the waste tanks at your last campsite, but if you didn't have a sewer hookup or used the facilities later, they need to be emptied. This can be done at a "dump station," which is a sewer inlet accessible to any RVer for the purpose of emptying waste tanks. They may be found at some campgrounds, truck stops, and certain municipalities have public dump stations.

Also, the agency may be able to provide you with a local map so you can easily find them and the nearest propane and public dump stations. Returning the RV is explained in more detail in Chapter 15.

As part of your trip planning process, allow several hours the first day for packing your camping gear, a major food shopping expedition, and setting up the galley. These are important to the success of your trip and you will want to get off to a good start.

Loading and Unpacking Tips

One of the important things you need to know is how to load the RV inside and out for proper balance. This is really not difficult, as it uses common sense. Proper balance will make the driving safer and easier. An improperly loaded RV will result in poor weight distribution which may greatly affect steering and braking, especially going around corners or curves. Store heavy items in lower compartments and as far forward as possible and light articles in upper ones. This will lower the center of gravity and minimize swaying or wobbling. Also, try to distribute the weight evenly between the right and left sides.

If there are a lot of people on the trip and you have heavy camping gear, it might be best to check the RV's weight at a weigh station. These can be found in the yellow pages under "Scales-Public." There is a plate on the driver's door that indicates the GVWR (Gross Vehicle Weight Rating), which is the maximum loaded weight you should carry, including fluids, cargo and passengers. Weigh the whole vehicle, then each axle separately to see how you are balanced. It is better to be safe than sorry. Weight is so important that I must remind you to leave things that are not necessary at home—another reason that good trip planning is a must. However, if you just have a normal amount of clothing and food, there is really nothing to worry about and no need to weigh the RV. If you have flown to your point of origin, you will have a pretty good idea of your weight situation and shouldn't have a problem. When in doubt, ask the rental agent.

There are several lockable storage compartments on the outside where you can put camping gear, barbecue and sporting equipment, suitcases, and other bulky items. As you fill these compartments try to balance each side of the vehicle for weight, but as you do, take into consideration how you are going to load the inside. Normally the inside storage compartments are placed so that proper loading will balance the RV, but make sure that compartments on either side carry approximately the same weight.

Another important thing to remember as you are filling any of the RV's interior storage compartments is to pack them tightly so the contents don't roll around. Not only is this important for heavy articles whose weight may shift, but it is especially important for food in the galley. We found that using small cardboard boxes turned open end out worked well to keep canned food and drinks from rolling around. As cans were used, we filled the empty space with cereal or snack boxes.

Most RVs will have an ample number of individual overhead compartments and we have found that assigning each person a compartment makes keeping the "house" neat much easier. One compartment near the front can be used for general items for the trip, such as books, travel guides, games, binoculars, and later, those treasured purchases. If you have brought along just the right amount amount of clothing, storage should not be a problem. Your RV will also have a large storage closet for hanging clothes, laundry bags, shoes, and other bulky articles. There should be storage pockets behind the front seats and in the cockpit where you can store maps, magazines, newspapers and any tourist information you will need.

Unpack and set up "house" before you leave the rental agency. This will make the trip much easier, and getting off to a good start is very important. Everyone in your family will feel right at home, and you won't hear "Mom, where are my crayons?" You can go nuts in a hurry if you haven't organized properly. Also, know what you will need at the store so that you can get that first big shopping done quickly. Use the checklists you will find in Chapter 10 and make up a master shopping list.

Getting Set To Go

Designate a Map Reader

As part of your overall trip planning, it is a good idea to designate someone in your party as the official map reader. Preferably, this will be the co-pilot who will be paying some attention to the roads, but a responsible teenager who has an interest could do it, too. Some people are better map readers than others, and since this is an important job, having a good map reader (or two) is essential. Before you leave the agency, get out the maps for your immediate destination and familiarize yourself and the co-pilot with the route numbers and names. Being able to read a map is very important, especially when you are driving in unfamiliar territory. Keep your maps handy in the front glove compartment or side pocket. As the trip progresses during the day, you will want to check your route periodically so you can be prepared for any road changes ahead and also to see if you are going to make your destination on time.

Set the Rules!

Set the "house" rules!! If you are traveling with children, establish right away the rules you expect them to follow. The adults need rules, too, so that everybody in your party knows what to expect and where the responsibilities lie. As in any discipline, being firm from the beginning will make a big difference. Make sure everybody understands the rules and the dangers involved if they don't obey. You certainly cannot let the kids do whatever they want or behave the way they would at home. Being in an RV and looking forward to a great adventure is very exciting, but driving an RV for the first time can be tricky and any distractions can be dangerous. See Chapter 13, Traveling with Kids, for some proven tips.

Teach Everybody about Safety!

Safe driving tips are covered fully in Chapter 12, but I want to discuss here some of the safety tips that everybody, including children, should know. The rental agent should have explained to you about the emergency exits, fire extinguisher, and safety alarms when going over the various parts of the RV. However, if not, find out before you leave the agency where the emergency exit, usually a specially marked window in the rear, is located and how it works. Without actually opening it, demonstrate to everybody in your party how to use it.

Also, make sure there is a charged fire extinguisher on board and show all hands where it is and how it works, too. Should you have a fuel or electrical fire, attempt to shut off the source of the problem first. For instance, if there is a propane fire, turn off the main propane valve at the tank, or in case of an electrical fire, unplug the power (Shoreline) if you are hooked up at a campground. The fire will now be easier to put out. An extinguisher can also come in handy if a fellow camper needs assistance putting out a fire caused by a faulty gas lantern.

The RV should have smoke, propane (LP-gas) and CO (carbon monoxide) alarms, and tell your party that if one of them goes off to wake everybody up immediately, as the situation could be very dangerous. Each one has a different tone. Emergencies and accidents do happen, so be prepared. Should a fire or accident occur, members of your party may become disoriented in the unfamiliar quarters. Tell everybody to keep talking so that you know where they are and will be able to find them or tell them what to do. At your first campsite, do a mock fire drill. A few moments of simple instruction could avert a tragedy.

More Safety Tips...

- When you are driving, the passengers shouldn't roam around the RV. A sudden swerve or stop could send them flying. If you need to get something or go to the bathroom, be sure to brace yourself. Otherwise, keep seatbelts fastened at all times, and remind the kids that the RV is not a rec room!

- Make sure the rear windows are tightly closed when you are underway, because this will prevent exhaust fumes from entering the RV.
- Don't cook while you are driving as hot foods could easily get knocked off the stove.
- Make sure the stove and hot water heater are off when you are traveling and the pilot lights are off during refueling.

Before you leave the rental agency, adjust both side mirrors, since you will need to use them right away. Set the mirrors so you can see what you need with a quick turn of your head. They should show the rear wheels in the bottom corner as well as a distance of at least thirty feet behind the RV. You can check for blind spots by having someone walk alongside the RV from the rear toward the front, at approximately the distance of the next lane in the road. When they disappear is where your blind spot begins. Repeat on the passenger's side, and adjust the mirrors accordingly.

You are now ready to leave the rental agency and begin your adventure!

Shopping

We have found that going to a supermarket to stock up on food and other necessities is a good place to start the vacation. Ask the rental agent if there is a big supermarket nearby. By doing a big shopping at the outset you will have a chance to set up the galley, get drinks and snack food that might come in handy right away, and really feel that you are ready to "go." There may not be a big store near your destination and you would then have to rely on expensive and limited camp or convenience stores. The success of any trip is in the organization, and shopping early makes a big difference! Shopping is explained in more detail in Chapter 10.

Name Your RV

Part of the fun of enjoying your new adventure is to name your RV. Here you are sitting high up above all those lowly cars with a big rig behind you. Probably this is the first time you have ever had this vantage point and the feeling is really awesome! Give your rig a pet name. If you are shopping or sightseeing and want to split up and meet back at the RV, you can say "I'll meet you back at the Road Warrior" or whatever you decide to name it. The RV is your home away from home—your wheel estate—and you are King of the Road. Pick a name that fits your mood or the purpose of your trip. Think big—this is your time to dream!

While you are at it, pick names for the driver and passengers, such as pilot and co-pilot, or skipper and navigator, captain and first mate, etc. During the trip you can refer to each other by these names—"Well, Navigator, what's the next route number?" or, "Skipper, when do you think we will make our destination?" This will bond the two of you and get you to focus on your vacation. The kids can be "crew" or "mates" and be made to feel part of the adventure and not just passengers. Everybody will enjoy the expedition more!

Your adventure has finally begun!

Chapter 8

Some Practical Camping and Travel Hints

When you are not an experienced camper, which we certainly weren't, you learn by trial and error. Lots of trials and lots of errors! I want to pass on some of the more unusual tricks and things we learned to help you on your trip. If you discover others, please send them to me so I can pass them on to other RVers in the future.

Toilet Paper Roll Trick. How do you keep towels or clothes that you have neatly clothespinned to a coat hanger and hung in the shower to dry from bunching up as you are driving? Simple, we discovered, but not until after some considerable thought. Take the cardboard core that the toilet paper (or paper towels) is wrapped around, slit it from end to end, open it up and slide it over the shower rod in between the clothes hangers or between the clothes hangers and the side of the shower. This trick keeps everything from becoming one big, soggy lump. You can use full rolls of toilet paper, too, if you have a spring loaded rod. Just put a rubber band around the paper.

Drying Sneakers and Shoes. There is nothing worse than the smell of wet sneakers! In Colorado we were caught in an especially heavy downpour and hailstorm. Although we were prepared for the rain with rain gear, our feet got soaked. Normal drying time inside the RV could have been days—if we lived that long! You can imagine the stench from six pairs of wet sneakers. My wife got the bright idea of putting them on the dashboard in the sun, where they dried in a matter of hours. We survived!

Laundry. We found the best time to do laundry was as we were preparing dinner. When the kids were with us, they would do the laundry and explore the camp store or the campground, I would plan the next day's travels, and the co-pilot would prepare dinner. That way we weren't all cooped up and going rammy. The campground laundry facilities are usually quite nice and uncrowded, and we told the kids to time the wash or dry cycles so they would get back to the machines right before they ended. Not only did this preclude someone stealing the clothes, but it also taught the kids responsibility. It worked well. Make sure they have enough quarters or dollar bills to complete the laundry!

The medium plastic trash bags with pull strings that we used for the camper's trash also made excellent laundry bags. Each person should have one, and they can be stored in the individual's compartment or in the closet. When dirty clothes are changed, they can be put in the bag immediately, instead of lying on the floor for days, as they do at home. Another good lesson!

Keeping the Camper Clean. You may not keep your house spotless, but you certainly will want to keep the RV in tiptop shape. Living in relatively cramped quarters can change your habits in a hurry! When you unpack your clothes, books, cassette recorder and tapes, etc., assign lockers or drawers to each member of the party for his/her belongings and make them responsible for keeping the assigned area neat at all times. There is nothing worse than getting out of the driver's seat and stumbling over several pairs of sneaks in the aisle, or trying to sit in a seat and have to move piles of clothes or games. Lay the law down from the beginning and it will certainly make your trip smoother and more enjoyable. After you have stopped for sightseeing or shopping, make sure everything is stowed away before you start up. The pilot, like the captain of a ship, has a lot of power in this area, and making the rules from the beginning will save a lot of shouting.

Another helpful hint in keeping the camper tidy is to clean the floors daily. Set up a regular time, perhaps after dinner or when you are breaking camp in the morning. Do it at the same time each day, so it becomes part of the routine. We found that a whisk broom worked well, but if you are going to a beach area, you may want to take a small dust buster to pick up all the sand. Cleaning won't take long but will sure make a big difference in your RV's appearance. If you have several children who are old enough, assign them the cleaning job on a rotating basis. The one who is "off cleanup duty" will be doing something else, such as helping with the hookups. Having the children doing something useful will make them feel like part of the team and responsible for the trip's outcome and enjoyment. Explain this to them on the first day, along with the rest of the rules, and your trip is bound to be more pleasant.

Some of the roads we traveled on out West were gravel or hard packed dirt and were quite dusty. We learned very quickly to close all the windows to keep the dust out, otherwise it will cover everything and be a real mess to clean up! Your RV should have a small piece of carpeting or a mat on the landing that can be used by everybody to wipe their feet. This will greatly reduce the dirt inside.

Trash should be disposed of daily, and a simple trick we learned helped keep the RV free of trash. We used a heavy paper grocery bag, folded the top down several inches for sturdiness, and put it in the stairwell so it wouldn't fall over. Inside the paper bag we placed the plastic bag with drawstring that the campground gave us. The bag can be closed when traveling and will not leak. During the day when we stopped to go sightseeing or shopping, we took the bag out of the stairwell so it wouldn't get kicked on the ground as we got out. Each morning we threw away the plastic bag in the campground's dumpster.

String Idea for Seatbelts. We are firm believers in having everybody wear seatbelts, but in the RV, the belts in the long couch kept falling underneath the cushions when it was made into a bed and it was very difficult to retrieve them in the morning. After nagging at the kids about wearing belts and having them complain of the difficulty in retrieving them, my co-pilot came up with the idea of tying a piece of string to each one before the couch was made into a bed. The belts were buckled together and pushed underneath the couch and the string was left accessible. In the morning the kids pulled the string as they made the bed back into a couch. Presto, the belts appeared. Problem solved!

A Sleeping Bag's Many Uses. Besides its use to sleep in, or perhaps as a backrest, the lowly sleeping bag has one other important function in the RV. Prop it in the doorway of the bathroom for ventilation while you are underway. It is the right size, won't roll around and can be easily moved when you need to use the bathroom. We have had RVs with bathrooms in the middle and side of the rear. Not only was it important to have the door stay open in the RV with the bathroom in the middle so I could see out the rear window, but also for air, as we hung clothes and towels to dry in the shower; they dried a lot faster and kept the RV smelling better, too.

Break up Your Trip. The biggest advantage of RV over car travel is the flexibility it gives you in several different areas. You have your own portable house. Can you imagine taking a long vacation with several kids and having to plan your daily routine around where to find a restaurant? Or, how about having to stop for snacks all the time? And don't forget the restroom stops! The joy and excitement of the trip can wear thin pretty fast. In the RV, on the other hand, you can stop for a meal at any time, and snacks and the bathroom are just a few steps away. The trips to the bathroom become much less important for "some reason."

Breaking up the daily travel into several segments serves two main purposes. First, it gives the driver a rest, and secondly, especially if you are traveling with kids, it breaks up the monotony. Utilize the breaks to walk around and stretch for a few minutes. This will revitalize you and get you ready for the next leg of the journey. An important part of the daily planning, explained more fully in Chapter 3, is to search out places of interest along the way in order to break up the trip. Doing this will give everybody a change of pace and give the tour director an opportunity to explain the next stop of the day, thereby giving everybody something to look forward to. The passengers will have time to describe each stop in their diary, thus not making it a chore, and consuming some potentially boring time between stops.

High Altitude Problems. If your travel plans include being in high altitude areas, be prepared for some physical changes. Philadelphia is pretty close to sea level, so when we spent our first night at over 7,000 feet, I was worried that the whole trip was going to be ruined. My heart pounded and did flips every once in awhile, and there was a strange feeling in my chest. Initially, I thought these palpitations were from having the jitters as a rookie RVer who had just experienced the excitement of driving the second most difficult road in Colorado. Not so, I was told. My co-pilot had a few symptoms, but the kids didn't seem to have any. Each person reacts differently, and if you know what to expect ahead of time it will keep you from worrying. My high altitude problems went away in a day or two as my body got used to the rarified air.

Traveling at high altitude also affects the driving performance of the RV and cooking, both of which are discussed in later chapters.

Chapter 9

Know Your RV

As mentioned in Chapter 7, the rental agent will have gone over the operation of all the RV's equipment with you before you left the agency. However, there is so much to learn, and much of it quite different from what you are used to, that this chapter will give you a more detailed explanation of the RV's equipment and can be referred to if you have a question. It is vitally important that you have a thorough knowledge of your RV's equipment and how it works, but there is nothing that is scary or terribly complicated about it. If I, as a nonmechanical person, can do it, then anybody can.

How the RV's Equipment Works

Air Conditioning

Most RVs have two air conditioning systems. One is the vehicle's system that is operated from the driver's seat just the way your car's is. On our summer trips out West we found this system to be adequate to cool the RV while we were driving. In fact, with the right combination of window ventilation, we found that we didn't even need the air conditioning at all except on a few very hot days. Do not use this system if the RV's engine is not running, as your battery will quickly be discharged. As in your car, the use of the air conditioner places an extra load on the vehicle's cooling system. If the engine starts to run abnormally hot, shut off the air conditioner until the engine cools down. In mountainous driving conditions, use of the air conditioner may make the RV go slower than expected, so you can shut it off to gain more power.

The other system is on the roof and is powered by starting the generator, or from the Shoreline if you are hooked up. You may use this system by itself, in conjunction with the vehicle's system when you are driving, or by itself if you are stationary. Some of these systems are dual heating and cooling. Make sure the air conditioner is set on "off" when you start the generator, then turn it on and slowly move to the desired setting.

See the section on use of the generator in this chapter for more information.

Batteries & Electrical System

Motorhomes have three separate electrical systems that will provide you with power when you are driving and camping. A thorough understanding of how they work is important for the successful operation of the RV's equipment and will keep you from running the batteries so low they won't function.

The first one is easy to understand as it is a 12-volt DC system similar to your car's, and is run off a battery connected to your RV's engine. This electrical system, called the "vehicle" system, starts your engine, and operates the brake and running lights and turn signals. When the engine is running the alternator produces electricity and recharges the battery.

The second electrical system, or "house" system, is also 12-volt DC, and gets its power from its own batteries (most RVs have two batteries hooked up in parallel) or from the power center converter when you are hooked up to the campground's electricity with your Shoreline. The Shoreline is a long extension cord tucked away in a compartment on the outside of your RV. When you do the hookups, you pull it out, add an adaptor if needed, and connect it to the campground's electrical outlet at your site. This "house" system supplies power to the exterior and interior lights, range hood fan and light, bathroom ventilator, furnace blower, water pump, refrigerator (if it operates on this mode), interior 12-volt receptacles, porch light, and monitor panel. The 12-volt receptacles can only be used with appliances designed to use this type of power. When you are hooked up to the Shoreline, the power center converter automatically converts the 120/220-volt power to 12-volt DC for use by those appliances that need it and also recharges the batteries. The batteries are also recharged by the RV's alternator when the engine is running, and when the generator is in use.

One of the different concepts of RVing that you will have to adjust to is the fact that the electricity from the 12-volt systems won't always "just be there" when you need it. We take electricity for granted at home, but on the road, the batteries can become discharged. The "house" batteries will discharge after 4-5 hours if the 12-volt electrical system has a heavy load and they are not being recharged by an outside source. For instance, if the refrigerator is on "battery" and you go sightseeing for a longer period of time than you expected, the "house" battery system could be dead when you return. Luckily, you won't be stuck, as the RV can be started by its other battery and the system can be recharged. This problem is also important to remember when you are staying in one place for several days without moving or without an external source of power. Keep this in mind if you visit relatives or are "boondocking" — camping without hookups.

To help overcome the problem of running the batteries down, you can buy an inverter, which hooks up to the battery bank and supplies AC power when you want to run appliances but don't have a Shoreline hookup or a generator. RVs in the rental fleets don't have these, so you will have to use the generator to get AC power if you aren't hooked up.

The third electrical system is a 120/220-volt AC system, similar to the one in your home, and gets its power from the Shoreline or the generator, and supplies it through the power center to the roof air conditioner, refrigerator, microwave, TV, exterior receptacles, and interior receptacles which are used for regular household appliances. Using this system will not only reduce the drain on your "house" battery caused by using the 12-volt system, but will also recharge it.

Batteries

Your RV will probably have two batteries, a main (vehicle) and an auxiliary (house) one. As I mentioned above, some RVs have two 6 or 12-volt auxiliary batteries hooked up in parallel for extra power. This is especially useful for campers who may spend a good deal of time away from an outside electrical source. For the RVer who will be staying at campgrounds most of the time, the main and auxiliary batteries are sufficient. I was not given a good explanation of their function on our first trip, but was told to "switch batteries in the morning." Knowing how they work would have been helpful, as I was constantly afraid of being without power in the middle of nowhere.

There is a battery monitor on the dashboard with green and orange indicator lights. When you start the engine the green light, or main battery indicator, should come on. If the battery has insufficient charge to start the RV, the orange, or auxiliary battery light will come on automatically, which means the auxiliary battery system has been activated to start the engine. However, if neither light goes on, both batteries are dead and you will need to recharge the auxiliary battery by plugging into an external 120/220-volt AC electrical source, or by running the generator. Use of the generator is explained later.

Besides being the backup for the main battery, the auxiliary battery's primary purpose is to take care of the living area's electrical needs when the RV is not plugged into an external power source. Please note, however, that all living area radios and tape cassettes (in-dash) are run off the main battery, so prolonged use while you are not hooked up to an external power source, or driving, can cause this battery to discharge. Some TVs in the newer models use a power inverter and can use 12- or 110-volt power. Again, just be careful not to drain the battery by using too many appliances for too long without being either hooked up or using the generator.

An indicator light on the monitor panel will tell you the condition of the batteries. Battery 1 is the main battery, and Battery 2 is the auxiliary one. To actually check the auxiliary battery, follow these steps:

1. turn off engine
2. unplug the exterior power source
3. turn on three lights or any 12-volt appliance—the battery must be checked with a load; a discharged battery will show a full charge unless some electricity is being drawn
4. press the Battery 2 rocker switch on the monitor panel to find out the strength of the battery

If all electrical systems are functioning properly, the batteries will be kept charged either by the alternator while driving, or by being plugged into an external power source.

On our recent trips I have not had to "switch batteries" in the morning as I did on our first trip. The new electrical systems take care of that switching for you and they also have a voltmeter which tells you if either battery needs recharging.

Dumping Procedure

One of the most intimidating aspects of RVing is the waste water dumping process. I am not mechanically inclined, to say the least, so having to follow instructions exactly in the proper order and understanding why they were done that way was totally confusing to me. However, I assume I am not alone, and even for those of you who are good at understanding the whys and wherefores of a process, it will be good to see how this one works.

Most RVs have two waste water holding tanks—one is the gray water tank for the sink and shower water, and the other is the black water tank for the toilet water. The two tanks can be dumped together or independently. Check the gauges on the monitor panel daily to see how full they are. You won't have to dump every night at the campground, as the tanks should be about 3/4 full for a proper dump. Depending on the number of people in your party and the frequency of use, you may be able to go two or three days without dumping. Carrying around more waste water than necessary, however, means a lot of extra weight and therefore, reduced fuel efficiency. This is especially important in mountainous driving. We made the practice of using restroom facilities at places we stopped, and this minimized the water usage. You can double check the black water tank level by looking down the toilet drain. Always keep an eye on the monitor panel! If you feel the tanks should be dumped but the gauges aren't registering 3/4 full, add water, then dump. This will provide enough water to ensure a complete flushing. In Europe, some RV models have portable toilets which can be emptied into a regular toilet or dump area designed for this purpose.

Besides dumping to empty the tanks when they are full, you will also need to think of odors, which can be a problem if you are not careful. Controlling odors in the black water (toilet) tank are described below, but odors can also come from the gray water tank. The problem may be caused by bacteria buildup from food particles and grease and oils, and usually occurs after a long storage. If you have this problem, there are special chemicals, such as Thetford's Grey Water Odor Control, designed to take care of it. These chemicals will break up the grease, help prevent future buildup, and deodorize the tank. You should not have this problem, however, if you are renting from a reputable dealer. Another cause of odors coming from the gray water tanks is "negative pressure" which can build up in the RV as you are driving. To alleviate this problem, put stoppers in the sink drains.

When you are ready to dump, follow these easy steps:

1. Remove the valve cap at the end of the dump valve outlet; (see Figure 11). Twist it counterclockwise and pull it off. Notice the nubs at the end of the valve and how the valve cap is attached with prongs.

2. Pull the dump hose out of its compartment. Note that one end has two prongs that lock around the nubs on the dump valve outlet. Attach one end to the dump valve outlet by twisting it clockwise and locking the prongs around the nubs and insert the other end several inches into the campground's sewer inlet. Some campgrounds and a few states require you to use a donut or sewer ring when dumping. The ring is a rubber gasket that fits into the sewer inlet and the hose fits snugly into it. It prevents sewer gas from escaping and infiltration of ground water and debris into the septic system. You can purchase one from a dealer or campground for a few dollars. Make the slope of the hose gentle and get the hose as straight as possible so the waste water will flow easily and not whip out of the sewer when you pull the dump valve. Place a rock or heavy piece of wood on top of the hose where it enters the sewer so it won't pop out.

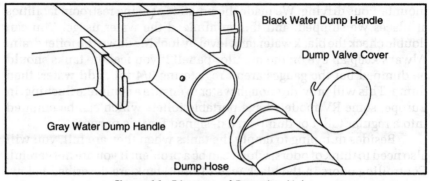

Figure 11, Diagram of Dumping Valves

3. Dump the black water (sewage) tank first. The sewage tank handle is the larger of the two. Pull it out until it stops—about two inches. As the sewage flows into the hose, make sure there are no leaks or spills. Check the connections to the dump valve outlet and the sewer, as well as the hose itself. Let the tank drain completely. After the flow has stopped, gently pick up the hose, starting near the valve outlet, and slowly move toward the sewer inlet. This process will cause any sewage remaining in the hose to flow out. The slope from the dump valve outlet to the sewer inlet is not usually great enough to do this without your help.

4. Close the sewage valve. Many people make the mistake of leaving the valve open all the time. This is wrong, since the system is designed to have water in it at all times. Sewer gas from the campground can also enter the RV if the valve is left open.

5. Next, dump the gray water tank (sinks and shower) by pulling out the smaller of the two handles. This will help clean the valves and dump hose, too.

6. Close the gray water tank valve by pushing it in.

7. Now rinse the sewage tank by running water through the toilet. Take a minute or so to do this and use several gallons of water. Open the sewage valve again, let the water drain out, and close the valve. This will clean the tank and the hose.

8. Run several more gallons of water through the toilet and into the tank. Having water in the tank will aid the breakup of future sewage. There are five to eight metal probes in the holding tank that are connected to the monitor panel; to tell you how full the tank is. If the sewage does not get properly broken up, waste material inside the tank will interfere with the probes and the

reading on the panel will be wrong. Also, the whole operation of the toilet may be adversely affected as it may become clogged. You can imagine what that means! Should this happen, fill the tank about half full and drive around for an hour or two. Step on the toilet flush pedal and look into the toilet to see if the clogged material has been loosened. Dump again.

9. Disconnect the dump hose from the dump valve outlet and walk it, hand over hand, back to the sewer inlet. This will drain any remaining water out of the hose.

10. Replace the dump valve cap securely. This often gets forgotten!

11. Rinse out the dump hose with fresh water and replace it in its compartment.

12. Replace the sewer inlet cap if there is one.

This process only takes a few minutes, but it took me quite a long time to figure out the proper steps, what order to do them in, and what would happen if I didn't do it right. Dumping is very easy if you follow these instructions.

Furnace

The furnace is operated in very much the same manner as the one in your house. If you are cold, turn up the thermostat. Well, it's not quite that simple, but almost. As the furnace is powered by propane, first make sure the LP-gas system is on. The furnace's blower is operated on the 12-volt system, so to keep the battery from being discharged the generator should be on or you must be hooked up either to the Shoreline or have the RV's engine running. Read the instructions for your particular unit, as operation varies from model to model. Generally, if you follow these instructions, your furnace will work:

1. Turn the manual shut-off valve on the furnace to the "off" position.

2. Set the thermostat slightly above room temperature. The blower will start. Let it run for several minutes to purge the combustion chamber.

3. After a few minutes set the thermostat below room temperature. The blower should go off.

4. Open the manual shut-off valve to the fully open position. This is a must for proper operation!

5. Set the thermostat above room temperature, and wait thirty seconds for the burner to ignite.

6. If the burner does not ignite, repeat this process. Also, check to make sure the manual shut-off valve is open, see if the propane is turned on and check the battery condition.

As a safety factor, if you run the furnace at night, leave at least one window or roof vent halfway open to allow fresh air in. This is necessary in case there is some malfunction which causes carbon monoxide to build up.

Generator

Most RVs in the rental fleets are equipped with a generator, which can be used instead of the auxiliary battery if there is no external power source available. The generator supplies 120/220-volt power and is run on gas drawn from the gas tank in such a manner that it will shut off before the tank runs dry. The generator must be used if you want to run the roof top air conditioner and there is no external power source, and it will also supply all of the RV's other electrical needs. By running the generator's power through the power center, the RV is able to operate its 12-volt appliances, too.

Depending on how your RV is set up, there may be a START/STOP switch on the inside of the vehicle to start the generator, or you may have to start it at the generator itself. The roof-top air conditioner and microwave should be off before you start the generator. Press this switch to START until the generator starts running. When you want to stop it, press the switch to STOP and hold it down until the generator stops running. Again, make sure the roof-top air conditioner and microwave are turned off before stopping the generator.

> Check the oil level in the generator after every eight hours of operation, and fill if necessary.

Just a word of warning about generators. If you buy, rent or borrow an older RV, do not use the generator for air conditioning at night, as there is a possibility of carbon monoxide poisoning. Many of the older units had the generator added in the aftermarket and the installation may not have been properly done. Factory installations, on the other hand, should be very safe. As of September 1, 1993, carbon monoxide (CO) detectors will be required in all new motorhomes. RVs in rental fleets are newer and will have properly installed generators as well as CO detectors, so this shouldn't pose a problem if you take safety precautions. Ask the rental agent if you are concerned. Should you need air conditioning, the best thing to do is use a campground's full-hookups. The furnace, on the other hand, can be used at any time because it is vented to the outside.

When operating the generator, do not open roof vents, windows or doors that could allow fumes to seep back into the RV. Also, make sure the exhaust outlet is not too close to a building, wall, fence, tree or bush that could deflect it back inside your RV or into a neighbor's RV or tent. If there is plenty of room for air to circulate near the exhaust outlet, you will be all right. Generators are noisy, too, so think of your campground neighbors when you want to run it.

Jack & Spare Tire

The rental agent should have shown you where the spare tire and jack are located, how to get them down and where to place the jack on the chassis. They are usually neatly tucked away underneath the RV, but it can be tricky getting them down from their hanger. If you are in doubt about the proper operation of the jack, read the instruction manual for your vehicle.

The procedure for changing a flat is basically the same as for your car, but because of the size and weight of the RV, it may be considerably more difficult. Make sure the brake is on and the RV is in "park," and place large stones or blocks of wood under the wheels to keep the RV from rolling. The jack base should be on very firm ground and you must be careful that passing traffic doesn't create suction and pull the RV off the jack. It is safest to pull off the road as far as you can but still have firm ground under the jack. All passengers should be out of the vehicle while you are changing the tire, as the slightest movement by somebody inside could cause the jack to slip.

After all these instructions, though, my advice is to find somebody experienced in changing tires on trucks or RVs to do the work. The job is difficult, especially if an inside tire is flat, and can be quite dangerous for an inexperienced person. First, look in your campground directory to find out if there is a service center located nearby. If there are no listings, call your rental agent and ask if they can help you locate the nearest service center on their list, or look in the yellow pages under "truck stops," "trucks-service & repair," the various RV categories, or call the local police. Another idea is to call a local campground to see if they have someone they can recommend. You might even try putting out a white flag to ask for help. A knowledgeable RVer or trucker may be able to assist, but this should be your last resort as you don't know who will stop. If you do do it yourself, take plenty of time, have patience, and read the instruction manual carefully! Station someone a good distance behind the RV to warn approaching vehicles of your problem.

Monitor Panel

This all-important panel is usually placed in a convenient location near the galley, as that is where it is handy to use it to test approximate tank levels and monitor the RV's other operating systems (see Figure 12 for a typical panel layout). The little round indicator lights will tell you how full your tanks are in 1/4 increments when you push the rocker switches. For instance, by pushing the rocker switch labeled LP-Gas, the indicator lights will tell you how full the propane tank is. The same is true with the fresh water and waste holding tank switches. Holding tank #1 is for the black water or sewage, and holding tank #2 is for the gray water, or the sinks and shower. The battery condition #1 is for the main battery, and battery condition #2 is for the auxiliary. The last operating switch is for the water pump, which is explained later.

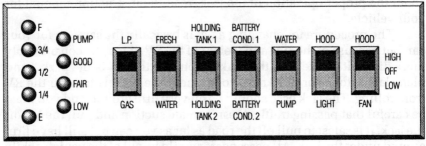

Figure 12, Typical Monitor Panel

Propane System

The LP (liquified propane) gas system supplies the fuel for the stove, refrigerator (while in the gas mode), furnace and hot water heater. The operation of each of these appliances is discussed individually. The motorhome's propane tank (some models have two tanks) is permanently built into the chassis and is located in a compartment on the outside with easy access for filling. Trailers, however, have removable tanks. When you are refueling the RV with gasoline or propane, this system must be turned off at the propane tank, as gas fumes could be ignited by a pilot light. Just turn the service valve.

I have found that a tank of propane will last about two weeks, but this may vary considerably depending on the number of people, and factors such as the number of showers, the amount of cooking, use of the furnace, etc. To check on your supply of propane, use the LP-Gas switch on the monitor panel, and if it reads 1/4, go outside to the tank and read the float gauge there. If the gauge reads approximately 10% of capacity, fill the tank at the nearest gas dealer. Look in your campground directory under RV service and supplies, or in a phone book under "gas companies," "gas-propane," or "propane." Some campgrounds sell propane, too. Propane tanks are filled by weight or by meter. The removable ones are filled by weight, and the motorhome's are metered. Many propane stations can fill both ways, and some cannot, so check with the station before you go out of your way to drive to it. Do not attempt to fill the tank yourself, as improper filling could be very hazardous. Of course, don't smoke when you are having the tank filled, and make sure all pilot lights are out and the service valve on the propane tank is closed.

If you smell propane, which has a very distinct odor, turn off the supply at the tank immediately, and air out the RV. Check all connections for leaks using a soapy water solution. If bubbles appear, you have found the leak. If you can't find it, take the RV to a service center immediately.

When you are not operating an appliance that uses propane, such as the hot water heater, turn it off. This will save propane and is safer, too. Never use cooking appliances for heating purposes as they need fresh air for safe operation. Lack of fresh air could cause asphyxiation if cooking appliances are used for an extended period of time. The flame on propane burning appliances should burn bright blue. If the flame is yellow or reddish, there is inefficient combustion, which results in carbon monoxide buildup. Have this situation corrected immediately!

Refrigerator

The refrigerator, although called by the same name as the one at home and performing the same important function of keeping food cold, operates in a completely different manner. You will need to know how it operates from the minute you begin your trip! The refrigerator will also have an ample freezer compartment that we found worked quite well.

There are two types of RV refrigerator systems. One will operate on either LP-gas or 120/220-volt AC electricity, and the other will operate on these as well as on 12-volt DC. The latter is called the three-way system. In the last few years, many motorhomes have been outfitted with only the 120/LP system. Using the 12-volt system isn't recommended unless the engine is running, as the batteries will discharge after a few hours. Use it temporarily if there is no other choice.

Motorhome refrigerators have no moving parts, unlike the one at home, and cool by chemical reaction and the laws of physics. The process is known as absorption refrigeration and relies on evaporation to cool the refrigerator's contents. Heat is transferred from the contents to the outside. Because this process doesn't cool by pumping refrigerant like your refrigerator at home, which cools the contents from around the box, it takes longer to cool, and it is necessary to understand how it works so you can maximize its capabilities.

A few dos and don'ts will help the refrigerator run efficiently. If the rental agency has done its job, the refrigerator will be precooled for you. If it hasn't been, however, allow several hours for it to cool before you put anything into it. After grocery shopping, put all the items into the refrigerator at one time instead of opening and closing the door several times. This will greatly help in the refrigerator's efficiency.

When you buy food, buy it as cold as possible, and don't expect the refrigerator to make a lot of warm food cold in a hurry. In other words, don't buy warm sodas and expect the refrigerator to cool them quickly like it does at home. Wipe off any moisture on the food, as the refrigerator's evaporation process will have to work harder if you don't. Also, any items that contain moisture should be sealed or placed in a covered container. Leave room for air circulation and don't over pack the refrigerator or block the cooling elements, as this will greatly reduce the efficiency. This is very, very important for good operation! For instance, if you have a six pack of soda, take the cans out of the cardboard wrapper. This will allow for better air flow and cooling.

We found that putting the next day's supply of items, such as soda, in the refrigerator the night before and replenishing them as the day went on, rather than overstocking at the beginning of the day, gave us cold drinks any time. This is much more efficient. When you have to get something out of the refrigerator, do it quickly so the cold air stays inside. I am sure you tell your kids at home not to stand in front of the refrigerator with the door open trying to think of what to get, and this is more important than ever in the RV.

If you have several kids who constantly need sodas or snacks, consider getting a small cooler (Styrofoam ones are cheap) for the day's supply. This way they won't have to continually keep opening the door and you will have more room in the refrigerator, too! Coolers are great if you want to stock up on fresh produce, seafood or meat, and don't have enough room in the refrigerator.

As part of your daily pre-travel check, you will switch the refrigerator from the campground's electrical hookup to LP-gas, and vice versa when you make camp. You can travel with the gas on, and will have to if you don't have a three-way refrigerator, but it will be used up faster and needs to be turned off when you get fuel. The RV's refrigerator has its own monitor panel that tells you what mode it is in. A green light tells you it is in the 120/220-volt AC mode, a blue light for the LP- gas mode, and an amber light for the 12-volt DC mode. When you switch to gas, make sure the LP system is on, otherwise, the refrigerator won't work.

Because this type of refrigerator works by gravity and not by a pump, it is important to have the RV level so the chemicals are evenly disbursed in the system, otherwise, the refrigerator will not work efficiently. Although modern technology has made leveling less crucial than for earlier models, it will still be important for cooking and sleeping, as I will discuss in more detail later.

We had a small bubble level at home, so we took that on our first trip, but on our latest ones, the RV has had a level in the refrigerator. Perhaps somebody left it there. You can buy a small level at a hardware or RV supply store if yours doesn't have one. Place it on a readily accessible spot in the refrigerator for ease of use. At least half the bubble should be within the guidelines.

For maximum efficiency when you are in a campground or stopped for a long time, try to park the RV so the refrigerator side is away from the sun.

To clean the inside of the refrigerator, use a mild detergent or baking soda on a sponge or non-scratch scrubber, and dry with a soft cloth. Never use abrasive cleaners.

Once you understand the principles by which the refrigerator works, it is as simple to use as the one at home.

Stove

The stove is very similar to the one you have at home. It will have several burners on top and an oven. Many of the newer RVs have microwave/convection oven combinations, so the gas oven is eliminated altogether. Unless you plan to do a lot of baking, this latest feature really makes sense. The only drawback is that it uses more electricity than a conventional oven.

The only difficulty we had with RV stoves was lighting the pilot in the oven. Read the instructions carefully, and allow some extra time when you first use it. I spent a lot of time trying to figure out how to do it, even after reading the manual, and went through quite a few wooden matches! The secret, I discovered, is to hold the match to the pilot until the thermocouple is warm and the pilot ignites, which may take 30 seconds to a minute. I was used to the instant pilot on my stove at home. The RV stove is designed so the pilot automatically goes out when the oven is turned off. This is important because all pilots must be out for safety reasons when you refuel.

When you use the stove, turn on the fan over the stove, or open a roof vent or window to allow fresh air to enter the RV. Using the stove consumes oxygen, so you need an additional supply. **Never, never** use the stove to heat the RV, as there is a chance of asphyxiation.

Toilet

RV toilets operate like marine toilets, but that won't help you if you have never been on a boat. When you look into the toilet you will see a long tube with a flap closure at the bottom. On the outside will be two pedals, a large one to open the flap, thereby flushing the toilet, and a smaller one to add more water. When you want to use it, fill the tube at least half way up. This keeps the sides cleaner. Afterward, push the flap pedal (large), which will empty the tube, then push the water pedal (small) to add water to the holding tank. Not enough water is used with the flush alone to push the solids along, so you must add extra water after the initial flush. It is necessary to have enough water in the holding tank to break up the solids and keep them in suspension so they don't clog the tank. When the tank fills up, the solids and water flush out together. Finally, close the flap and add several inches of water, but not so much that it will spill out when you are underway. I have found this makes a seal and keeps out odors. By doing this you won't think you are going through pig farm country!

If you use chemicals to control holding tank odors, use only those recommended for RVs, as they are specially formulated for this purpose; do not use those from a grocery store. The chemicals can be purchased at the campgrounds or at RV service centers. Read the labels of any product you are considering. Until recently, most of the odor control/liquifying products were formaldehyde based. However, as we have become more environmentally aware, manufacturers have developed products using enzymes and/or bacteria to do the same thing as formaldehyde, which is a poison. Another environmentally sound reason to use these products is that they predigest the wastes, which makes it easier for the community's sewage system to handle them. Waste coming from an RV is much more concentrated than waste from your house and may overload the sewage system's ability to properly treat it.

The one drawback to the enzyme/bacteria products is that they are less effective in temperature extremes. If it is below freezing or very hot, you may have to switch to a formaldehyde-based product. Should you need to switch, empty your holding tank and fill it three-quarters full with fresh water and drive around for awhile to help rinse it out. Dump and repeat. Different chemical products usually don't mix, and you want to make sure what you are using is going to be effective.

Also, don't use bleach, as it will damage the rubber seals of the toilet and dump valve. There is special toilet paper for this type of toilet that breaks down more easily, but I have never used it. When buying toilet paper, use only brands that are labeled "biodegradable," as they will be less likely to clog the system. After finally learning the procedures for operating the toilet that I have described here, I never had a problem.

There is a possibility that when you are hooked up to the campground's water supply there may be too much water pressure for the toilet, and the tank may fill up and overflow during the night. Check the toilet after an hour or more of nonuse to see if it is filling up. If it is, turn the outside water off when you go to bed.

Water Systems

The fresh water in the RV is supplied from one of two sources: a tank on the inside, or from the campground's water source. Either one will supply all your water needs. The first source is called the internal or gravity system and has a tank beneath a sofa, dinette, kitchen cabinet or bed. The rental agency should have filled this tank before you picked the RV up, and you will be able to go quite awhile, perhaps the whole trip, without refilling it. The tank in the Class "C" is usually 30-35 gallons, while that in the Class "A" is 50-100. This system is used whenever you are not hooked up to a campground's water supply. To operate it, turn on the water pump by using the switch on the monitor panel, and you are all set.

The second system is the external, or city, one, which you activate when you hook up to the campground's water supply. This system uses a separate fill receptacle from the internal system. The receptacle is usually located near the Shoreline storage compartment. A check valve causes the water to bypass the water pump, storage tank and toilet, and goes directly to the RV's piping. When water is called for, it is supplied, just like in your house. Before you hook up to the city water, turn the water pump off.

Water Heater

The water heater draws its water from the RV's storage tank or from the external water supply if you are hooked up, and heats it by propane. I was the first person up every morning, so my initial duty of the day was to go outside and turn on the water heater. Within minutes we had enough hot water for showers and cooking.

To light the heater, turn the control knob to "pilot," depress the reset button and light the pilot (long wooden kitchen matches come in handy here). Hold the reset button down for about thirty seconds to make sure the pilot is fully lit. If the pilot doesn't stay lit, relight the pilot and hold the button down longer. Once the pilot is lit, turn the control knob to "on," and you should have hot water in a few minutes. For best results, set the temperature dial midway between warm and hot, and you will have ample hot water. Close the access door so the pilot doesn't blow out. Some of the newer RVs have direct ignition that allows you to start the water heater from inside the motorhome. This is a very nice feature as it saves a lot of steps, and is really great if it's cold or rainy. Also, you don't have to show your neighbors what you look like before you are fully dressed and ready to face the world!

Turn off the water heater when you are driving. Not only will you save propane, but for safety's sake all gas sources must be off when you are refueling. The gas fumes could be ignited by a lit pilot.

Water Pump

While you are hooked up to the campground's water supply there is enough pressure to supply all your water needs without the water pump. If you are not hooked up, however, the pump, which works only on demand, needs to be turned on if you need water for any reason. Simply push the water pump switch on the monitor panel to "on" when you need it, and "off" when you are finished. When you are going to be away from the RV for an extended period, turn the pump off, as a slow leak could activate it and discharge the battery. The pump runs off the 12-volt DC system.

You may notice a rat-a-tat-tat sound when the water pump is on—don't worry, that is normal. This is air being bled from the lines. It took us quite awhile to figure out that there wasn't something drastically wrong and the pump was about to die on us. If you don't turn it off and are driving merrily down the road, it may suddenly do that for no apparent reason. This is probably caused by a slow leak.

Should the pump continue to operate whether a faucet is on or off, check the "fresh water" indicator on the monitor panel. The water tank may be empty or there could be a leak in the system. If there is one, report it to the rental agency.

Other Things You Need to Know

Electrical Leakage

While I have already discussed the RV's electrical system itself, I want to briefly mention what happens if there is current leakage coming from the RV park's electrical hookup. It is possible to receive quite a shock after plugging into the park's power source when you touch part of your RV, say the bumper or step, for instance. This is caused by faulty grounding in the park's electrical hookup. The problem is overcome by using a shock shield which acts as a ground fault interrupter (GFI). The shock shield, which is an adapter that connects the park's electrical hookup to the RV's power line, constantly monitors the current flow to the RV, and if leakage exists that poses a ground fault hazard, will automatically shut off the current to your RV in 1/40th of a second.

The shock shield is more than a ground fault interrupter, as it also acts as a surge protector. Even if you use indoor surge protectors for your refrigerator, VCR, microwave and computer, you can never be absolutely sure if they will work when the moment arrives. Power surges (common in RV parks) can virtually destroy these appliances, especially new ones that use sensitive semiconductors. When the power surge comes, the shock shield will turn off your electrical system. You simply go out and turn it back on again. If it refuses to turn on, wait a few minutes and try again.

As far as I can determine, current leakage appears to be extremely rare, and should have been corrected by the time you hook up. However, there are power surges. For normal vacationers, I would not worry about these problems at all, but if you are taking an extended trip or full-timing and have high technology equipment, it would be wise to invest in a shock shield.

High Altitude Driving

Just in the same way your body needs to adjust to the high altitude, so does the RV. If you are planning to drive into a high altitude area, make sure the rental agency knows this and can have the RV engine tuned accordingly. Otherwise, the RV will not get the proper fuel mixture and will struggle and sputter in the mountains, and the end result will be a fouled carburetor, terrible gas mileage and lost vacation time while you get repairs. Vehicles in fleets near high altitude areas will be ready for this type of driving.

The cause of this problem, as you can well imagine, is that the high altitude causes a change in the air density, and therefore, the ability of the carburetor to give the engine the proper mixture of air and gas. The air/gas mixture you have been using closer to sea level will be too rich for high altitude driving and will result in reduced combustion efficiency and fuel economy. The carburetor should be set higher in order to produce the right mixture. A good mechanic can do this quite quickly, and the results will be gratifying, although you won't be able to appreciate a properly tuned engine unless you have had one that wasn't! Also, the octane rating of the gas can be reduced one point per each 2,000 feet above the 4,000 foot level. This will give you good fuel efficiency and performance.

Leveling

Although leveling the RV is not terribly difficult, it can be a trying ordeal for the rookie RVer, as it may entail pulling forward and backing up several times in a campsite. While campground owners try to provide level sites, many times they just can't due to the terrain. There are two main reasons for the RV to be level: one, for the proper operation of the refrigerator, as I mentioned above, and two, for ease of cooking and sleeping. Nothing like trying to cook something in a frying pan and having all the ingredients slide to one side! Sleeping with the RV at an angle isn't much fun, either. After several nights on the road you should have a pretty good idea of how level you need to get the RV. Somehow you develop a special sense of balance. If you are unsure of how level you are, do this simple test we used: take a frying pan partially full of water and set it on the stove. You will easily see if you are level.

Some privately owned RVs have levelers built into the vehicle that will automatically level it on any terrain no matter how bad a parking job you have done. The rental units don't have them, so you will have to take some time practicing pulling into a site and making sure you are level.

Locking Up and Keys

While keeping your RV locked at all times should go without saying, I want to reinforce this point very strongly. Many people don't lock their homes, even in this day and age, but at least they know their neighbors. On the road you won't know your neighbors, so, be wise, and lock up at all times, even if you are going to be away for just a few minutes. Locking up means more than just locking the door; it also means securing any window that someone could reach or climb through, as well as locking the outside compartments. You don't want your trip ruined by a thief, and the problem can be avoided with a few precautions. The pilot should be in charge of making sure the RV is secured before the party leaves it. Make a habit of checking the doors and windows as soon as you begin the trip!

Have you ever locked yourself out of your car? That is really embarrassing, but usually help can be found nearby at a garage, locksmith, or the police. However, imagine doing it miles from anywhere with no phones nearby! This could be a real disaster, to say the least. My advice is to ask the rental agent for a spare set of keys, or, if none is available, go to the nearest hardware store and make it and give it to the co-pilot. Check the keys to make sure they work before you leave the store, as I have had many keys made that didn't work. Always carry the spare set in a purse or bag that will be taken with you, and not in something that may be left inside the RV. You will really feel stupid if you lock two sets inside! The pilot and co-pilot should each carry a set, not only in case of loss, but also if you split up for some reason and go back to the RV at different times.

Service & Repair

Hopefully you won't need any service or repairs on your trip, but it is always good to know what to do if you need help. The rental agent should have given you instructions on what to do when you picked up the RV. (Review Chapter 7, Picking Up Your RV—Getting Started, for more information.) In this chapter I want to briefly discuss what you should do before you call for help. Just like calling the doctor for a sick child, you will need to try to figure out what the problem is so you can explain it. Read the instruction manuals first, see if you can fix the problem, or at least get an idea of what is the matter.

When you call, the rental agency should have a list of service and repair shops near where you are. The campground directories will also have listings of repair facilities, but according to your contract, you should call the rental agency first unless the problem is under the discretionary minimum. If your problems occur at the most inopportune times like mine always seem to do, it will be right before the service center closes or on Sunday. It never fails! Call the service center ahead to see if they can take you.

On our last trip, we had a problem that led to two master's degrees in creative problem solving for the co-pilot and me. A fuse blew when the windshield wipers were in use. Under normal conditions this would not have been a big deal, but we didn't have any spares and I couldn't even find the fuse box! I had read the instruction book, too, but the box was not where it was supposed to be. The RV had a wraparound windshield, and due to the position of the wiper arm, the blades also wrapped around the curve of the windshield. However, the motor was not strong enough to pull them back to the center of the windshield if there was not enough water to make them run smoothly. The first time we blew a fuse was late on a Saturday afternoon shortly before most stores were closing. It was fortunate that we were near a town, or we would have been in real trouble. We had a terrible time finding a garage open that had the fuses we needed and would take the time to put them in. I bought an assortment of fuses just in case I needed them, as I saw the potential for serious problems.

Within half an hour of leaving the garage the wipers stuck again, and the newly installed fuse blew. Now, at least, I knew where the box was—under the driver's dash. This model RV, however, didn't have a driver's door, so to get to the fuse box I had to lie down on my back on the seat, and slide headfirst to the floor so I could get my arms in position to pull the fuse. Not only did I have to pull and replace the fuse, but I had to hold a flashlight! This was the beginning of my education at the Harry Houdini School of Twists and Turns.

We knew what caused the problem, so we figured that if we could keep the wipers from wrapping around the curve, we would be OK. The co-pilot came up with the brilliant idea of tying string to the controlling wiper arm so this wouldn't happen. At first she held onto the other end of the string, and every time the wipers started to wrap around, she pulled the string. This worked very well, but after awhile, she decided that she could tie it to the side mirror and wouldn't have to hold it. The type of string we had stretched when it got wet, so you can imagine the result! The co-pilot had to go back to holding it and really earned her degree from the Rube Goldberg School of Advanced Engineering! Finally, I solved the problem by putting in a bigger fuse.

As a precaution against having problems like this on the road, pick up a small box of assorted fuses at the beginning of the trip. It will only cost you a few dollars, but will save plenty of headaches if you get stuck!

Smoke & CO Alarms and LP-Gas Detector

I am sure you have heard the expression "trial by fire" to test someone's fortitude. In my case it was "trial by noise," at 2 a.m., needless to say. At home, the smoke alarm batteries always seem to die in the middle of the night setting the alarm off, and I have to roam around to find a stool so I can stop the beep-beep-beep.

This can happen in an RV, too, and it did on our last trip. Suddenly, in the middle of the night, the alarm went off. Which alarm was it? The smoke, propane or CO (carbon monoxide)? After a few seconds of getting myself oriented, I saw the propane alarm's blinking light, and of course, heard the noise. I didn't smell propane, which smells like rotten eggs, so I assumed I didn't have a gas leak. The rental agent had told me about the alarm and what to do. I followed his instruction—press the button for a few seconds, then let go—no luck. The beep-beep continued. As I have learned from putting together Christmas toys, when all else fails, read the instructions. By now, I was fully awake and quite aggravated, but I had to get the noise to stop and also see if something was wrong in the RV. After about fifteen minutes of finding and reading the instructions and fiddling with the propane unit, I finally got the beeps to stop. The alarm had gone off for some reason, but I never did figure out why. We had the furnace on, which is vented outside, but exhaust fumes, sewer gases or a sudden drop in power can also set off the alarm.

The LP-gas detector is located near the galley and close to the floor so it can detect any gas infiltration. It is powered at all times unless your RV has a master cut-off switch. This switch should be on ON. If there is a gas leak, some detectors will automatically shut off the flow of gas at the tank, and the alarm will go off and won't stop until the gas fumes are gone. The newer RVs don't have the automatic shut-off, since it malfunctioned too often. When the alarm sounds, get your family out of the RV, open all doors and windows, quit smoking immediately and manually turn off the LP supply at the tank just to double check. Do **not** turn ON or OFF any electrical switches or equipment, as a spark could cause an explosion. The detector has a reset button which will stop the alarm for one minute. If the gas is still present, the alarm will sound again. There is a self-check circuit in the detector, which will go off if the circuit fails. The tone is a short beep between long intervals, and is a much different sound than the alarm. Earlier RVs we had rented didn't have this detector and they are certainly a good safety device.

The above discussion may seem a bit scary to those readers who have not used propane before, but, really, it is a very safe and predictable fuel when handled properly. After a short while you will be as comfortable using propane as you are with putting gas in your car or using gas to cook. Remember, propane has made motorhoming possible!

Smoke alarms have been standard equipment in RVs for quite a few years, and are also an important safety device. A fire can spread very quickly in an RV and you will need as much warning time as possible so you can get out. Our one incident with the smoke alarm was caused by a mug of hot tea being set under it and setting it off. They are heat as well as smoke sensitive.

Carbon monoxide (CO) is a deadly byproduct of combustion. You can't taste or smell it, but it can kill you, so take the proper precautions to avoid any problems. I have mentioned the precautions necessary to take under the discussion of operating the RV's furnace, generator, and stove earlier in this chapter. The detector should be at an adult's eye level, and is either operated by batteries or wired into the RV's 12-volt electrical system.

These alarms are only as good as their maintenance. For battery operated units, make sure the batteries are fresh. Sometimes they are wired into the 12-volt DC system, but here again, this battery must be functioning properly and not run down. I prefer the direct wired method, as with the smoke alarms in my house you can forget to change the battery. Should the RV's electrical system fail, you will have to take extra safety precautions anyway.

As part of the safety instructions to your travel companions, make sure that everybody is awakened if an alarm sounds. Don't try to be a hero and search out the cause by yourself and not alert the others, thereby losing precious warning time. The result could be tragic.

Weight, Height, Length & Fuel Capacity

The rental agent should have told you what the loaded weight capacity (GVWR) of the RV is, as well as the height and the fuel capacity. The GVWR, or gross vehicle weight rating, is usually listed on a plate on the driver's door, and is the carrying capacity of the RV, including fluids, cargo, and passengers. For safety's sake, it is important not to go over this limit. By the way, while I am talking about weight, you should understand the weight of the fluids you are carrying, as they will have a bearing on fuel economy as well as safety. Use these figures when estimating your load:

Water	8.4 lb/gal
Gasoline	6.3 lb/gal
Diesel	6.6 lb/gal
Propane	4.3 lb/gal

If you plan to do a lot of mountainous driving, carrying around hundreds of extra pounds can affect your fuel economy and speed, and cause unnecessary strain on the engine, so it is important to make some calculations in your trip planning and limit the amount of extra fluids you will carry with you. Not only should you know the capacity of your fresh water tank, you should also have some idea of the capacities of your waste holding tanks, gas tank, hot water tank, and propane tank (usually 19 pounds). Look in the manuals for tank capacities. As an exercise some night, calculate the weight of the fluids you are carrying. Multiply the capacity of each tank by the appropriate weight from the table above—the results will surprise you! Eliminate as much excess weight as possible for mountain driving—it will make your trip much easier!

By keeping track of your fuel economy daily you will have a pretty good idea of what it is under various driving conditions and how much gas you will need for the day's run. This is very important for good trip planning. Don't cut it too close on fuel, however, as getting help on the road can be a real nightmare!

Knowing the height of your RV is also critically important for the safety and enjoyment of your trip. Besides avoiding problems with bridges and tunnels, you will need to pay attention to bank and gas station canopies, toll booths, tree branches, and going through fast food drive-ins. If you have anything attached to the roof, such as a boat, luggage container, or a TV antenna, find out how much additional height this adds to the height of the vehicle. Make sure your co-pilot knows this figure and is on the lookout for road signs.

The length of your RV is important to know when you are looking for campsites, as some campgrounds, especially those on public lands, cannot take RVs over a certain size. If you plan to take a ferry, for instance in Alaska, British Columbia or Europe, length is important to know when making the reservations, since the ferries have space limitations. The price of the ferry will depend on the length, too. Also, some roads don't allow RVs over a certain length because of the narrowness of the road and the hairpin turns. When we visited Glacier National Park we were one or two feet under the maximum length, and as we drove through, I understood why they had limitations. Don't push your luck!

Windows & Vents

Windows in an RV are either jalousie or slider, and the important thing to learn about is how the slider windows lock. I have seen several varieties of locking mechanisms, so look at your vehicle's windows to see how they work. Practice locking a window to make sure you are doing it right, and show all members of your party how it is done. There are screens on the windows, so you can let fresh air in and keep bugs out! Patch any holes if you are camping in bug country. You can buy a screen repair kit at the hardware store, or use tape to cover the hole if you can't get to the store. Bugs will find holes, no matter how small!

Your RV will have two or three roof vents that are opened by a hand crank. Open these if you stop to sightsee or shop, and when you are in a campground, as they are a major source of ventilation. Close the vents when you are underway, as the force of the wind can rip them off or bend them so they won't work. When it was really hot driving, we opened the driver's and co-pilot's windows and the vents an inch or so to help create a draft and cool the RV. This worked pretty well, and we didn't have to use the RV's regular air conditioner often, even in very hot weather.

As I mentioned in an earlier chapter, make sure the co-pilot understands how the various RV systems work in case something happens to you. Spend an hour or two going over the operation of all the equipment, as well as driving techniques. Have the co-pilot do some test drives. In case of emergency he or she will know what to do and won't panic.

Chapter 10

Food & Cooking

The memories of campground cooking from my boyhood travels quickly disappeared when I saw our RV's well appointed galley! No roughing it here—it was almost like home. All the appliances were downsized, but fully functional, and there were plenty of cabinets and a pantry to stow supplies. There was even a microwave. No longer did I have to worry about setting up a camp kitchen every day, cooking on the Coleman stove, trying to light a fire to barbecue (I never made it to Boy Scouts), or boil water to wash dishes. I didn't have to worry if it rained, either. The RV was like a turtle with a house on its back. Self-contained and ready to go!

To some people a vacation means the end of cooking—they want to be waited on hand and foot. Well, you can eat out every meal on an RV trip if you want to, but it will surely spoil one of the most enjoyable parts of the trip — new experiences in eating. Dining out will also force you to look for restaurants and rearrange your travel plans accordingly. This gets to be very inconvenient and a big waste of time. Just imagine trying to find a greasy hamburger stand in the middle of some beautiful mountain range! It's lunch time and the kids are hungry. You'll learn fast!

One of our outstanding reminders of the benefit of travel flexibility in an RV was in the mountains near Glacier National Park, Montana. It was nearly lunch time and we were on the beautiful Going to the Sun Highway heading toward a spot about an hour away where we were going to eat and do some sightseeing in the afternoon. There had been a sudden rain storm and drop in temperature. Driving around a bend we came upon a sparkling mountain stream dashing down a ravine next to the road, a thick stand of trees, and a beautiful rainbow. A perfect picture! We couldn't pass it up. There was a convenient turnout at the side of the road next to the ravine, so we pulled off, cooked soup and hot dogs, and enjoyed the scene. If we had been heading for a restaurant, we would have stayed a few minutes, then pushed on. Instead, we were treated to a magnificent rainbow in a beautiful setting — and had a meal, too! Being able to fully enjoy a setting like that makes the trip ever so rewarding.

When you are well prepared, the speed of making meals and the variety of dining options, let alone the travel flexibility eating in gives you, will make cooking in the RV a very enjoyable part of the trip. You know how long it takes to get food at a restaurant. Cooking in the RV saves a lot of time, and if you save only half an hour every day on a two week trip, you have gained a full day of sightseeing!! Let's not forget the cost, either. Eating out is at least double the cost of preparing your own food, and this can add up to a significant amount on a long trip. Don't get me wrong, we did eat some lunches out, but they were to sample the local specialties. Part of the fun of traveling is to eat the local fare, and when we shopped, we looked for regional foods to try.

The challenge of preparing simple, yet very satisfying meals was an added and unexpected pleasure to the overall RV experience. We liked to arrive at the campground before dark, set up, then make dinner and relax and reminisce about the day's adventures or what we were going to see the next day. While the co-pilot was making dinner, I had a chance to do the next day's trip planning. If we had gone out for dinner and come back after dark, getting into the campsite and doing the hookups would have been more difficult, and I would have had much less time to do the planning.

The following lists will guide you in setting up your galley. If you rent the kitchen equipment from the rental agency, get a list of what they will supply when you make your reservation, and supplement it with items from these lists. Some items may be brought from home, and others can be purchased when you do your initial shopping.

We have refined the lists after several trips, and while you may be able to get away with basic equipment, you will inevitably need to supplement what the dealer provides if you decide to rent their "convenience kits." If you have enough time, send out a box or trunk with supplies to the RV dealer, or a friend, if you have one nearby. For a short trip, say a week or ten days, you may be all right without the full complement of supplies, but they will be quite necessary on a longer one. The number of people in your party is also a factor in making this determination, as cooking becomes more complex with more mouths to feed.

Another major consideration in pulling together this part of the travel planning is whether you are going to be starting your trip close to home or from a faraway departure point. Organizing the galley is much easier if you will be leaving from close to home, as you can load the things in your car and unload them at the rental agency, or drive the RV home and load up. Just keep this caveat in mind when you are doing your planning: you will be cooking on the road and can't run to the nearest convenience store if you have forgotten an ingredient.

The typical "convenience kit" supplied by the rental agencies will contain the following items needed in the galley:

- Knives, forks, spoons
- Dinner plates, saucers, bowls, coffee cups, tumblers
- Frying pan, large & small pots with lids
- Carving knife, spatula, serving spoon, steak knives
- Tea/coffee pot
- Can opener, cork screw
- Dish cloths, potholders
- Serving dish

Compare this list to the one we have developed below, and outfit your galley as you see fit. One easy way to make your own additions to the list of kitchen supplies is to go through your kitchen cabinets and drawers and write down what you use most often. Keep it simple, though!

Kitchen Supplies

Basic Galley Supplies

- ☐ aluminum foil
- ☐ baggies—large size zip-lock or twist tie
- ☐ can opener
- ☐ clothespins (clip)—6 per person—use for: drying towels (clip on hanger), drying clothes, closing packages (chips, etc.)
- ☐ dishcloth, sponge, scrubber, handi-wipes, etc.
- ☐ dish towels (2)
- ☐ divided tray for silverware
- ☐ drainer or colander
- ☐ ice cube trays (if not provided)
- ☐ kitchen scissors
- ☐ long wooden matches—use for lighting pilots and barbecue
- ☐ paper plates & cups
- ☐ paper towels & napkins

- [ ] plastic containers with lids—for leftovers—can also be used in microwave (if OK for microwave use)
- [ ] plastic cutting board (8"x10")
- [ ] plastic trash bags (medium), pull-tie closure
- [ ] plastic wrap
- [ ] potholders (2)
- [ ] rubber bands—including a thick one for opening jars
- [ ] Scotch tape
- [ ] small dish drain rack that fits in one side of sink (this is a big help!)
- [ ] soap—dish, laundry & hand
- [ ] string/twine

Table Service

- [ ] **Dinnerware:** (in general, 1 per person + 1 extra service) dinner & luncheon plates, cereal/soup/salad bowls, cups/mugs, glasses (plastic is best).
- [ ] **Miscellaneous dishes:** platter, serving bowl, 2-3 smaller serving bowls for dips/sauces/condiments, butter dish.
- [ ] **Flatware:** (1 per person +1 extra): knives, forks (salad forks optional), spoons, soup spoons, steak knives, serving spoons (2).

Cooking Utensils

- [ ] large bowl—for mixing, serving salad, etc.—we found a large 8 cup Pyrex measuring bowl with handle served multiple uses
- [ ] long fork
- [ ] grater—unless you use this a lot, get a flat one with several grating surfaces on one side; it takes up much less room, although it is slightly less efficient
- [ ] sharp knives—utility (paring) & small carving
- [ ] ladle
- [ ] measuring cups, measuring spoons
- [ ] peeler/corer
- [ ] potato masher
- [ ] slotted spoon
- [ ] spatula

☐ large spoon
☐ tongs—spaghetti, salad, BBQ
☐ wooden spoon

Pots & Pans

☐ frying pan with lid—10" is ideal
  Lid can be round cookie sheet that doubles as an oven tray.
  Electric would be handy.
☐ spaghetti pot—aluminum, not one that is heavy
☐ 2 sizes of sauce pans with lids
☐ cookie sheet for oven
☐ tea/coffee pot

Miscellaneous Supplies

☐ candleholder & candles
☐ charcoal & lighter
☐ clips to hold down tablecloth
☐ cookbook and recipes
☐ cork screw
☐ egg beater/whisk—most beating can be done by hand
☐ hibachi
☐ skewers—if you do a lot of shish kebob
☐ vinyl tablecloth for picnic table

Food

Create a master shopping list by starting with any items from the above list of kitchen supplies that you either haven't brought from home or rented in the convenience kit. Put a check mark next to each one as a reminder. Next, go down the shopping list below and check off the items you need and add them to the master list. The yellow tablet I recommend you bring will come in handy for your shopping lists. Tape a blank sheet inside a cabinet door to use for marking down items to be purchased.

Basic Supplies

- ☐ baking soda & baking powder
- ☐ butter or margarine
- ☐ condiments—ketchup, mustard, relish, mayo, soy sauce (fast food packets are handy), vinegar, salad dressing, BBQ sauce
- ☐ cooking oil & non-stick spray
- ☐ flour
- ☐ Kleenex
- ☐ sugar—small bag/jar can be brought from home
- ☐ salt & pepper (Morton's twin paks); season salt
- ☐ spices and herbs—take small packets of what you use in baggies or containers that seal well and can provide permanent storage
- ☐ toilet paper

Drinks

- ☐ milk—don't buy gallon containers (they take up too much room for the refrigerator to work efficiently)
- ☐ juice—buy first one in glass/plastic bottle to reuse with frozen concentrates or dry packets
- ☐ sodas
- ☐ bottled water—we have never had trouble with campground water, but in some places it might taste funny to you; don't drink that sparkling crystal clear stream water!; the bottle can be useful if you are going on a hike
- ☐ coffee/tea
- ☐ cocoa

Breakfast

- ☐ pancake mix
- ☐ syrup
- ☐ cereals
- ☐ eggs
- ☐ bacon/sausage
- ☐ pastries/donuts/muffins

Lunch

- ☐ bread/rolls
- ☐ lunch meat/cheese
- ☐ tuna/Spam/ham/chicken/crab spread
- ☐ dried soup mixes—easier to store than canned
- ☐ jelly
- ☐ peanut butter
- ☐ lettuce
- ☐ tomatoes/onions

Snacks

- ☐ candy/gum
- ☐ carrots/celery
- ☐ chips/pretzels
- ☐ cookies
- ☐ crackers/cheese
- ☐ dried fruit
- ☐ fresh fruit
- ☐ ice cream (ice cream sandwiches and bars, popsicles)
- ☐ marshmallows
- ☐ nuts
- ☐ popcorn

Dinner

We have found it really successful to plan and shop for four or five dinners at a time. With a party of five or six, however, you may only have room for four meals. Create your menu around the following basics:

meats
rice/pasta/potatoes
vegetables
ingredients not in stock

Meal Planning Guide

Use the following chart as a dinner planning guide and build your shopping list around it:

	Meat	Starch	Vegetable	Other	Dessert
1.					
2.					
3.					
4.					
5.					

Restock:

Items under "other" might include fruit, fixings for salad, muffins, biscuits and the sauces and gravies that go with your meat or starch selections.

Make several photocopies of the chart in Appendix 11 and use it to plan your meals. When you shop, be sure to buy all the ingredients needed, since you can't just "unhook" to go get something you forgot. You will find using this method greatly simplifies the meal planning process. When you are at home it is so easy to go into the freezer, refrigerator, or pantry and be able to use a large variety of supplies. But in the RV, you won't have a large quantity of ingredients from which to draw, so you have to be more organized—plan ahead!!

Planning meals like this can be a real adventure. Since the whole family is somewhat forced to go grocery shopping together, this is a good way to keep everyone interested.

Helpful Cooking Hints

There are many things we learned on our trips that made cooking easier and more fun for everyone. Don't forget, you are on vacation, and the whole idea is to experience new places and enjoy the trip, and not be bogged down in "housework." Save gourmet meals for your fully stocked kitchen at home. The RV galley is small, so keep it simple. Many people have said to us "I'm on vacation, I don't want to cook!" They just don't realize that RV/camping cooking is part of the experience, and by using different approaches to cooking, the whole family will enjoy the new "food experience." We developed many shortcuts that made the food preparation process quicker and easier, and added a whole new dimension to the regular menu used at home.

- Don't bake—sample fare from the local bakery for a real treat
- Make and freeze individual hamburger patties
- Cook a large amount of ground beef; use 1/2 and freeze 1/2 when cooled; freeze in a thin layer in a plastic bag; can be made into meat sauces and will keep and thaw easily. Great for sloppy Joes, too!
- Buy fruit and produce on the road—it is fresh, cheap and delicious. It is really fun to eat local varieties. Of course, be sure to wash it.
- Boil hot dogs in soup—they cook the same as in water and add extra flavor to soup
- If the weather is nice, cook on the grill and eat at the picnic table. Eating out is nice if it isn't too dark or buggy!
- Buy pancake mix that needs only water or milk added
- Stir-frys are quick and easy
- High altitude cooking is a lot different!! At high altitude (3,000 feet or above) water boils at a lower temperature, due to the lower atmospheric pressure, and it seems to take forever to cook anything. Remember, it is the heat, not the boiling, that cooks the food! A general rule at 5,000 feet or over is that cooking time takes 50% longer and more water will be needed, due to increased evaporation. It could take even longer, so allow extra time and check periodically. After a little trial and error, you will be able to judge the amount of time needed. Baking is quite different, too, but packaged mixes and cookbooks usually give high altitude directions. The reason for this is that foods containing leavening agents will rise faster. To get a properly baked product, you will either have to reduce the

amount of flour, sugar, baking soda or baking powder or add slightly more liquid.

- Cold meals are wonderful on hot days! Canned meat/fish make great salads with leftover rice or pasta and vegetables. We usually cook as much pasta as the pan will hold, since it will reheat by a quick dip in boiling water. Rice will reheat the same way (if there is no microwave), so make at least two meals worth. Remember these "extras" when planning meals.

- Canned meats, chicken, tuna, shrimp, etc. are excellent additions to packaged rice or noodle mixes and make a complete, easily prepared meal. Just follow the directions and add the meat or fish during the last five minutes of cooking. Some tasty examples we like: noodles with sour cream and onions with tuna fish; Creole rice with shrimp; rice with broccoli and cheddar cheese with chicken.

- We also used a lot of different flavors of Hamburger Helper. The kids loved it on the road, but wouldn't touch it when we got home!

By planning ahead in your shopping and cooking, you can save a lot of time preparing the food. And, any time saved on a vacation is very valuable!

Other Helpful Hints

- Scrape all excess food into the trash bag; food scraps and oils that get into the waste holding tank can create unpleasant odors

- Rinse dishes in cold water first, so the hot water rinse will be cleaner. A dish drainer that fits in the other section of the sink lets you stack the dishes so they can be quickly rinsed off by a spray or a panful of clean water. Wash glasses first, as water is cleaner and do dirty pots and pans last

- Instead of turning on the water heater to wash a few dishes, heat some water on the stove. Be careful to mix with cold water in the sink or dishpan so it's not too hot. This will save propane

- Make ice cubes at night and put them in baggies in the morning. This will give you an ample supply. You may have to limit the amount of ice in drinks, unless you have a big supply

- Eat breakfasts in shifts—while one shift eats, the other takes showers. This really speeds up the breaking camp process and keeps the kids out of the cook's way!

- As you use up your supplies, the carefully stowed items will start to roll around in your galley unless you figure out a way to keep it neat. We used small cardboard packing boxes from the grocery store to create dividers for the food supplies, and kept some empty boxes for "filler." Extra rolls of towels can be used, too
- Funnels can be made out of tablet paper or foil
- If the utensils rattle around in the drawer, line the drawer with several layers of paper towels
- Don't place things on the counters when you are underway as they will slide around; place them in one side of the sink and use a dish towel to keep them from rattling
- Use a frozen juice can or tin can for fats and oils—let it cool before putting into refrigerator
- If you bring spices or other ingredients from home, many of them can be repackaged in smaller containers. Old spice or condiment containers are excellent for this purpose. Some smaller items can be put into zip-lock bags. Be sure to label them!
- Your RV oven, microwave and refrigerator will be smaller than the ones at home, so cooking dishes and food containers may not fit; use medium size pots and cookware
- For our European visitors, or in case your travels take you to a country that uses the metric system, see Appendix 12, Metric Conversion Tables, for equivalents useful in cooking

This book is intended for the novice RVer who will be taking a vacation, not the full-timer who has plenty of time to entertain and cook elaborate gourmet meals. Your primary goal will be to see the country and begin to learn about the RV lifestyle. Cooking on a tour should be kept to the basics—keep it simple, add a good dose of variety, and enjoy the trip! When the pace allows you to be more leisurely or there is a special occasion, you can spend more time cooking and entertaining.

Cookbooks for the RVer

There are several cookbooks for RVers that we have used—three general ones, and two gourmet. Woodall's *Campsite Cookbook* and *Favorite Recipes from America's Campgrounds*, and the *Good Sam RV Cookbook*, are good basic camping cookbooks. The gourmet cookbooks, *Dining With Zock, A Complete Guide to RV/Tailgate Cooking* and *The Happy Camper's Gourmet Cookbook* will be most welcome when you want to add some pizazz to your on-the-road cooking and entertaining. Both books have comprehensive checklists and tips, as well as delicious recipes, to help you prepare for the ultimate in RV gourmet dining. When you want to go all out for family, friends or that special occasion, these books will save the day. Eating may never be the same again! Information on all the cookbooks mentioned is in the Directories, Guides & Publications section of Appendix 13.

Once we learned the fundamentals of shopping, setting up the galley, and meal planning, we discovered that RV cooking became a very enjoyable part of the travel adventure. Following our tips and using the checklists will help your meal preparation tremendously. Being able to eat when and where you want, and having the ability to prepare any type of meal makes RV cooking a key factor in a successful trip.

Chapter 11

The Campground

My image of a campground was formed during my childhood trip out West in the late fifties. Most campgrounds seemed pretty run down and not too clean. There were no facilities except rustic showers and outhouses. There were no amenities whatsoever, and there was no place nearby to get food. Mosquitoes, flies of all sorts, and other creepy crawlies were the main inhabitants. I dreaded getting into camp each night as we had to unpack the station wagon, set up the tent, air out the bedding and clothes that hadn't dried, and try to set up a makeshift kitchen. Heaven help us if it was raining! In many places we were warned to put our food up in a tree to keep it away from bears. My youthful imagination saw bears behind every tree waiting to grab me (or my sister!). After a few nights of this the adventure of camping quickly disappeared. So much for the "good old days!"

Today's Modern Campgrounds

Times have changed in camping since my first trip many years ago, almost as radically as they have in space exploration. Modern campgrounds have developed into self-sustaining vacation communities with excellent facilities and a wide range of amenities, including well-stocked camp stores, laundries, pools, horseshoe pits, fishing, boating, hiking, nature walks and other activities for the whole family. Some of them even have daily activity programs, area tours, and evening entertainment. Today, the ultimate in camping is the RV resort with golf, health club, tennis, whirlpools, cable TV—all at prices much lower than hotels or motels. RV camping has now become a viable vacation alternative for a large segment of the American public, not just for the adventuresome or those who can't afford a fashionable seaside or mountain resort area.

Finding a Campground

Your first day on the road will culminate with having to find a campsite. This will be the first test of your tour director skills, so hopefully, you will have gotten at least one of the campground directories mentioned in Chapter 6, picked out a campground near your destination — and made a reservation! Your trip would be off to a terrible start if you arrived late in the day and found the campground full and had to spend time trying to find another one. With a reservation, you will be assured of a campsite and can do the initial grocery shopping and still have time to learn how to make camp. After the first night, however, you will discover that the beauty of RV travel is not needing reservations, thereby allowing you to have a very flexible travel schedule. The exception to this rule we have found is that reservations are needed at many of the National Parks, near popular tourist attractions during the high travel season, and around major holidays, such as July 4th, Memorial Day and Labor Day. If the campground is full, ask if they have an "overflow area" that you can use. This is usually a field with no hookups, but sometimes the campground will supply electricity.

Besides needing extra time for shopping on your first day, you should be prepared to spend time setting up camp and learning how to do the hookups, so don't arrive at your destination after dark, if you can possibly avoid it. Try to arrive during daylight so that you will have time to make camp, finish stowing the camping gear, do some exploring, cook dinner, and plan for the next day's trip. Campers tend to go to bed early, so this doesn't leave much time for all the things you need to do.

Depending on the part of the country you are traveling in and the number of campgrounds there, as well as the season, you may or may not have to make reservations. After a few days on the road you will get a feel of how to tell the need for reservations—just ask the campgrounds how fast they are filling up and do they recommend reservations, or ask fellow campers how they found conditions where they came from. If the situation is tight, be wise and make reservations. Should you make reservations and then find that you can't keep them for some reason, call and cancel them so another camper can take your spot. Try to call by 4 p.m., as from this time on is when campgrounds seem to get the big rush and may need your place.

I always made reservations as early as possible if we were going to be around a popular National Park or other major attraction. When we were going to be in a fairly remote area with few campgrounds, I called in the early afternoon to see how fast they were filling up. I told them I might make it to their area and just wanted to see how full they were. If it looked tight, I made a reservation. However, with the large number of campgrounds in most areas today, reservations are not usually necessary, and if there is not a crush of campers, having no reservation allows you greater flexibility in your schedule. If you plan to arrive after 5:30 p.m., check with your proposed campground earlier in the day to see if they recommend reservations. Some campground's don't accept reservations, and if there are a lot of campers, try to get to the campground between 4 and 4:30 p.m., since this is when they start to fill up. Once you are registered, you can continue to sightsee. Part of the fun of RVing is wandering at your own pace, and if you come upon a great spot and want to spend a few extra hours, you will have to find a campsite closer than expected.

Whether you are going to make reservations or are just planning your next stop, look at the directories to see if they have sites for your size RV and the hookups you need. We have always had RVs that were 22'-27' and have had no problems from a size standpoint, but I have noticed that some campgrounds have limited availability for RVs over 30' and some campgrounds on public land can accommodate only small RVs. If you are driving one of the larger ones, be sure to check the availability of appropriate sites.

If there are several campgrounds near your destination, evaluate them by seeing if they provide the facilities and amenities you need, then drive by and pick out the one you like the best. If you need peace and quiet, don't stay near a major highway or the railroad. Brochures or ads may glorify them, or they may be next to a noisy road, so be choosy!

You don't always have to stay at a campground. Many states and provinces allow you to park overnight at rest areas along their major highways. The recently published *Rest Area Guide to the United States and Canada* describes the rules and regulations of using these rest areas for camping, and offers a wealth of other useful driving and tourist information. This handy book lists all the services offered at the areas, as well as hours of operation, phone numbers for emergencies and road condition information. In Europe, you may also park in most legal parking spots for 24 hours. Check with local authorities if in doubt.

A word of caution is necessary here. Many states do not permit or encourage overnight camping at rest areas. One of the compelling reasons behind this prohibition is the people who use these rest stops for illegal activities, therefore making them unsafe for campers. Do not use the rest areas as a substitute for campgrounds, but only as an emergency backup. Camping at rest areas is not what RV camping is all about, anyway. There is nothing like the feeling of security you have at a campground.

Registration and Campground Terminology

Once you have decided on a campground, pull up to the office and register. They will ask you the size of your RV, the license number, the number in your party, how long you are going to stay, if you belong to a club, and the hookups you want. As I mentioned in Chapter 6, Campground Information, the camping fees are quite nominal, but the fee structure varies from campground to campground. The base fee may be calculated on two or four campers, a family, or everybody in an RV. It may also not include hookups, with additional cost for each one, or it may include full hookups, with deductions for the ones you don't want. If charges are made separately, the charge is usually $1 for each utility, and $1-1.50 for each additional camper. There may be extra fees for showers, toilets, or use of the recreational facilities.

Most campgrounds accept credit cards, and some accept personal checks, but don't count on the latter. A sizeable percentage of campgrounds in some parts of the country, however, don't take credit cards, either. This is especially true of the smaller, non-chain affiliated ones. Before you start your vacation, survey campgrounds in your directory to see what their policies are. You may need to take more cash and use your credit cards less. If the campground is affiliated with a chain or RV club, such as the Good Sam Club, you may be entitled to a discount. If you are not a member of the Good Sam Club, you can join at any of their affiliated campgrounds. The cost is nominal and will pay for itself in a few days.

Here is where you need to understand campground lingo. What are "hookups" and which ones do I need? What's a "pull-thru?" Full hookups include water, sewer, and basic electricity for the RV, but not the 220-volt power for the air conditioner. If you don't need sewer or electric hookups, the camping fee will usually be reduced $1-2. Campgrounds usually charge $1-2 extra for electricity for the air conditioning; however, on our trips out West, all taken during the summer, we needed the A/C only once. By the time we arrived at our campsite the RV was cool from traveling and the sun was going down, so there was no heat gain, and as long as we opened the windows, we were quite comfortable. You may need the A/C, however, if you are in an area that is hot and humid.

Depending on the number of people in your party, you may not have to dump every day, so you can take a site without the sewer hookup, and the campground may charge less. However, should you need to dump and there are no sites available with sewer, the campground should have a dump station, or there may be a public one nearby. If you need to use the laundry, toilets, showers, or certain recreational facilities, ask the management to give you a site as close as possible to them so you don't have a long walk. Last but not least, before you leave the office, ask when the camp store, pool or other facility you need closes so you won't be disappointed.

"Pull-thrus" or "drive-thrus" are sites where you can pull the RV straight in and then drive forward on the way out. This is more important for those towing trailers or cars, as it eliminates the need for that wonderful spectator sport—backing up. If your RV needs a pull-thru, you may want to make reservations, since sites are often limited.

The campground office will give you a map of the facility and tell you where the showers, laundry and other facilities you need are and how to get to your site. They will also give you a campground brochure with their camping rules and a plastic trash bag for use in the morning. While you are there, pick up any travel brochures, maps and local travel-related newspapers, as they are a great source of things to do in the area that you might not know about otherwise. The campground people should be able to answer any questions you may have about sightseeing opportunities, museums, churches, local shopping and routes to the next destination. Don't be afraid to ask!

Getting Level

After you have checked in, drive to your site very slowly, because there may be lots of children wandering around the campground, and prepare to pull in. Survey the site first so you can see how level it is, if there are any obstacles, and where the hookups are.

Designers of campgrounds certainly aren't rocket scientists, as you will find out fairly quickly. The layout of the sites generally makes it easy for you to pull in and have the hookups close at hand, but you may find they are on the side away from where you need them. In this case you will have to back in, or if you are lucky, drive around to the other end of the site and pull in facing the opposite way. This won't be possible, however, if the campground is laid out with two sites facing each other.

I have found a few sites so poorly laid out that the sewer and the water and electric hookups, which are usually together, were so far apart that they couldn't be used without extension cords or long sewer hoses, and in some cases, the dump hose had to be run underneath the RV. This is not the norm, though.

Rookie RVers should get out of the vehicle and inspect the site carefully with the lookout, paying close attention to obstacles, location of the hookups, and any possible difficulties in getting level. You have already learned how to get level, but a little practice may be necessary to get level **and** have the hookups readily accessible—at the same time!

Your first night on the road will teach you the importance of having the RV level. I have mentioned it before, but this will be your first test. For your refrigerator to operate properly the RV must be level. This is especially important on the first night, as you will have just filled the refrigerator and it will have to be operating efficiently to cool everything.

Can you imagine sleeping on a slant? Well, you will be if you aren't level, so spend time mastering the techniques of getting level even if you have to pull in and out of your site several times. After a few days you will become proficient at leveling and should be able to tell if you are level from the pilot's seat. I was able to tell pretty well by looking at the terrain how to pull into the site so that I would be level with a minimum of jockeying, but some sites are tough.

Should you find your campsite unsatisfactory, or if you see an available one with a better view, ask the campground manager if you can switch. They are usually happy to oblige.

Setting up Camp

Now that you are in your campsite, you are ready to make camp. If you are traveling with kids who are old enough to help you, the first night is the time to show them how to do the hookups. If this is your first time RVing, you will have to practice what you have learned in this book, so go slowly and have them watch you. From then on, you can assign each of them a task which will make them feel part of the team and keep them from competing with one another. I am sure you will have to settle cries, such as "Dad, Johnny's not doing it right!" or something like that, but you will have to teach all the kids to let the others do it as best they can and not fight over it. Nobody wants fighting kids in the campsite next to them, so, if there is a problem, have the kids come to you.

If the children fight over the tasks or if they don't seem to get the hang of it, don't yell at them, but gently explain how to do it. They will all be overly excited about helping, but need a firm, gentle, guiding hand in learning something new. Remember, patience is a virtue! Competent helpers will make camp setup much faster and more pleasant. Rotate the hookup tasks, so the kids don't feel that they are stuck with the same one.

Doing the hookups is really quite quick and easy. Take the water hose out of the outside compartment, screw one end to the campground's faucet, and the other to the RV's water intake receptacle. Make sure that you are using the "city hookup" or the external water supply one and not the internal fill connection. I made that mistake once and very shortly had enough water spouting out of the receptacle to take a shower! The city intake should be well marked. Turn the water on and check for leaks.

Many times I found that one end of the hose or the other leaked badly, and except for the replacement of an absent washer on one occasion, there was usually no remedy—the connections were just not very good, so don't worry if this happens to you. If the leak is too bad, turn off the water at the campground's faucet before going to bed. Otherwise, you and your neighbors may be camping in a mud puddle. Having an adjustable wrench is very helpful in these situations.

Next, pull the RV's electrical cord (Shoreline) out of its small compartment and plug it into the campground's 120-volt receptacle. If you need 220 power for your air conditioner, the campground will loan you the proper adapter. All RVs have grounded 115-volt electrical systems, which means you must use a three-prong plug for the electrical hookup. A few of the older campgrounds still have ungrounded outlets, so you will need a two-prong adapter with a pigtail that can be attached to the water faucet or outlet grounding screw to make a ground connection. Failure to make a ground could cause shock or electrocution if there is an electrical problem, so be sure to have one. With this hookup completed, the RV will no longer be operating off its batteries.

A brief explanation about the number of amps is needed here. Campgrounds will have at least 20, and probably 30, amp service, while new ones and older ones that have upgraded will also have 50 amps. RVs are now requiring higher amperage due to the increased electrical amenities, such as coffee makers, electric heaters, microwave/convection ovens, washers and dryers, dishwashers and TVs. Some of the campground directories list the amps, so if you need to use a lot of electricity, check this out in advance. Even if the campground has 50 amp service it does not mean that all sites have it. If you need it, call the campground to make sure they will have a site for you. In an older campground with lower amperage, you may not be able to use all of the appliances at once without blowing a fuse, and you may need an adapter to properly hook into their electrical system.

The last of the hookups is the sewer hose. You learned how to do this in Chapter 9, so review that chapter if you need to. Take the hose out of its compartment, attach one end to the RV's dump valve and put the other about six inches down inside the campground's sewer inlet. To keep the hose from popping out, I usually try to place a heavy rock on the hose where it enters the ground. The hose can pop out when you dump if the end is not securely in place. To keep the campsite sanitary and not smell up the place, proper setup is important.

Now light the propane hot water heater and you will be all set for cooking and showers. Don't forget to turn it off before you go to bed, as leaving it on overnight will waste a lot of propane.

Once your utilities are hooked up, you should take a few minutes to check over the outside of the RV. Inspect the tires and lugs, and clean the windshield, headlights and rear window if they need it. The tires should be inflated to the maximum that is printed on the sidewall. Checking to see if they are properly inflated can be difficult and should be done when they are cold. Many RVers as well as truckers hit the tires with a heavy club—if it bounces back, the tires are OK. Do any maintenance at night so that you won't waste time in the morning.

While the pilot is handling the outside chores, the co-pilot can get the inside organized. The first thing to do once the RV is in place, is to open the roof vents and side windows. This will get the air flowing and help keep the RV cool for the evening. Turn the refrigerator from gas to electric and light the oven if you are going to use it. Any bedding or clothing that needs to be aired out can be taken outside.

Now that you are set up you can wander around the campground, pick up supplies, newspapers and souvenirs at the camp store, do the laundry, or use the recreational facilities. We've enjoyed many walks along rivers or on mountains near campgrounds, as they are often located in areas with these activities in mind. One of the camper's golden rules is to respect the environment, so as you enjoy the recreational facilities—be a good camper and leave them the same way you found them! This is also the time when you can meet your fellow campers. You will find they are very friendly and will want to know where your home is, what your itinerary is, and inquire about your rig. They are a good source of travel information about routes, sites to see and campgrounds. RVers love to swap tales! If you have had any problems with your RV, seek out someone with a similar rig.

You may want to take showers after you get set up, and if you don't want to use the RV's, go to the campground's. Take along just the toilet items needed, a change of clothing, flip-flops, soap, towel, and last but not least, shampoo. How many times did we hear from the kids about showers without shampoo! The kids had cheap plastic containers with holes for their toilet items so that they could be taken into the shower. Have a covered soap dish for each sex so that they can take showers simultaneously in their respective shower rooms. We found it was quicker and easier to have them take showers in the campground than hang around the RV and tie up the bathroom endlessly. If you are boondocking, it will save on your precious water supply. It cuts down on the noise, too! One precaution to take here, however, is to be careful with your clothes and valuables when you are in the shower.

Campground Etiquette

Campground etiquette is so important to the enjoyment of the camping experience, that it is good to learn what is expected and teach it to the kids the first night. The old habits from home of running around like wild hooligans won't be appreciated by your fellow campers. The campground should have given you a set of their rules when you registered, so read them over carefully and explain them to the kids, giving them plausible reasons why the rules need to be obeyed. One basic rule I have never seen written down, but should always be obeyed is "don't walk through someone else's campsite!" This is their turf, so stay off.

Although they will vary from one campground to another, the basic rules of camping apply. My main concerns have been over noise the kids (mine or others) made, quiet hours and pets. As I mentioned earlier, campers like to get up early so they can get on the road, which means they like to go to bed early, too. Most campgrounds have quiet hours beginning at 10 p.m. and ending at 7 or 8 a.m. This can be especially confusing if you have changed time zones. Since part of the enjoyment of RVing is to forget what day it is, you will also lose track of the time of day. If you do have kids with you, try to wind them down before 10 p.m. One good method is to tell them about tomorrow's trip and explain what they will be seeing. Let them ask questions. This will make them feel part of the trip and they will look forward to these evening "briefings."

Another type of annoying sound is caused by generators. I just want to remind you that they are quite noisy, and also their exhaust creates pollution that may bother other campers. Unless you desperately need it, shut it off, especially at night. If you arrive at a campground at night, dim your lights as you drive to your site and make as little noise as possible.

Campers may often stay more than one night and will want to keep their same site; so if you see a chair or some other object in a site, it has already been staked out. Most campgrounds have assigned sites, but this bit of camping courtesy will eliminate any confusion.

If you travel with a pet, especially a dog, just remember that other campers may not appreciate your sweet "Poochie-Poo" as much as you do. Some are scared of dogs, and others may be allergic to dogs or cats. First, do not leave it unattended in the RV, as it may get too hot or the dog may bark and annoy others. Second, walk your dog on a leash and use a pooper-scooper! Not only will this keep the campground clean, but you also won't have to worry about dog fights or your dog biting a neighbor. Being thoughtful of your fellow camper really means a lot in close quarters with strangers, let me tell you!! You should expect the same courtesy in return.

Breaking Camp

In the morning allow about an hour and a half to break camp from the time you get up until you hit the road again. This may seem like a lot, but by the time you take showers, get dressed, get breakfast cooked, eaten and cleaned up, rearrange the beds and stow the bedding, go through your daily pre-travel checklist (see Appendix 7), and review the day's travel plans, this time is barely ample. Without kids, of course, you can probably cut this by half an hour. You will find the few minutes it takes to go through the pre-travel checklist time well spent and it could possibly save unnecessary repairs or possible injury. Can you imagine leaving the campsite with the dump hose still connected to the sewer? Or the roof vents or antenna still up? Assign people in your party certain responsibilities and check with them that everything has been done. That way not only do you not have to do it all, but it also gives them a sense of being part of the team—and something to do! Following set procedures, just like pilots do in airplanes, will make your trip as trouble free as possible.

Unhook the water hose last, since you may need it to wash off the dump hose or around the sewer inlet. After you have turned off the water at the source, open a faucet in the RV to relieve the line pressure. Don't forget to replace the plug in the intake receptacle!

You'd think the steps to break camp would be obvious, but it took me quite a few days before I got the routine right. There was so much to do, and so many "helpers," that it took awhile to get the sequence of breaking camp in proper order.

As you are about to leave the campground, walk around your site to pick up any litter, put your trash in the plastic trash bag the owners provided you and place it in their dumpster—don't leave it at the campsite! Many campgrounds are now recycling, so if yours does, sort the appropriate materials and put them in the specific containers. Before you pull out of the site, make sure everybody is ready and safely seated with belts on. If you didn't have a sewer hookup and need to dump, use their dump station or ask if there is a public one nearby. You are now ready for the day's adventures!

Chapter 12

Safe Driving Tips

One of the things that concerned me the most after we decided to take our first trip in 1986 was "What is driving a big rig like?" Luckily, my Lincoln Town Car was pretty big, but the RV we were renting was about ten feet longer and quite a bit higher and wider. I spoke to several friends who either had RVs or had driven them, so I was somewhat relieved by their answers—but not completely! Only on-the-road experience will give you the necessary confidence, but my friends' assurances that RV driving was really quite simple were well founded...with one notable exception—backing up!

Hopefully, the rental agency will give you a trial run and teach you some of the basics of driving an RV. An RV should always be driven defensively, so drive at a safe speed for the road conditions, allow plenty of time to change lanes, watch changing traffic patterns, and know your RV's limitations. The driving tips that follow will give you everything you will need to know, but on-the-road experience is the best teacher.

Learning New Driving Techniques

Your RV is a large vehicle, and because of its size, weight and limited visibility, driving requires different skills than a passenger car does. Due to the size of the RV, you quickly become aware of going under bridges or low hanging tree branches, turning corners and parking. The geometry equations for driving have changed, and for the first time, you have to consider height. Motorhomes weigh 4-5 times more than your car, so braking, lane changing and acceleration habits have to be readjusted. In addition, visibility in an RV is considerably different than in your car, so you will have to use side mirrors for parking and lane changes and probably a lookout for backing up. Once these elementary skills are learned, however, driving an RV is really quite easy. Follow the tips I have outlined below, and you will be an RV pro in no time!

The Importance of a Co-pilot

As I mentioned earlier, the co-pilot is a very important member of the RV's crew for a number of reasons. First, safe driving means advance planning, and the co-pilot can read the map, discuss alternatives and navigate so the pilot will know when to make a route change and how far away places of interest are. Knowing where you are going will save hasty last minute decisions. The co-pilot can also watch out for merging traffic, rest areas, pertinent road signs, such as route numbers, bridge heights, no propane allowed, etc., and be the lookout for cars or obstacles when you are changing lanes, cornering or backing up. With the co-pilot's help you will be able to plan ahead, which is an important element of defensive driving.

The co-pilot will also review the day's itinerary as you go along and inform the crew of what lies ahead. This is an important part of the trip planning process that I discussed earlier. In addition, the pilot and co-pilot, especially, will have to communicate effectively and make decisions together. This will enhance the enjoyment of what you are going to see.

One of the aspects we like about motorhomes is that the passengers can get up and move around while you are underway. The co-pilot can get drinks and snacks for the pilot so you can just keep rolling along without interruption. This is so much easier than traveling by car!

As the day's travel draws to a close, the co-pilot can look in the campground directory and see what campgrounds sound interesting and discuss the pros and cons of each with the pilot.

Driving for Co-pilots

Here I want to give a boost to those who don't expect to drive but may become RV drivers for the first time—really, it's quite easy, so don't be afraid! Even if you don't plan on driving, the driver may be injured or get sick and you may be pressed into the pilot's seat, like it or not. The best thing for you to do is pay close attention to the explanations of the various equipment on the RV before you leave the agency, then watch the pilot closely and ask basic questions about driving. If the pilot doesn't want to answer at first, don't nag as he or she may be trying to hide the jitters. At some point early in the trip ask to do a test drive, perhaps in a vacant parking lot or on an untraveled back road. Get a feel for how the RV handles and how it relates to the road, and what all the gauges mean. Practice a few turns, parking and backing up, and have the pilot explain the basic driving techniques to you. In the campground, watch how the hookups are done and how to check the engine fluids.

With some on-the-road pilot training and learning the following tips, you will become familiar with the rig and ready to drive when the occasion arises.

Getting a Feel of the Road

One of the first things you should do after leaving the rental agency is to get a feel for how the RV relates to the road. It is much bigger than your car, so you will need to find out how to center it on the road for safe driving. The best way I found to do this was to sit in the driver's seat and pick a reference point on the dashboard and/or windshield and line it up with the middle stripe of the road. I then looked out the driver's side window to see how far I was from the center line. The reference point could be a seam in the vinyl, the edge of a speaker, or a piece of tape used as a marker, and should be where you can see it at a glance while driving. Depending on where the reference point is, the "target" stripe in the road may be to the left, right or dead on to the reference point on the dash. Your vehicle should be six to eight inches from the edge of your lane, and after you have learned to center it, you can double check by looking in your mirrors. Once you have this technique mastered, driving the RV (forward!) will be almost as easy as driving the family car.

Having learned this technique of centering the RV on the road, I asked my co-pilot to tell me how far I was from the right edge of the road, and thereby saw how the RV related to it. This will be extremely important when you pass another vehicle. Now that you have mastered centering the RV in the road, you should feel pretty comfortable driving in traffic. Just remember, because of the size of the RV compared to your car, allow extra room to corner, change lanes, or pass another vehicle.

It's Higher, Wider, Longer & Heavier!

An RV is much higher, wider, longer and heavier than a car, and with the long side, reacts differently in the wind. Because of these factors, you will have to think farther ahead and drive defensively, as more room is needed to maneuver, accelerate and stop, and you will have to learn how the RV handles under various road and weather conditions. You will also have to watch out for low-hanging branches, bridges, tunnels and gas station and fast food canopies. The center of gravity is higher in an RV, so going around curves will not be the same as in a car.

Length becomes a factor if you are parking or driving on an incline, such as a driveway, or pulling off the road. On an incline, once the front end goes up, the rear goes down, and may scrape the pavement and do serious damage to the undercarriage. This can really be a problem if your RV has a long overhang beyond the rear wheels. If at all possible, drive onto an incline at a diagonal.

The RV's weight will affect nearly all aspects of driving, and is explained in discussions of those aspects. The table below will give you an idea of the approximate weights of various sizes of RVs. The Gross Vehicle Weight Rating (GVWR) is the maximum weight the RV can be when fully loaded. (Cars, on the other hand, usually weigh between 2,000–4,000 pounds.)

Weight Range for Various Size RVs

    27' 11-12,500 pounds GVWR
    32' 13-15,000 pounds GVWR
    36' 14,500-19,000 pounds GVWR

Pretend you are in a bus, not your car, and learn the handling techniques described in this chapter. After awhile, driving your RV will be second nature and you can concentrate on the rest of your trip.

Use Your Mirrors

Right from the outset you will have to learn to use both side mirrors frequently to check on traffic behind you. This is important if you want to change lanes, enter a highway, or know if you are holding up traffic. At the beginning of your trip ask one of your passengers to tell you how far the closest car behind you is so that you can judge that distance in your mirrors. You have a long rig behind you and the mirrors can distort distances, so it is necessary to learn to interpret what the mirrors are telling you. (Only when you see that first gray hair or wrinkle on your face do mirrors lie!) Frequent use of the mirrors will become second nature very quickly as you learn the necessity of checking on traffic conditions. There are two types of mirrors, flat and convex, and they may be combined. The convex one will be a round bubble at the bottom of the flat mirror. The flat mirror will give you good perspective in the distance, while the convex one will let you see vehicles in the next lane and closer to you, but is not good for judging distances.

Be Friendly!

RVers are quite friendly people. As you start passing other RVs you will notice that many of them will wave to you—a nice form of camaraderie.

Usually, I have found, drivers of one class RV will wave only to those RVs of the same class.

Let People Pass!

One of the cardinal rules of RV driving is to let other vehicles pass! For whatever reason, you may be going slower than other vehicles, so don't cause a line behind you like ants to a pile of sugar. Periodically look in your mirrors to see if there are any vehicles behind you that might want to pass. There are two methods I have found to indicate to drivers behind you that it is all right to pass. One is to pull slightly to the right and cut your speed a little; the other is to wave them around you. For either method, tap the brakes slightly several times to indicate that you acknowledge they want to pass. This will tell them that you are ready and now it is up to them to pass. Remember, they can't see around you, so your actions are important to them. Part of the fun of RVing is to poke along, but don't ruin the driving for others. Just pretend the shoe is on the other foot!

Curves Can Be Dangerous

Be careful on curves. As I mentioned above, the RV will handle differently than your car, especially on curves. Going around a few curves will give you an idea how the RV handles and you will see how the weight, center of gravity and size affect the steering capabilities. Once again, this is not terribly difficult and a little practice will make you feel comfortable with driving. Of course, speed and road conditions will greatly affect how the RV handles, so pay attention to them!

When you enter a curve or an exit ramp, slow down before you get there, as the higher center of gravity will affect the steering ability of the RV. Remember, the posted speed limits are for cars, so for safety go at least 5 mph slower than the limit and don't brake when you are in the curve. Notice if the RV leans when you are in the curve, and be careful if you have to brake hard, as it will lean even more due to the high center of gravity.

Cornering

Cornering is another problem you will need to master in a hurry. Not only is the RV much longer than a car, but also the back end extends past the rear wheels and will follow you around the corner like a long tail. Take a look at a bus or a straight body truck going around a corner, and you will see what I mean. You just cannot cut the corner the way you would in a car, but need to make a wider turn in order to keep from jumping the curb. Take corners slowly and with caution. Quite often there is a curb and some traffic or utility poles on the corner, so be sure to have your co-pilot watch for these. Use your right-hand mirror if you are making a right-hand turn so you can see how much clearance there is. As you make the turn, notice how the rear of the RV swings out—but be careful not to oversteer. You will also need to watch traffic and get your reference points to the road in line, but after a few corners you should be OK. Of course, use your turn signals so people behind you will know what you are doing.

Passing and Stopping

Passing and stopping are other skills you will need to learn quickly, especially if you will be on a superhighway early in your trip. Learning the road reference points mentioned earlier is critical to mastering passing skills. Due to the RV's length, maneuverability, and acceleration speed, passing takes more time and skill than in a car. Make sure there is plenty of clear highway ahead. Of course, don't pass on curves or hills unless there is a special passing lane.

When you want to pass, put on your turn signal and look at your side mirrors. Remember that you may be pulling into a lane of traffic that is moving faster than you are, so allow plenty of room between you and following traffic. Make the lane change slowly in order to give a vehicle behind you a chance to honk if you are too close. Also, be careful if you are pulling to the left, as there may be a blind spot near the driver's door. After you have gotten ahead of the vehicle you are passing, again put on your turn signal and look in your side mirror. At this point note the position of that vehicle in the mirror. For the first few times you pass someone, it is best to post a lookout in the rear of your RV to tell you when you have properly cleared the passed vehicle. When they give you the OK, again note the position of that vehicle in your side mirror and move into that lane. This is another very important reference point you will need to learn. After a few passes it will become old hat and you won't think about it.

A final word of caution is about the suction created when you are passing, or being passed by another large vehicle. You have probably experienced this in your car when you have been passed by a truck. Now you are a large vehicle and may help create the suction. If this occurs, both vehicles will tend to move in towards each other. Pulling slightly to the edge of the road is a good safety precaution if you are being passed by another RV or a big truck. The more distance you have between the two vehicles the less suction there is. As speed increases, so does the suction. I have never found this to be a problem—just a slight sideways movement—but it could be at high speed and especially with crosswinds. If you obey the basic rules for speed in an RV you should never have a problem.

Stopping an RV is fairly simple if you follow standard driving precautions. Because of the weight and size of the vehicle, it cannot maneuver or stop in the manner and distance your family car does. Excess speed and poor road conditions will compound this problem, so it is very important at the beginning of your trip to learn how your RV stops. Practice a few stops under different driving conditions and road surfaces to see how the RV handles. This testing, along with the other driving tips mentioned, will give you a good idea of the RV's capabilities. Under normal driving conditions, allow at least one length of the RV between you and the vehicle ahead of you for each 10 mph of your speed. Increase this distance if the road or weather conditions are bad. Don't forget—you have a lot of rig behind you!

Parking

Parking an RV is probably the next trickiest thing to backing up. In some states, especially those where RV travel is common, you will find well demarcated areas for RVs and parking will be fairly easy. Most tourist areas will have an area with large spaces set aside for RVs, so all you will have to do is pull in. Leaving the parking space is more difficult, and it is wise to post a lookout, either outside or in the rear of the RV to tell you if everything is clear. Just remember that the rear will swing around more than you are used to in a car, so pull far enough out of the parking place next to you so you don't turn too sharply, oversteer, and back into the vehicle next to you. Once you have mastered the geometry, this phase of parking will be second nature. On our last trip I was pulling out of a parking place behind our daughter's house, didn't back out far enough, hooked the bumper of the car next to me as I straightened out and crushed my side reflector light. So much for my high marks in geometry!

In some areas you will have to parallel park. Many people don't like to parallel park a car because they can't get the geometry right, so if that is your case, don't plan to parallel park an RV! Otherwise, the geometry is the same as in a car, but you must be careful of the swing of the front and rear. Once again, it is wise to post a lookout. You will really have to be careful of telephone poles and signposts at the curb.

If you are in an area that does not cater to RVs, try to find a parking space that is away from the cars, where you can take up several car spaces. These spaces will be narrower and shorter, so you will stick out in the lane unless you park at an angle. As you park, think of what you will have to do to get out and make sure you can't get boxed in. Look at how the rest of the parking is configured, not only near you, but also at the end of the lanes where you will have to turn to get out of the parking area. Even out West where RVing is common we had to park at the edge of the parking lots when we went grocery shopping. I guess shopping center owners think RVers don't have to eat! On our trips we never got boxed in, but I was very careful where I parked.

> Remember: your wheels should be turned toward the curb when you are parked, especially on an incline. This will give additional help to the parking brake.

Braking

Braking in an RV is quite different than in your car, so learning new braking techniques under various driving and weather conditions is very important for driving safety. The weight and center of gravity of the RV will affect how it handles under all conditions, so before you have gone too far on your trip, do several tests on the braking ability of the RV. The amount of time it takes to slow down is considerably longer than in your car, due to the increased weight.

For going down a hill, especially a long one, you will need to learn new braking techniques. Because of the weight and type of brakes the RVs have, make sure you slow down before you start your descent. As you go down the hill, reduce your gear to low. The transmission will automatically be in second until your speed drops to 30-35 mph, then it will drop to low. Avoid prolonged continuous use of the brake pedal, as that will cause the brakes to fade from overheating and you may lose control of the RV.

The accepted method of braking procedure on a hill is for light to moderate, intermittent pressure on the brake so that you don't start to pick up too much speed. Between gearing down and braking you should not pick up much speed. However, if you do start to pick up more than 3-4 mph over when you began your descent, brake a little harder to reduce speed to 3-4 mph less than when you started the descent. This method should help reduce the possibility of brake fade. Since the more speed you pick up will take longer to slow down and your brakes may fade, the best policy is to monitor your speed closely as you start to descend. If the brakes don't slow you down fast enough or start to feel spongy, pull over to the side of the road for a few minutes and let them cool off. Car drivers aren't used to this problem, so it is good to be aware of it.

Should you need to stop suddenly, pump your brakes to warn vehicles behind you, as they may not be able to see what is happening in front of you. If there is time, put on your flashers to indicate to those following you that there are traffic problems ahead. Just pretend you are on an expressway in your car wondering why the big bozo up ahead is going so slowly. Wouldn't you like to know there were problems ahead?

I cannot overemphasize the importance of weight, speed and road conditions on the braking, stopping and handling ability of your RV! Pay very close attention to the road conditions and learn how the RV reacts to them under varying circumstances.

Watch Your Gas Gauge!

As your trip progresses, keep an eye on the gas gauge from time to time. Since the RV will typically get 8-12 mpg, it will consume fuel faster than your car. This is especially important if you are driving in the West where the distances between gas stations can be great. If you are starting a stretch that may not have a gas station, fill up, even if you are half full. Part of the fun of RVing is to get off the beaten path, but this also means that some of the elements of civilization—like the gas station—will be missing. In our wanderlust I have taken many a wrong turn or unexpected side trip and often these led to mile upon mile of desolate driving. Some of the scenery we have found has been worth the escapade, but the thought of running out of gas was always in the back of my mind.

If you are doing mountainous driving, keep in mind that fluids weigh a lot (gas, 6.25 lb/gal, diesel, 6.6 lb/gal, and water, 8.4 lb/gal) and that you will have to carry this weight up the mountain. This consumes more fuel and slows down the RV. A few hundred pounds of extra weight can really mean a lot on mountainous trips, so check your gauge before you start the climb and figure out how far it is to an area where you can get gas. Don't fill your tank, but allow a considerable margin for error, and remember that mountainous driving will reduce your mpg. We did a lot of mountainous driving in Colorado, Montana and Wyoming, and I guess the gas consumption increased 10-15%, which wasn't as bad as I had expected. Gas mileage is pretty good going down the mountain!

Refuel before entering a city or other congested area. Not only will gas stations be more difficult to find, but maneuvering around the pumps, canopies and cars will be tricky as well.

At the end of a day's run, calculate what your gas fuel consumption was, then figure out your mpg. To do this accurately you will have to fill up the tank. Use Appendix 10, the Daily Travel Log, to keep track of the mileage and fuel consumption. Depending on the type of terrain covered you will be able to determine the gas mileage you can expect on future runs. This knowledge will be especially important in desolate areas and during mountainous driving. After a few days of these calculations you will be pretty comfortable estimating fuel consumption and how this relates to the gas gauge.

Do Safety Checks

As a general safety precaution, each time you stop for a driving break walk around the RV. Check tire inflation and inspect underneath for anything that may have come loose and for fluid leaks. Occasionally, I left the hot water heater on and didn't realize it until several hours later. One time I heard a loud hissing noise, which turned out to be air leaking from a front tire with dirt in its valve—and not a rattlesnake! Luckily, I got the dirt out and filled the tire with air, but this could have been a serious problem if we had been far from a service station and I hadn't made a check. When you stop for gas, check the transmission and engine fluid levels, and clean the front windshield, rear window, and the mirrors. Before getting gas, turn off all pilot lights and open flames, as they could cause a fire or explosion if there were a gas spill. Relight the pilots once you have pulled away from the pumps. If you are towing a trailer, boat or car, check the couplings, hitch and safety chains, and the electrical and brake connections.

Every couple of nights when you are parked at the campground, turn on the engine and see if all the running, brake, driving lights and turn signals function properly. Even if you don't plan to drive at night, you might have to in case of a delay or emergency, and you want to be sure all systems are "go."

Beware of Tunnels and Bridges!

Several of the most hair-raising incidents on our trips occurred going (or trying to go) through tunnels and bridges that were not meant for RVs. This is another important reason to have an experienced map reader as the co-pilot. Once you get off the main highways you will need to pay attention to tunnel or underpass heights and the width of bridges and other narrow areas. Back East in our metropolitan area these were not problems, at least in a car. However, out West these problems occur frequently when you are off the beaten path.

The problem is "trying to get there from here," as the saying goes. My first experience with this problem happened soon after we crossed into Utah and wanted to head south on route, let's say 8137. That seemed like the shortest and perhaps, only route to easily get to where we wanted to go. I looked at the sign, and that was the route number all right, so down the road we went. After many miles of driving through ranches we came to another sign that reaffirmed that we were going in the right direction. This was OK until we came to what I can best describe as a bridge similar to the one depicted in Thornton Wilder's *The Bridge of San Luis Rey*. Just imagine a narrow, rickety, swinging bridge. Well, it didn't swing, but it sure would have if I had continued over it as I had planned. It was so narrow I had to fold in the side mirrors! I just assumed this was typical Western driving!! A daredevil I am not, and with six lives at stake I backed off the bridge. Luckily, I had only gotten about half the length of the RV onto the bridge, so backing off wasn't too much of a problem. After I turned around one of the kids said, "Hey Dad, the sign says 'limit five tons, no RVs.'" I am forever thankful my kids can read, but why can't they read these signs sooner?!

We retraced our steps to the interstate and looked at the map again. I should have been right, so what went wrong? Since we couldn't figure out what had happened, we continued heading west to the next exit, and there, lo and behold, was route 8137 again. This route didn't have grass growing between the ribbons of concrete like the first one did, so we took it and got to our destination in good time. What we hadn't understood about the road numbering system was that in Utah, and perhaps other states, the ranch roads had similar numbers to the state highways, but had an R, for ranch, before the number. I am a quick learner and didn't make that mistake again!

One of our travel guidebooks mentioned a beautiful lake in a crater near Mt. Rushmore, South Dakota, so we decided to find it. When we left Rushmore, I asked one of the Park Rangers if an RV could get to the lake, as I knew from reading the material there were tunnels on the route. The Ranger said, "Yes," so off we went. After many miles of climbing winding roads toward the crater and passing through several tunnels, we came to one that said "Caution, Height 10'6." I stopped dead. How was I going to get our 11' RV through the tunnel? After some serious consideration I decided I wasn't, so I began the arduous task of backing down a narrow, winding road. Luckily, the cliff was not on my side of the road. At that point I wouldn't have minded hitting something, but I certainly didn't want to fall off a cliff. Cars came both ways and carefully navigated around me, looking up at the idiot driver in wonderment. Fortunately, I had plenty of helpful lookouts, and after about a mile and a half, came to a hairpin turn that had some extra shoulder so I could turn around. My average speed must have been 1 mph!

When we got down to the bottom of the hill one of the kids said, "Look at the sign I told you about." Sure, enough, it warned of the low tunnel height. Do adults pay attention to teenagers? Never! I don't remember the admonition on the way up the mountain, but he did, as he knew just where to look for the sign on the way down. Once again, this is a good reason for the co-pilot to pay attention to the road signs as the driver has a lot to look out for and might miss an important one. This is so much more important than in a car that I must keep emphasizing it. Preview your route and then tell everybody to pay attention to the signs. Pay attention to the kids, too!

The only route east from Zion National Park goes through a tunnel, and that was the direction we wanted to go. After bad experiences on two of the previous trips, I thought I was pretty smart. I read the map **and** asked the ranger. He even measured me with a special pole. All systems "go!" I was following a big tour bus, so I figured I was OK. If it could do it, I certainly could. Right? Half way through the tunnel I heard this ungodly scraping noise and saw sparks flying behind me. My first thought was that I had ripped off the roof air conditioning unit. Expensive, yes, but we didn't need it. I pulled over to the side as soon as we got out of the tunnel and found that the side mirror had been cleanly sheared off. With another week of travel this was going to make a big difference. It could have been worse, but I don't know how the bus made it and I didn't. Anyway, pay attention to the **sides** of wherever you are driving, as well as the height, and you will avoid some of my mistakes.

Vapor Lock

I had heard about vapor lock and even had it once on a long trip in my 1965 Porsche. After having driven for several hours I had stopped for a soda at a turnpike rest area, and when I tried to start the car, nothing happened. Somebody more mechanically inclined than I suggested that I wait awhile and let the engine cool down some more. Another person suggested that I pour fruit juice over the engine. At the time this latter suggestion didn't make sense, but having learned more about the problem, that fellow wasn't too far off.

My ability to describe vapor lock in layman's terms may oversimplify it, but at least you will understand what it is and what to do about it. Vapor lock is the inability of your engine to start due to a lack of fuel in the carburetor and fuel pump. It occurs during summer driving and is caused by higher temperatures in the engine compartment, which heat up the fuel more than in the winter. This leads to excessive fuel expansion and vaporization. The vaporization and expansion put positive pressure on the fuel pump, and as heat becomes greater in the fuel supply lines, it overcomes the pressure and creates vapor lock. The engine just can't get rid of it. With the extra pressure and the fuel vaporized away, your engine is unable to start. Depending on the chemical makeup of your fuel, it will vaporize at different temperatures. Many fuel dealers try to get the right blend for the summer, but there are a lot of factors that go into the vaporization equation. This problem has been made more difficult in recent years as gasolines have been reformulated to reduce certain emissions. The new oxygenated blends have a greater tendency toward vapor lock, as they will boil and vaporize more easily. This may be more of a problem at high altitudes, as the atmospheric pressure is less and fluids boil at lower temperatures.

I never had this happen to me on our trips, but on one trip, in particular, every time I stopped for gas and unscrewed the gas cap I got a loud hissing sound as the pressure was released. If this happens to you, don't worry. You have done nothing wrong and if your RV is properly tuned for the driving conditions and the gas blend is right, you won't get anything more than the hissing.

Vapor lock conditions won't affect your driving and will occur only when you stop. I have never heard or read a technical explanation of the hissing sound except that a mechanic at a gas station told me that it was part of the vapor lock process and caused by the fuel mixture and heat, but not to worry. So I didn't!

However, what do you do if your engine won't start? In retrospect, the suggestions given to me years ago will work. The idea is to let the fuel system cool down so that any fuel in the fuel pump and carburetor won't be vaporized. First, open your engine compartment to let air blow over the engine. Second, pour water over the engine, especially the fuel pump. Be sure not to get any wires, spark plugs or the distributor cap wet or you will have other problems! A quart of water should do. Third, wait awhile. If the engine won't start now, pour some more water over the fuel pump, wait a few minutes, and try again. When the engine is sufficiently cooled down, it should start. However, if it doesn't start at this point, get a small amount of gas and pour it into the carburetor. Do it slowly so you don't flood it. This should prime the system again and get you going.

Don't Speed!

Speeding is unsafe in your car, but it is much worse in an RV because handling is considerably more difficult due to its size and weight. Driving the recommended speed limit for RVs gives you more time to react in critical situations. Stopping distances are also much greater than for your car, as I mentioned earlier. Besides the dangers of speeding, fuel consumption is greatly increased the faster you go over the optimum speed for the RV. Check the recommended speed with the rental agent; I have found traveling at 50 mph or under is best for normal conditions. However, go slower as road or weather conditions worsen. Just remember to let people pass. You may think you are going the speed limit, but you aren't! I have driven comfortably at 55 mph on superhighways with little traffic, but you really don't get there any sooner by driving faster, so slow down!

Be Careful in Windy Conditions

Wind conditions can greatly affect how your RV handles. Just think of yourself as a big sail on a boat (don't forget, you are driving a land yacht). Your car is quite aerodynamic, but the broad side of the RV can really catch the wind. In most instances you will experience nothing more than a slight sideways push, and that shouldn't bother you, but when you see signs that warn of windy conditions, heed them and slow down! There are certain areas that are naturally windy due to the terrain. Excess speed multiplies the force of the wind dramatically and makes steering more difficult. You might not even feel crosswinds in your car, but you certainly can in an RV. I have seen several big RVs that have been blown off the road in these windy areas and it is not a pretty sight, so I hope a word to the wise is sufficient. Some parts of the country are more susceptible to these winds than others, but don't worry about going to them, just be prepared for the driving conditions. In other areas if it becomes very windy and you are being buffeted, the best advice is to pull over to the side of the road and wait out the storm.

Backing Up!!

I was quickly able to adjust all my car driving skills to those needed for the RV—except backing up. My friends had told me it would be different and the salesman at the RV center we went to when we planned our first trip told us it was pretty easy. And salespeople, as we all know, don't lie! However, I remembered renting a truck to pick up some antiques a few years before our first trip. At the rental agency I managed to back about five feet before I hit a large post guarding the gas pumps. That was my first experience with blind spots. With this episode in mind, I was ready to tackle the RV! I vowed nothing would get the better of me.

In your car you depend on the mirrors and what you see if you turn around. The RV's mirrors will tell you part of the picture, and you may be able to look out your window and see part way down the RV. But how about the rest of the side, the co-pilot's side, or worse yet, behind you? What's above you? Here is where lookouts really come in handy. In most cases, when I needed to back up in a parking lot a lookout in the rear of the RV was sufficient. Of course, this depends on where the rear window, if any, is placed. However, backing into a campsite or a tight spot is much easier with a lookout outside and behind the RV on the driver's side. Other RVers may try to guide you, but they can be confusing and should be tactfully ignored; you need to know the principles of backing up and use any input from bystanders only for gauging your distance from an object. Quite a few RVers who own large rigs have a backup system with a TV monitor in the cockpit. That really must make backing up easy!

The best procedure is for both the driver and lookout to get out of the vehicle and survey the terrain. Don't just tell someone to go out and look. Tell them exactly how to direct you. First, tell them to look for obstacles and the amount of clearance, especially overhead branches or parts of buildings; next, tell them where you want them to stand so that you can see them in your side mirror and what hand motions you want them to make; make sure that they are clear of the RV so that you won't run over them! The lookout plays a very important part in the teamwork that is needed to become a pro at backing up, so proper instructions from the beginning are essential.

I have never been good at backing up a car, so I approached doing it in an RV with much trepidation. Even though the geometry of backing up is the same as in a car, the sheer size of the RV can throw off your sense of direction. You can't see, so you have a feeling of helplessness. Which way will the rear zig if I turn my steering wheel to the right? What do those wild hand motions indicating I should go to the left mean? Which way do I turn the wheel to make the rear go in that direction? How do I back-and-fill? How will I ever get level in the campsite? Help!!

Got the picture? Arms flying in all directions, hands spinning around the steering wheel, your head turning around in circles like a duck's, and finally, yelling, which you instructed the lookout never to do, as it attracts onlookers, then... crunch...! Watch your temper!

All these potential problems raced through my head as we began our first day on the road. I was King of the Road, remember? Needless to say, I avoided getting into any situation that might have forced me to back up. Chicken? You bet! I must have taken up half a football field when we finally stopped to load up on groceries! "Take no chances, have no problems," became my instant motto.

Our first night was to be spent at my brother-in-law's cabin on a mountain 2,000 feet above Boulder, CO, which itself is 5,000 feet above sea level. Boulder is only twenty-five miles from where we had picked up the RV, so I hadn't had much driving experience as we started the long climb from Boulder up Flagstaff Mountain. I had heard about switchbacks, but where I come from back East with few real mountains and good roads, I had never driven on one. I got a cram course (I was going to say crash course, but that might have sounded scary) in a hurry. As the co-pilot and kids kept yelling "Look at the beautiful view...the red-tiled roofs..." or whatever, I was becoming a bus driver that Greyhound would be proud of. Actually, I mastered the geometry of driving on these switchbacks more easily than I had dared to dream and managed to pull into my brother-in-law's drive in one piece. My heart beat had doubled, but I told myself it was just the altitude. I was still King of the Road! King of the hill, too! I came, I drove, I conquered!

I didn't know anything about leveling, but I parked at what I thought was level. Our first night on the road was spent sleeping at a good list to port!

My brother-in-law had left for work by the time we departed the next morning, so I had plenty of room to maneuver. With some novice lookouts, I made a few back-and-fills, and we were off! So were a few branches. Oh, well, I figured, they were half dead anyway. I felt pretty good that the RV had survived its first backup with me as the driver!

The old adage "practice makes perfect" doesn't hold true for backing up an RV. Believe it or not, this is a team sport! Just remember, it is like backing up a BIG car, except you have a BIG blind spot. However, practice can make you pretty good at it, and with a good lookout, following these backing up tips, taking plenty of time, and a good dose of patience, you will survive.

Follow these practical tips and you won't be classified as a rookie too long and feel embarrassed when you pull into a campsite. Inspect the site and instruct the lookout how to guide you. Once you start to work as a team you will need to know how to respond to the lookout's hand signals. If the signal is to get your rear to the right, turn your steering wheel to the right. Don't make sharp turns as you may oversteer and the RV will swing too far in one direction. Also, make sure you pay attention to how the front of the RV swings as you back up. Take it slowly, watch your lookout and keep an eye on the front. If you get too close to a tree or other obstacle, pull forward, straighten the RV and try again. If for some reason things aren't working out, don't start shouting at each other. Simply reverse roles—let the driver become the lookout.

If you have to back up at night, be sure to use a flashlight and practice the signals before you start maneuvering. Go very slowly, as it may take the lookout longer to check all the obstacles.

After a few backups you will feel like an old pro. Now you can regale in those "remember when" stories as you watch rookies learning the ropes. Both you and the lookout will feel a sense of accomplishment. When you get the confidence go to the aid of a rookie, you've really made it!

Running off the Road

If you need to pull off the highway suddenly, check the shoulder to see if it looks firm enough to hold the RV's weight. However, if you run off the road, don't brake, as the change of surface may cause you to go out of control, but do slow down as quickly as possible. Also, your center of gravity is much higher than your car's, so don't go off at an angle or into a dip, as this could cause you to turn over. Come to a complete stop unless the shoulder and road are even, in which case you can proceed cautiously back onto the highway. If you stopped, slowly pull back onto the road and regain normal speed. If you are pulling off the road because of a problem, put on your hazard lights to alert drivers behind you that you are having trouble and pull as far off the pavement as possible. Your RV is much wider than a car, so you want to leave plenty of room for other vehicles to pass you.

Blow Outs and Changing a Tire

Blow outs are infrequent, but you should be prepared in case one happens. When it does, drive as straight as you can, slow the RV down, but do not slam on the brakes, as braking will cause the RV to veer to one side and you may lose control. Once the RV is under control, slowly pull off the road and stop, making sure that you are far enough off the road and on firm ground that you can work safely on the tire. Put on the hazards, set out flares or reflectors and tie a white handkerchief in a visible spot to alert passing drivers of your trouble. Part of RV courtesy and mutual aid is to stop if another camper seems to be in distress. Hopefully, someone will stop to help or make a phone call for you.

At this point, the best thing to do is call your rental agency and have them locate a road service company for you, as well as get any specific instructions or authorization you might need. Changing a tire on an RV is more difficult and dangerous than on your car, so it is better to leave it to more experienced hands. The agency should be able to find one near you, but if they can't, look in your camping guides under "road service or truck repair," in the yellow pages, or call the local police. Also, truck stops may have a towing and repair service or know the nearest one.

The Good Sam Club started an Emergency Road Service (ERS) for its members in 1984. If you are a member, and have this service, which costs extra, call them for towing or repair facilities anywhere in the country. They will contact and dispatch the repair service for you.

In Europe, call the ADAC, the German Automobile Club, which is the equivalent of our AAA. The club has a lot of English-speaking members thanks to the large number of American servicemen there, so you won't have any trouble communicating.

But, if there is no choice, you must change it yourself. The rental agent should have shown you where the jack and spare tire were and how to get them down from their holding clamps. In Chapter 9, Know Your RV, I gave a brief explanation of how to use the jack. However, look in the instruction manual for your particular RV to get the accurate safety instructions!

A brief word of caution is needed here: jack the RV up just enough to get the tire off, and allow room to get an inflated one on; the higher you go the more danger there is that your RV could be blown (or sucked) off the jack by passing traffic. If your RV has dual rear wheels and the flat is on the inside, skip the jack and drive the good tire onto a piece of wood or stone just high enough to get the RV off the ground, then change the flat tire. Of course, before you start jacking, make sure the parking brake is on and put blocks under the other wheels so the RV won't roll. If the tire is too heavy or you can't figure out what to do, wait for help. There is certainly no sense in getting hurt.

One of my friends who is in the trucking business told me it is nearly impossible to tell visually if you have a flat on an inside tire, as the outside tire will bear the weight and make it look inflated. You can check by hitting them with a stout stick or a heavy tool. If there is a difference in sound, you have a flat.

Keeping Alert

Driving an RV can sometimes be tiring, due mainly to the way you must sit to steer, so learning how to keep alert is important. I have found the seats to be very comfortable, even for long distances, but I was not used to the position needed to drive, and discovered some "new" muscles. One good way to overcome this problem is to break up your trip into segments, as I mentioned earlier. Whether you stop for gas or sightseeing, stop at least every two to three hours and take a few minutes to stretch and get the kinks out of your neck, back and chest. The co-pilot and crew will appreciate it, too!

A few simple exercises that can be done while you are underway will also be rewarding. I quickly found that rolling my neck around and from side to side, then massaging the muscles, helped relieve the neck strain I developed. Try shrugging your shoulders up and down, then back and forth about five times each hour. This exercise will help relieve sore shoulder and upper torso muscles. Another on-the-road relaxation technique I learned was to do isometrics by holding my hands on either side of the wheel and squeezing toward the center, and conversely, by pulling out. These exercises were very effective in relieving the neck, shoulder and upper body strains that developed while driving.

After a few days, doing these simple exercises became second nature and I did them routinely for the duration of the trip. Those "new" muscles I discovered didn't seem to bother me as much after awhile, either. My body was also probably getting adjusted to the steering position. Keeping fit on the road made driving less tiring and the whole trip more enjoyable. If you start to feel stress and strain, pull over for a few minutes and do some exercises. You will soon feel revitalized and be ready to go again.

Overheating

Overheating always happens far from anywhere, so the best thing you can do is watch for signs of the engine running hot and know what to do. Going up long hills is one of the most frequent causes of overheating, as there is extra load on the engine, transmission, and cooling system. As you start up a hill, gear down so the engine doesn't strain and overheat. One of the items on the daily checklist is a check of the engine's fluids. If your radiator is full, you should be OK, even on a long mountain climb in hot weather. But, there is always the chance of a pinhole in a hose, or a leak somewhere, or, the engine just may be too hot. If your warning light goes on or the temperature gauge starts to climb into the hot zone, your engine is getting too hot.

Follow these steps to cool it off: first, turn off the vehicle's air conditioning (not roof-top) and turn on the heater to high. This will give the cooling system a rest and drain some of the heat away from the engine. If the engine is still overheated after a few minutes, pull off the road in a safe spot, put the transmission in neutral and race the engine for a minute or two. Doing this increases the fan speed and will move more air through the engine compartment and hopefully, cool it down. If the engine still remains too hot, turn off the ignition, raise the hood, and wait for it to cool down. After five or ten minutes, carefully remove the radiator cap to check the fluid level, and fill if necessary. When you take the cap off, wait 10-20 seconds in case the pressure inside blows hot fluid out. This happened to me once, and I got a face full of hot antifreeze. I was really lucky that I was wearing glasses!

Winter Driving

RVing is being enjoyed year-round, even in the coldest climates, as more and more people change their vacation habits. Historically, people have taken long summer vacations and a little time off around the holidays. Today, however, more people are moving away from extended summer vacations and are taking long weekends or mini vacations throughout the year. With all the comforts of home, RVs become mobile chalets during the winter and give people the opportunity to take fall foliage tours, a quick trip to see friends, relatives, kids in college, or to participate in such popular outdoor activities as skiing, ice fishing, snowmobiling and ice skating. Sightseeing can be a real pleasure during the winter, too, as the vistas take on a totally different dimension, and with fewer vacationers crowding the roads and places of interest, you may be better able to enjoy what you have come to see. Rental rates are much cheaper, too! National Parks are a favorite wintertime destination for thousands of travelers, as their majestic beauty changes with the seasons.

Just think, after a brisk outdoor activity you can return to your RV and get a mug of hot cocoa or a bowl of steaming soup to warm you up, pull off several layers of clothes, and relax! What would you be doing if you were in your car? You'd have to scrape frost off the inside of the windows, drive to see if you could find a restaurant that was open, and peel off layers of clothes as the car warmed up. There's nothing like a home on wheels!

Many of the country's campgrounds stay open to cater to winter vacationers, but some of their facilities may be closed. Call ahead to see if they are open and if they have the facilities you need. Some of the campgrounds are near winter-fun destinations, such as ski resorts, and provide winter activities like hot tubs, sleigh rides, and wintertime excursions. Other RVers like to escape from the cold, and head to warmer climes to fish, play tennis and golf, or relax by the pool. No matter where you go during the winter, but especially in the colder areas, it is wise to make reservations, as the availability of alternate sites may be quite limited. If you are going to be where it is cold, confirm that your site has an electric hookup when you make the reservation.

Winter driving and camping require some changes from what you do the rest of the year. Besides taking extra care in driving, winter RVing requires different procedures for dealing with water and waste, and precautions in heating the RV. Before you go on a trip, check with the rental agency for their suggestions for the conditions you will be facing and read the owner's manuals for proper operation of equipment. The following helpful tips will make your winter trip safer and more enjoyable.

Driving

Driving on ice and snow is much more difficult in an RV than in a car. Follow the same precautions you would in a car, but remember that you have a much larger vehicle. Get a feel for the road under various conditions, as acceleration and braking will be quite different than in dry weather. Take tire chains along and make sure you know how to put them on. The weight of the RV will be helpful on icy roads, but go slowly and use lower gears.

Heating the RV

Heating the RV is essential to your enjoyment of the trip, just as it is in your house. Make sure the RV uses propane, not butane, because butane will not work below 32 degrees Fahrenheit. A motorhome's furnace will use about 1,000 BTUs per foot of length per hour when it is on all the time. A twenty pound cylinder of propane will yield between 345,000 and 390,000 BTUs. Remember, however, that the furnace will cycle on and off, and therefore, use less gas, but you don't want to press your luck and run out, so keep close track of your LP-gas supply!

Never, NEVER, **NEVER** use the stove, oven or catalytic heater for heating your motorhome, because they will consume the oxygen in the RV and replace it with carbon monoxide. The RV furnace is safe because it gets its air from the outside and vents the products of combustion outside. When you are cooking or baking, always open a window or roof vent as a fresh air source, and there will be no danger from fumes. If you need supplemental heat, buy an electric heater that operates on less than 15 amps.

If you are boondocking—that is, not hooked up to an outside electrical power source—remember that the furnace blower runs off your 12-volt battery and can discharge it in about eight hours if it runs continually. However, as I mentioned about the LP-gas supply, the furnace will not be running all the time, so the battery will last longer than eight hours without being recharged.

Fresh Water

Unless you have an RV that is totally set up for winter traveling, you will not have the fresh water system that you do when it is warmer. You will have to take showers at the campground and cook, wash dishes and flush the toilet with water you take with you. It is probably safer to use a portable water source anyway, just in case you lose your heat for some reason. The RV rental agency should be able to supply you with the necessary water jugs, but ask them when you make the reservation.

Waste Water Tanks

The black and gray water holding tanks will need special RV nontoxic antifreeze to keep them from freezing. As your trip progresses you will be adding water to these tanks, so make sure you keep the right amount of antifreeze in them.

> If you will be driving in snow or slush, your dump valve covers may become frozen shut. Either cover the valves with a waterproof material, or if they do become frozen, thaw them by pouring warm water over them.

Picking a Campsite

When selecting a campsite, pick a sunny one rather than a shady one, preferably near a wind break, and face either end into the wind.

Winter Camping Tips

- A CB radio could be very helpful if you get into trouble and need to call for assistance. Perhaps you could arrange for a short-term rental of a cellular phone; this could be especially important for women driving alone who may not want to broadcast their distress on the CB.
- Take along heavy-duty jumper cables in case you (or someone else) can't get started.
- Add a shovel, sand or kitty litter, and a long, heavy-duty extension cord to your supply list.
- Extra blankets and candles could also come in handy if you lose power.
- Take a big sheet of plastic to sit on in case you need to put on the chains.

- A general driving rule that should be observed during all seasons is to put on the running lights at dusk and in rain or fog. An RV is a big vehicle, and with reduced visibility it is important for other drivers to be able to see you from quite a distance.

- Take an extra supply of warm clothes, including warm boots, in case you get wet, or if there is a problem and you have no heat or have to walk a long distance for help.

Taking some extra precautions during winter RVing is necessary for a successful trip. It would be terrible to get stuck somewhere when it's 10 degrees Fahrenheit just because you didn't follow winter camping procedures. The benefits of taking a trip at this time of year are countless, and you should plan a winter RV vacation if you have the time to get away.

I have taken a lot of time to describe the various driving situations you will face, as I feel the rookie RVer should have a good idea of what to expect before the trip begins. By quickly learning these safe driving techniques you will have command of the road and be assured of having a safe and enjoyable trip. Only on-the-road experience will give you the necessary practice, but by taking it nice and slow when you start out you will find that driving an RV is really quite simple. My tips, coupled with some instruction from the rental agency and on-the-road experience, will quickly make you a pro.

Chapter 13

Traveling With Kids

Traveling with children or grandchildren can be a truly rewarding experience—if you do it right! An RV vacation gives the family uninterrupted quality time together and will create memories that will last forever. A special bonding takes place between parent and child as you share experiences, play silly games, sing songs, and enjoy an educational vacation. There is nothing better than seeing kids' reactions to what they are doing and sharing in their excitement. You will feel a great sense of fulfillment as a parent or grandparent while you act as tour director, opening up the world to your children.

An RV vacation is certainly much easier than packing everybody into the family car, having to worry about finding a restroom or a restaurant, and living out of a suitcase. In an RV, with all the comforts of home, the kids will be able to get up for a snack or use the bathroom, take a nap in a bunk, or just get up to stretch.

Getting There Should Be Half the Fun!

While the flexibility of RV travel alleviates many of the problems of traveling with children, there are several secrets you should learn that will really make the vacation enjoyable for everybody. The first secret, and the one that you must keep in mind once you have decided to take a trip, is that getting there should be at least half the fun. The kids need to be involved in the trip, beginning with the planning. While traveling, they must be made active participants and know that this is **their** trip and that they are not just baggage. By keeping them involved, you will have a lot more cooperation and an eager crew looking forward to the next stop on **their** vacation adventure.

In Chapter 3 I mentioned how to involve the children in the planning process: ask for their input and discuss travel information as it comes in; listen to what they have to say and pick sites they express a desire to see. Doing this will get them interested in the trip before it begins and they will feel they contributed to its success. This is part of the psychology of travel, and how you use it during the trip will greatly affect the outcome.

If you plan it right, your trip will be a learning experience for everybody. As part of the planning, look for things that will teach history, geography, geology, nature, awareness of the environment, etc. When you stop to see a site, explain its significance to the kids. As you drive along, discuss what they are about to see. This will make the trip meaningful to them.

Keep Them Occupied!

The second lesson you will need to learn is to keep the children occupied while you are traveling. This is so much easier in an RV than in a car! However, the long hours spent getting from one place to another can be trying on any family, so plan some fun along the way. Most kids have short attention spans, so you will need to take a wide variety of things for them to do. Don't forget you will have to carry **everything**, so keep toys and games light and small.

Some of the obvious items to take are: playing and flash cards, diary, pens, pencils, crayons and drawing tablets, travel games, and hand-held puzzles (a Rubik's cube is great!). Also important are electronic games, sporting equipment, cassette recorder (include the headsets!) and tapes, and those "special things" they can't be without such as stuffed animals, dolls and action figures.

Toy stores have a variety of travel games and books which will keep the kids occupied for hours. Rand McNally publishes an excellent series called Backseat Books with such titles as *Kids' U.S. Road Atlas*, *Are We There Yet?*, *Best Travel Activity Book Ever*, and *On Vacation*, and an activity book with stickers called *Around the U.S.A.* They are packed with puzzles, games and other activities to keep children occupied. Having some sporting equipment, such as a frisbee or small football, is important as you will want something they can do outside when you stop for a break. This will work off some of their excess energy and settle them down for the next travel segment.

Teaching children who are old enough how to read a map can serve several purposes. First, when they become good enough at it they can become an assistant navigator; second, looking at the map will give them something to do and they will learn about the road systems, how to read signs, and how to judge distances. Have them keep track of your travel progress on the map using colored markers. You can ask them, "Are we there yet?" and they will have to find your location and tell you. This will sharpen their observation skills and keep them from asking you that nagging travel question.

Another idea to keep children occupied is to let them pick out a postcard every day depicting a place you have been and let them write their impressions on it. Not only does this reinforce the experience, but it gives them two things to do: look for the postcard and write on it. These can be made into a special album when you get home. If you have a cassette recorder, you can make an on-the-road taped "letter" to a friend or relative describing what you have seen or done. Just think how exciting it would be to get such a "letter!"

We have always felt very strongly about having the kids sharpen their writing skills on our trips. Not only does this help with their creative writing, but it also develops their powers of observation, and gives them something to do in between stops and as they unwind before bedtime. Buy each one a diary or spiral notebook so they can record their special memories. Have them write down or draw in their diary what their impressions were. The little ones can dictate their thoughts to you and embellish the diary with illustrations.

To keep all of us occupied on the road, we like to make lists of car license plates with unusual phrases, odd place names and unique store signs. There are a number of excellent books on the market that are exclusively written about traveling with children. I would suggest buying one, as they are full of tips, songs, and games that will give everybody something to do.

Anticipate Their Needs

Another key travel secret is to anticipate the children's needs and make adjustments before problems arise. If they are on a schedule for school activities, naps or eating, try to stick as closely to them as possible, at least for the first few days of your trip. Break up the day's tour by stopping frequently to maintain their routines, and if you see them getting too wound up, shift the trip's focus for awhile. This may entail changing the activity they are doing, stopping to sightsee more frequently, or letting the kids out of the RV to run off some of their pent up energy.

More Travel Tips...

- Set the rules for expected behavior at the outset of your vacation. Everybody will be excited to partake in an RV adventure, but if the children get too rambunctious you can't just tell them to go to their room!

- Depending on the number of kids and beds available for them, plan to rotate the sleeping arrangements, at least for the first few nights on the road. This will keep them from fighting over who gets what spot. After a few days and the novelty of being in an RV has worn off a bit, they may all agree on set sleeping arrangements. For variety, let them sleep under the stars if the weather is good. Just make sure they are quiet, as campers go to bed early and don't like being disturbed.

- Rotate seating arrangements as well. Depending on the interior configuration of your RV, there will be a dinette, a couch, and perhaps an easy chair, so the kids can read, lie down or do activities. By frequently rotating where they sit you can keep an eye on what they are doing and monitor their behavior. Switching seating will also give them a chance to look out different windows.

- As I mentioned in an earlier chapter, teach them about safety, especially staying seated while the RV is underway.

- Assign them rotating tasks, such as helping with the hookups, doing laundry, getting milk or the newspaper from the camp store, sweeping out the RV, or throwing out the trash. This will give them some responsibility and a sense of self worth, and they will feel they are an important cog in the success of the vacation.

- Make sure the door is doubled locked while you are underway. That way there is no chance of a child accidentally unlocking the door and falling out.

With the proper planning and constant monitoring as you travel, you will never hear, "There's nothing to do" or "I'm bored," those insidious phrases most parents hear at home, or that wonderful on-the-road phrase, "Are we there yet?"

Chapter 14

Emergencies, First Aid & Security

Emergencies & Safety

Unfortunately, emergencies do happen, and it is wise to be well prepared for them—have the right tools and know what to do. Most of the emergency situations have already been covered in previous chapters. Just be prepared for the unexpected—flat tires, mechanical breakdowns, fires and medical emergencies, and make sure everybody in your party knows what to do. Show them where the fire extinguisher, tool kit, first aid kit, jack and spare tire, flashlight and important papers are, and how to contact people in case of trouble. Always have the rental contract readily available!! Develop a plan of action with the group so that everybody knows what to do in a crisis. Use Appendices 4 and 5 to record information that will be useful to you in case of medical emergency, and if you have any non family members with you, be sure the medical release form, Appendix 3, is filled out so you can give it to the doctor or hospital.

If you have an accident or breakdown, call the rental agency immediately and report the situation. Have the following information handy to give to them:

- ☐ your rental contract number
- ☐ your location and phone number
- ☐ the nature of the problem

Through their network of service and repair facilities, the rental agency should be able to get help to you quickly. However, if you need to be towed, have them authorize it first. Usually the agencies will authorize you to make repairs up to a certain dollar limit without contacting them, but be sure to follow their guidelines for handling repairs in your contract. Sometimes they specify the type of tire, battery or other part needed, and will not reimburse you for other brands without express authorization. Save your receipts, too!

First Aid Tips

Animal bites. If you are bitten by any wild animal, wash the wound thoroughly with lots of soap and warm water to kill any virus, then go directly to the nearest medical clinic or emergency room of a hospital. Wild animals may carry a variety of diseases harmful to man, so immediate attention is important. You'll need a tetanus booster if it's been more than five years since your last one, and probably some antibiotics, too.

Baking soda. Baking soda has many uses, so be sure to pick some up on your first shopping trip or take a baggie with several tablespoons full. Make a paste and apply it to burns, hives, poison ivy, insect bites and stinging nettles; it also soothes and relieves itching.

Bee stings. If you are allergic to bee stings, by all means take along a bee sting kit. It may save your life! The kits have Benadryl and an injection of adrenaline that will help counteract the affects of the sting. For those of us who are not allergic to it, use Benadryl ointment, or make a paste of meat tenderizer (MSG), apply it to the sting, and take aspirin, Tylenol, or some other over-the-counter analgesic. Putting ice on the sting and elevating the limb, if possible, will help. However, if you are stung several times and start feeling woozy, take some antihistamine, like Benadryl, and seek immediate medical help. This happened to me once when I was alone, and it was quite scary. I immediately went to a neighbor's house in case I passed out or had to be taken to the hospital, and it took me over a day to recover.

Dehydration. One thing all travelers must be aware of is the possibility of getting dehydrated. Perhaps you have decided to go on a hike to look at some scenic beauty and have been away from the RV for quite awhile. If you have been sweating or it is hot and dry, you may become dehydrated. Of course, the best thing to do is take a water bottle along with you and drink periodically, and also drink some liquid before you leave. Stay away from alcohol and caffeinated beverages, as they actually deplete body fluids. Beverages with sugar are best when you are trying to get yourself "recharged."

Medicines. Heat, light and humidity can affect your medicines, so packing them properly for your trip is very important. If you have to repack medicine for the trip and it was originally packed in a dark container, pack it in another dark container. With any capsules that have gelatin shells, don't use cotton balls in the container as they will absorb water and this may dissolve the gelatin. Use silica gel packets to absorb moisture. Many drugs will break down chemically due to moisture and become ineffective, so keeping them in good condition is important. Keep prescription labels on the containers so you know what is in them, and make sure they are child-proof if there will be children around.

Snake bites. Snake bites can be life threatening, so the best thing to do is get immediate medical attention. There are snake bite kits available, but using them may cause more problems than the bite itself, unless you are an expert. I tend to steer very far away from snakes, and they don't like humans either, so, if you come upon one, remain still, and hopefully it will slither away. If you are bitten, note the markings and coloration of the snake so the doctors can determine what antidote to give you, and get to the hospital or emergency center as fast as you can. Contrary to popular belief, few snakes in the United States are poisonous, and only water moccasins (cottonmouth), copperheads, coral, and rattlesnakes pose a threat.

Sprains. Sprains can easily happen on trips because you are doing things you would not normally do and in a manner that is reminiscent of an indestructible six-year old. Jumping from rock to rock while hiking or crossing a stream, slipping on loose gravel on a trail, or falling off a log while pretending to be Little John are common causes of sprains. If you do get a sprain, just remember the acronym RICE, which stands for rest, ice, compression, and elevation. The objectives are to reduce swelling and relieve pain. Wrap the sprain in an elastic bandage and apply ice for 30 minutes; remove ice and bandage for 15 minutes; repeat the process as long as necessary to reduce the swelling and pain. Keep the sprained area elevated above your heart, as this will help the fluid drain and reduce the blood flow to the area, which will minimize the swelling. Take it easy once you start to feel better, as it can take months before a sprain is completely healed.

Sunburn. The culprit here is ultraviolet radiation (UVR). If you are going to be at high altitudes, beware, as UVR increases 4-5% for every 1,000 feet of elevation. To avoid problems when going out in the sun, wear a hat and sunblock with at least an SPF of 15. The sunblock absorbs the

UVR. You can get a first or second degree burn quite easily! However, if you get sunburned or other types of burns, immediately hydrate the affected area using a cool wet towel. Leave it on for a few minutes, as this will help to stop the burning process and will start to cool the affected area. Also, take two aspirin, acetaminophen (Tylenol), or ibuprofen, which will help retard the burning. Easily made home remedies are very helpful in soothing a sunburn, if you have the ingredients with you. A compress moistened with tea (one with tannic acid) will also help, as the tannic acid is a good soothing agent. A paste made of baking soda is another successful remedy. Vinegar can also be used to soothe sunburn. For other types of burns, or if blisters develop from a sunburn, cover affected area with an antibacterial ointment to prevent infection.

Ticks. Ticks can transmit two diseases to humans that should concern campers who walk in the woods or in tall grass—Rocky Mountain spotted fever, which can occur throughout the United States, but is concentrated in the Southeast, and Lyme disease, which is concentrated in the Northeast. Rocky Mountain spotted fever can be fatal, and Lyme disease can cause serious ailments. Prevention will save you a lot of problems.

If you walk in the woods or tall grass in areas where these diseases are prevalent, wear a hat, long-sleeved shirt, long pants, light colored socks, and tuck your pants inside your boots, as well as put on insect repellant that states that it is effective for ticks. Repellants containing DEET are good and can be applied to your clothes. If your pants don't tuck into your boots, you can use masking tape or rubber bands to help form a seal. Light colored clothing is best, as the ticks stand out. When you return to the RV, inspect your clothes and hair, and moist spots such as your groin, underarm and behind your knee. Ticks seem to like these areas!

In March, 1992, New York State banned insect repellants that had more than 30% DEET, citing possible health hazards. In response, manufacturers developed products combining less DEET with a fly repellant that is safer and effective against flies as well as mosquitoes, gnats and ticks—a great combination! DEET Plus, by Sawyer, is one of these new products.

Early detection and removal of a tick is important, as it takes 24 hours for a tick to transmit the infection. Should you find a tick on your body, the best thing is to remove it as carefully as possible. Ticks breathe through tubes in their body, so dab gasoline, rubbing alcohol, or liquor on it with a cotton ball. This should smother it and it will back out of your body and you can gently flick it into the toilet. If the head breaks off, pull it out carefully with tweezers, being careful not to crush it or damage the skin around the area, as that may allow the tick's disease-carrying blood to enter your body. Finally, wash the area with soap and water and apply antibiotic ointment. Treatment of Lyme disease, even with antibiotics, is difficult, at best, so prevention is certainly preferable.

Security on the Road

Just because you are on vacation doesn't mean you are free from trouble. In fact, you may be a prime target. You are not in your usual surroundings, you are happy-go-lucky and in a rush to do a lot of things and may not be as careful as you would be at home. You also have with you the accoutrements of a tourist : cameras, audio equipment, bikes and other recreational equipment, all of which may be left unguarded or in plain sight on a seat in the RV. One of the things to remember while you are touring is not to have a false sense of security, and to take some basic precautions to thwart a burglary. Some preventive measures will go a long way toward making your trip trouble free. The key is to recognize what the real dangers are and try to avoid them.

Some of the preventive measures are quite obvious, such as not leaving your keys in the ignition. If you do that at home the only thing the burglar gets is your car. On the trip, however, you would lose your transportation and your house on wheels! Don't leave portable items outside your RV while you are away or asleep. Stow them in the outside compartments, or inside and out of sight. Keep your passport, camping carnet, and other important documents with you at all times! Losing them could be a real disaster.

We usually didn't have trouble keeping things out of sight in the RV, as we made a practice of keeping it tidy. Every once in a while, however, one of the kids would run out and leave a camera on the seat, so we had to drill it into them that this was a bad habit and that if a burglar saw the camera and broke in he would then look for other items. The basic idea is to discourage the burglar from wanting to enter the RV in the first place!

The biggest potential safety problem that we have faced was caused by open windows. Most of the RVs we have rented have had sliding windows with screens, and if they are left open, it is a simple job to push in the screen and climb inside. One of our motorhomes had a co-pilot's door with a window, so a burglar could easily have pushed the screen in and turned the door handle. If you are going to be away from the RV for awhile, leave the roof vents open, but shut the sliding windows! Close the blinds and curtains, too, so a potential burglar can't see what's inside.

Park your RV in a well lit area or where there are plenty of people around to notice anyone breaking into it. A burglar needs time and certainly doesn't want to be seen in the act. Use your common sense and make it as difficult as possible for someone to break in. More than likely they will move to another target. Everybody in your party should be instructed in what precautions to take and why, as the slightest slip-up could cause terrible problems. A brief discussion of security procedures the first night out is a good idea. As with health, prevention is the best choice.

Chapter 15

Turning In The RV

Just imagine, for a moment, that you are on your honeymoon and have just arrived at your destination, a lovely, secluded villa. You are on cloud nine, ready to enjoy this special moment in your life. You open the door... the place is dirty, the bed isn't made, there is leftover food in the refrigerator, and the toilet isn't flushed. Your dreams are dashed! Well, having an RV returned dirty isn't quite that bad, but you will certainly be breaking a cardinal rule of RV renting if you take your vehicle back that way. The next vacationers may be waiting at the agency to start their dream vacation, expecting to leave shortly after you arrive. Normally, the agency can get the RV ready to go after a wash, inspection, and engine checkup. However, if it is left dirty and the sanitary tanks have to be dumped, the extra time to get it ready could be quite lengthy.

So, to be fair to the agency and the next renter, RV rental agencies take a security and/or refundable cleaning deposit in case they have to spend time cleaning the vehicle. Don't be surprised if the cleaning fee is $100 or more. It takes time to do the cleaning and it is a great inconvenience for all concerned. Please leave the RV the way you found it!

What the Rental Agency Expects

Before you leave on your trip, find out from the agency what they expect upon return. Find out when the RV is to be returned, what the late charge is if you are a few hours late, how full the gas tank should be, where the nearest propane and public dump stations are, and exactly in what condition they want the RV. They may have this spelled out on a separate sheet, but if they don't, take notes. Late charges can run $20-25 per hour, but make sure this is written down so there are no arguments when you return. The rental agency will also charge you if the holding tanks have not been emptied and the propane tank is not refilled, so take care of this before you return.

Besides taking the RV back clean, it should be back on time, or as close to the designated time as humanly possible. Again, the next vacationers may be waiting, and if you are late, that will throw their travel schedule off. So, put yourself in their shoes. If you are going to be late, call the agency and give them the expected time of arrival. That way they can advise the next renter and shuffle their own maintenance schedule.

Getting Ready to Return the RV

To make the return of the RV as easy as possible on you, plan to pack as much as you can the evening before. Check what you are packing against your packing lists. Allow extra time when you break camp on your last morning to complete the pack-up job, do the dump, and fill the gas and propane tanks, as it always takes much longer than you think. The following list will remind you of what needs to be done to the RV:

Returning the RV Checklist

- ☐ Sweep out the interior
- ☐ Empty ash trays
- ☐ Clean the sinks and bathroom, including shower & toilet, but don't use abrasive cleaners on the fiberglass. You don't need to kill yourself, but clean up the hair, makeup and toothpaste spills, etc. and make it look nice
- ☐ Clean the stove, oven & refrigerator
- ☐ Throw out the trash
- ☐ Fill the propane tank
- ☐ Empty the gray and black water tanks and leave dump valves open
- ☐ Fill the gas tank to required level
- ☐ Clean and sort any rented equipment
- ☐ If you had a pet on the trip, be sure to vacuum up all the hair
- ☐ Check all the storage compartments inside and out, including glove compartment, and seat and door pockets, to make sure you haven't left anything
- ☐ Make a list of repairs needed for the rental agent

Make a list of anything that went wrong with the equipment that needs to be fixed by the rental agency before the next vacationer's trip. Remember that thud, thud, thud you never paid any attention to? If your door lock doesn't work properly, as ours didn't on our last trip, and you don't report it, the lock may not get repaired and can cause problems and aggravation for the next renter. Our windshield wipers didn't work properly either, and without being repaired, could have become a very dangerous driving hazard. Most of these things can be quickly repaired, but the rental agency may not know about them unless you tell them. A report will be very helpful to them in maintaining the quality and safety of their fleet. The next renter will appreciate it, too!

Allow Time to Pack & Get to the Airport

When you begin your trip, ask the agency how long it takes to check out and how long it takes to get to the airport or train station. Add to this time the amount of time you will need at the airport or station, and a pretty good margin for error in case of miscalculations, bad weather conditions, accidents or other unforeseen tie-ups. Make sure your last campground isn't so far away that you have to speed to return to the rental depot on time. That way you will end a very wonderful vacation on a nice note without unnecessary stress, flared tempers, and the mad rush to get home.

Don't forget to make arrangements to send your trunk back home! Once you have returned to the rental agency, you will have to repack it and call the shipping agent. Use the packing list you had when you came out so it will be the same weight and take extra labels for the return shipment. Check with the rental agency before you begin your trip to see if they will let you leave the trunk until it can be picked up.

As soon as you return to the rental agency, make arrangements to get to the station or airport if the agency can't take you. If you have to call a cab, do so right away, unless you have to wait a long time to check out. The agency can do this for you, but make sure that it is done amidst all the turn-in confusion.

After our first trip, we cut the last day pretty tight and barely made it to the airport on time. There were six of us, so the women headed for the plane to hold the seats while the males handled the check-in. We made it, but might have been bumped from the plane if we hadn't done it this way. With such crowds at the airports these days and the airlines' overbooking policies, it is wise to allow plenty of time.

You are now on your way home at the end of a wonderful adventure. Like any good vacation, however, it won't end the minute you set foot inside your house. For years to come you will be reminiscing about the trip, showing friends your pictures or "special treasures" and dreaming about your next vacation as King of the Road!

Appendix

1. Cost Estimator

Cost of transportation to point of departure:

$ _____ per person x number of people   = $ _____

Cost of RV per da/wk x number of da/wk   = $ _____

Cost of CDW/VIP/ PAI $ _____ x no. of days = $ _____

Cost of convenience kits $ _____ x # needed = $ _____

Vehicle prep charge   = $ _____

Estimated mileage _____ x $____ per mile =$ _____

Rental sales tax (include all items above)   = $ _____

Gas: Mileage _____ /_____ mpg x $_____ gal. = $ _____

Food: $_____ per day x number of people   = $ _____

Campground: $_____ per day x number of days = $ _____

Sightseeing $_____ per day x number of days = $ _____

Miscellaneous: souvenirs, gifts, taxis, etc.   = $ _____

Total cost of vacation: = $ _____

2. Names & Addresses of Friends

Name _____

Address _____

Name _____

Address _____

Name _____

Address _____

Name _____

Address _____

Name _____

Address _____

Name _____

Address _____

Name _____

Address _____

Name _____

Address _____

Name _____

Address _____

Name _____

Address _____

3. Medical Consent Form

Whereas, _____(name of child) _____ (age) is our child by birth, legal adoption or guardian rights; whereas, said child is traveling with _____ and _____ (name(s) of responsible adult(s)) on a trip from _____ to _____ (dates).

Whereas, it is our desire and intent to ensure that said child will receive any necessary medical treatment, and to authorize the adult(s) who will be accompanyng said child to consent to the rendering of such treatment in the event reasonable attempts to contact us and obtain such consent are unsuccessful.

Now, therefore, we do hereby convey, in the event all reasonable attempts to contact us at the below-listed telephone numbers are unsuccesful, to _____ and/or _____ (name(s) of responsible adults(s)), authority to procure and consent to any necessary emergency medical care (including rendering of prescribed medicine or surgical treatment) needed while said child is in the custody of the responsible adult(s) mentioned above.

To our knowledge _____ (name of child) is known to have _____ (name of disease or condition) and is on _____ (name of prescribed medicine). He/she is also allergic to the following: _____ (medicine or environment).

The following additionl information may be needed by any hospital or doctor not having access to the child's medical history:

Insurance company: policy #
_____

Physical impairments
_____

Blood type   Date of last tetanus shot
_____

Doctor's name   *phone*
_____

Address
_____

Doctor's name   *phone*
_____

Address
_____

Dentist's name   *phone*
_____

Address
_____

Specialist's name   *phone*
_____

Address
_____

_____	_____
Parent/Guardian	*Parent/Guardian*
Street address	*Street address*
City *State* *Zip Code*	*City* *State* *Zip Code*
Home phone	*Home phone*
Business phone	*Business phone*
Alternate Contact Phone	*Alternate Contact Phone*
Witness	*Witness*

4. *Important Information*

1. Take a copy of your medical insurance claim form

insurance company's phone (   )
_____

policy number
_____

2. Auto insurance company:
_____

agent's phone (   )
_____

3. Credit card   **Number**   **Exp. date**

_____   _____   _____

_____   _____   _____

_____   _____   _____

_____   _____   _____

_____   _____   _____

4. Prescriptions & Medical Information

glasses
_____

contact lenses
_____

medicines
_____

_____

_____

allergies
_____

blood type   *social security #*
_____

5. In Case of Emergency...

Emergencies can happen on the road, so it is wise to have the necessary contacts in one spot in case you need them.

Personal Physician _____

Phone ( ) _____

Personal Physician _____

Phone ( ) _____

Specialist _____

Phone ( ) _____

Dentist _____

Phone ( ) _____

Relative _____

Phone ( ) _____

Neighbor _____

Phone ( ) _____

Lawyer _____

Phone ( ) _____

Office _____

Phone ( ) _____

Veterinarian _____

Phone ( ) _____

_____

Phone ( ) _____

6. Questions to Ask When Renting an RV

1. What classes and sizes of RV are available?
2. What is the rent? Daily? Weekly?
3. How many free miles are included?
4. What is the excess mileage charge?
5. Is insurance extra? How much is it?
   a. CDW
   b. VIP
6. Do you rent convenience kits? How much are they?
7. Do you rent: TV, lawn chairs, bicycles?
8. Does your orientation include a road test?
9. What is the reservation deposit required?
10. When is the balance of the rental due?
11. How much is the security deposit?
12. What is your cancellation policy?
13. How much is the prep charge?
14. Can you store our trunk/luggage?
15. Do you have a pickup/drop-off service?
16. How much extra is the one-way cost?
17. How does your repair network operate?

Have them send you:

1. Rental brochure with rates, insurance, convenience kit and floorplan information
2. Reservation confirmation

7. Daily Pre-Travel Checklist

Exterior

- ☐ Close waste water valves; disconnect dump hose and replace covers securely
- ☐ Disconnect electrical hookup
- ☐ Disconnect water hookup
- ☐ Turn off propane at tank unless used for refrigerator
- ☐ Turn off pilot on hot water heater
- ☐ Check tire pressure & lugs
- ☐ Check engine oil & radiator fluid levels
- ☐ Check windshield washer fluid
- ☐ Check generator oil level (if used)
- ☐ Clean mirrors, headlights, windshield & rear window
- ☐ Make sure all compartment doors are securely shut
- ☐ Remove any blocks under the wheels
- ☐ Secure awning
- ☐ Retract doorstep
- ☐ Walk around campsite to make sure it is left clean

Interior

- ☐ Empty the trash
- ☐ Lock refrigerator & switch from electric to gas or 12-volt battery
- ☐ Turn off pilots for oven & stove
- ☐ Close roof vents
- ☐ Close jalousie windows most of the way

continued...

- ☐ Close any open rear or side (rear) window
- ☐ Make sure all food, clothing, bedding, toiletries & personal items are tightly stowed away & all cabinet doors closed
- ☐ Check holding tank levels on the monitor panel & dump if necessary
- ☐ Check water level on monitor panel & fill if necessary
- ☐ Turn off water pump
- ☐ Turn off furnace
- ☐ Check LP-gas level on monitor panel
- ☐ Check battery charge gauge on monitor panel & switch mode of battery operation if necessary
- ☐ Check fuel level
- ☐ Lower TV antenna & secure TV for travel
- ☐ Securely close & double lock entrance door
- ☐ Plot your course for the day
- ☐ Adjust mirrors
- ☐ Fasten seatbelts!

You can divide up these responsibilities and have an operations pilot and an interior co-pilot.

8. Before You Leave Home Checklist

- ☐ Stop mail and newspapers or make arrangements to have them picked up daily

- ☐ Make arrangements to have someone take care of the plants

- ☐ Make arrangements for pet care

- ☐ Set timers on several lights

- ☐ Empty kitchen trash

- ☐ Remove food from refrigerator

- ☐ Turn down thermostat to lowest possible setting

- ☐ Unplug appliances, TV, radio, computers, etc.

- ☐ Turn off hot water heater and gas to stove

- ☐ Alert friends & neighbors of your schedule

- ☐ Leave a house key with a trusted friend or neighbor

- ☐ Ask police or sheriff to check your home periodically

- ☐ Have someone move cars around in your driveway

- ☐ Have lawn mowed, snow shoveled or leaves raked

- ☐ Leave itinerary or contacts, including phone numbers, with friend or relative

- ☐ Have house sitter open & close drapes and shades twice a day

- ☐ Lock all doors & windows, including garage, and immobilize sliding glass doors

- ☐ Store valuables in a safe-deposit box

- ☐ Leave family contact numbers with a neighbor

9. Travel Information Centers

Call the travel centers in the states, provinces or countries you are interested in and ask them for their vacation information kit, including maps and any camping information. Allow several weeks for delivery.

United States

Alabama	(800) 252-2262	Nebraska	(800) 228-4307
Alaska	(907) 465-2010	Nevada	(800) 638-2328
Arizona	(800) 842-8257	New Hampshire	(603) 271-2666
Arkansas	(800) 628-8725	New Jersey	(800) 537-7397
California	(800) 862-2543	New Mexico	(800) 545-2040
Colorado	(800) 255-5550	New York	(800) 225-5697
Connecticut	(800) 282-6863	North Carolina	(800) 847-4862
Delaware	(800) 441-8846	North Dakota	(800) 435-5663
Florida	(904) 487-1462	Ohio	(800) 282-5393
Georgia	(800) 847-4842	Oklahoma	(800) 652-6552
Hawaii	(808) 923-1811	Oregon	(800) 547-7842
Idaho	(800) 635-7820	Pennsylvania	(800) 847-4872
Illinois	(800) 223-0121	Rhode Island	(800) 556-2484
Indiana	(800) 289-6646	South Carolina	(800) 346-3634
Iowa	(800) 345-4692	South Dakota	(800) 843-1930
Kansas	(800) 252-6727	Tennessee	(615) 741-2158
Kentucky	(800) 225-8747	Texas	(800) 888-8839
Louisiana	(800) 334-8626	Utah	(801) 538-1030
Maine	(800) 533-9595	Vermont	(802) 828-3236
Maryland	(800) 543-1036	Virginia	(800) 847-4882
Massachusetts	(800) 447-6277	Washington	(800) 544-1800
Michigan	(800) 543-2937	Washington, DC	(202) 789-7000
Minnesota	(800) 657-3700	West Virginia	(800) 225-5982
Mississippi	(800) 647-2290	Wisconsin	(800) 432-8747
Missouri	(800) 877-1234	Wyoming	(800) 225-5996
Montana	(800) 541-1447		

Canada

There are Canadian Tourist Offices located in many cities in the United States and abroad. In the United States: Atlanta, Boston, Buffalo, Chicago, Cincinnati, Cleveland, Dallas, Detroit, Los Angeles, Minneapolis, New York City, Pittsburgh, San Francisco, Seattle, and Washington, DC. In other countries: Frankfurt, London, Mexico City, Paris, Sydney, The Hague, Tokyo, and Seoul. For tourist information about a particular province, use the following numbers:

Alberta .... (800) 661-8888
British Columbia .... (800) 663-6000
Manitoba .... (800) 665-0040
New Brunswick .... (800) 561-0123
Newfoundland & Labrador .... (800) 563-6353
Northwest Territories .... (800) 661-0788
Nova Scotia .... (800) 341-6096 (US only)
                                        (800) 565-0000 (Canada)
Ontario .... (800) 668-2746
Prince Edward Island .... (800) 565-0267
Quebec .... (800) 363-7777
Saskatchewan .... (800) 667-7191
Yukon .... (403) 667-3053 (US)
                                        (800) 661-0494 (Canada)

Mexico

Mexican Government Tourism Offices
Chicago .... (312) 565-2786
Houston .... (713) 880-5153
Los Angeles .... (310) 203-8151
Montreal .... (514) 871-1052
New York .... (800) 44-Mexico (639426)
Toronto .... (416) 925-0704
Washington, DC .... (202) 728-1792

European Tourist Offices

British Tourist Authority .... (212) 986-2200
French Government Tourist Office .... (212) 757-1125
German National Tourist Office .... (800) 637-1171
Italian Government Tourist Office .... (212) 245-4822

10. Daily Travel Log

Date: _____ Weather: _____

From: _____ To: _____

Left: _____ Arrived: _____

Odometer Out: _____ Odometer In: _____

Miles Traveled: _____

Campground: _____

Comments: _____

_____

_____

EXPENSES

Fuel _____

Groceries _____

Restaurants _____

Activities _____

Souveniers _____

Camp Fees _____

Miscellaneous _____

Total _____

FUEL CONSUMPTION

(1) Mileage this fill-up _____

(2) Mileage last fill-up _____

(3) Miles traveled _____

(4) Gallons of fuel purchased this fill-up _____

MPG (line 3/line 4) _____

TODAY'S ADVENTURES:

_____

_____

_____

_____

_____

_____

_____

11. Meal Planner

Use the following chart as a meal planning guide and build your shopping list around it. Depending on the number of people in your party, you may only want to plan for 3-4 days at a time.

Meat	Starch	Vegetable	Other	Dessert
1.				
2.				
3.				
4.				
5.				
6.				
7.				

Restock:

_____

_____

_____

_____

_____

_____

_____

12. Metric Conversion Tables

In order to assist the many foreign travelers who have come to see this beautiful country of ours, the following conversion tables may come in handy. You may need them, too, if you go to a country that uses the metric system. **Note**: some measurements are approximate for easy conversion.

Temperature

Degrees Fahrenheit		Degrees Celsius
212	*(boiling)*	100
110		43
100		38
90		32
80		27
70		21
60		16
50		10
40		4
32	*(freezing)*	0
20		-7
10		-12
0		-18

To convert degrees Fahrenheit to degrees Celsius use the following formula: subtract 32 from the number of degrees Fahrenheit and divide by 1.8 (for example: 85° F-32 /1.8 = 29° C).

To convert degrees Celsius to degrees Fahrenheit use the following formula: multiply the degrees Celsius by 1.8, then add 32 (for example: 20° C x 1.8 + 32 = 68° F)

Oven Temperatures

300°F = 150°C	400°F = 200°C
325°F = 160°C	425°F = 220°C
350°F = 180°C	450°F = 230°C
375°F = 190°C	500°F = 260°C

Weights & Measures

Liquid Measures

1/4 teaspoon	= 1.25 mil.
1 teaspoon	= 5 mil.
1 tablespoon	= 15 mil.
1/4 cup	= 60 mil.
1/3 cup	= 80 mil.
1 cup	= 250 mil.
1 pint	= 0.5 liters/500 mil.
1 quart liquid	= 0.9 liter
1 gallon (US)	= 3.8 liters
1 Canadian/Imperial gallon (British)	= 4.5 liters
6 US gallons	= 5 Canadian/Imperial gallons
1 liter	= 2.1 pints liquid (US)
1 liter	= .888 quarts liquid (Imp.)
1 liter	= 33.92 oz, 1.06 quarts liquid (US) or 26 gallons

Quarts to Liters	Liters to Quarts
1 qt = 0.95 l	1 l = 1.06 qt
5 qt = 4.75 l	5 l = 5.30 qt
10 qt = 9.50 l	10 l = 10.60 qt
50 qt = 47.50 l	50 l = 53.00 qt

Gallons to Liters	Liters to Gallons
1 gal. = 3.8 l	5 l = 1.3 gal.
3 gal. = 11.4 l	10 l = 2.6 gal.
5 gal. = 19.0 l	20 l = 5.3 gal.
10 gal. = 38.0 l	50 l = 13.2 gal.
20 gal. = 76.0 l	100 l = 26.4 gal.

To convert **liters to quarts**, multiply by 1.06; to convert **liters to gallons** (US), multiply the number of liters by .26 (for example: 50 l x 0.26 = 13 gal); to convert **gallons to liters**, take the number of gallons and multiply by 3.8 (for example: 10 gal x 3.8 = 38 l).

Dry Weights

1 ounce (oz.) = 28 grams
1/4 pound (lb.) = 115 grams
1/2 pound = 225 grams
1 pound = 454 grams (.45 kilogram)
2.2 pounds = 1 kilogram (1000 grams)
1 stone = 14 pounds
1 gram = .035 ounces
(or about a paperclip's weight)
100 grams = 3.5 ounces
500 grams = 17.5 ounces
1 kilogram (kg) = 2.2 pounds

To convert **kilograms to pounds**, take the number of kilos and multiply by 2.2; **pounds to kilograms**, multiply the number of pounds by .45 (for example: 100 lb x .45 = 45 kg); **grams to ounces**, multiply the number of grams by .035.

Pounds to Kilograms	*Kilograms to Pounds*
1 pound (lb) = 0.45 kg	1 kg = 2.2 lbs
5 lbs = 2.3 kg	5 kg = 11 lbs
10 lbs = 4.5 kg	10 kg = 22 lbs
50 lbs = 23.0 kg	50 kg = 110 lbs
100 lbs = 45.0 kg	100 kg = 220 lbs

Cooking Equivalents

Unsifted Flour

1 tablespoon = 8.5 grams
1/4 cup = 35 grams
1/3 cup = 45 grams
1/2 cup = 70 grams
1 cup = 140 grams

Sugar (white)

$$1 \text{ teaspoon} = 4 \text{ grams}$$
$$1 \text{ tablespoon} = 12 \text{ grams}$$
$$1/4 \text{ cup} = 50 \text{ grams}$$
$$1/3 \text{ cup} = 65 \text{ grams}$$
$$1/2 \text{ cup} = 95 \text{ grams}$$
$$1 \text{ cup} = 190 \text{ grams}$$

Length & Speed

1 inch (in.) = 2.5 centimeters
1 foot (ft.) = 0.3 meter
1 yard (yd.) = 0.9 meter
1 mile (mi.) = 1.6 kilometers (km)
1 millimeter = 0.04 inches (or less than 1/16 inch)
1 centimeter = 0.4 inch
1 meter = 39 in./1.09 yards/3.28 feet
1 kilometer = 0.62 mile

Miles to Kilometers	*Kilometers to Miles*
1 mi. = 1.6 km	1 km = 0.62 mi.
10 mi. = 16 km	10 km = 6.2 mi.
20 mi. = 32 km	20 km = 12.4 mi.
30 mi. = 48 km	0 km = 18.6 mi.
50 mi. = 80 km	50 km = 31 mi.
100 mi. = 160 km	100 km = 62 mi.

To convert **kilometers to miles**, multiply by .62 (for example: 50 km x 0.62 = 31 miles). To convert **miles to kilometers**, take the number of miles and multiply by 1.6 (for example: 100 miles x 1.6 = 160 km). To convert **meters to yards**, multiply by 1.1. For **yards to meters**, multiply by 0.9.

13. RVer's Resource Guide

Campground Chains

Privately Owned

Best Holiday Trav-L-Park Association
1310 Jarvis Avenue
Elk Grove Village, IL 60007
(708) 981-0100
For reservations:
(800) 323-8899 (ask for Best Holiday)
An association of over 75 parks located near major attractions.

Kampgrounds of America (KOA)
PO Box 30558
Billings, MT 59114
(406) 248-7444
Founded in 1962; international system of franchised family camp-grounds; largest system of privately owned, full-service campgrounds in North America with nearly 600 locations.

Leisure Systems, Inc.,
Yogi Bear's Jellystone Park Camp-Resorts
6201 Kellogg Avenue
Cincinnati, OH 45228
(513) 232-6800
(800) 558-2954 reservations & resort information

Founded in 1969; international system of franchised family camp-resorts with a Yogi Bear theme; approximately 70 camp-resorts; special amenities and recreation for the whole family; most have pool, miniature golf, game room, playground, video theater, snack bar, laundry and retail store.

Membership RV Resort Chains

Camper Clubs of America (CCA)
4012 Hillsboro Road
Nashville, TN 37215
(615) 297-0959
(800) 234-8749 US & Canada

Founded 1990; company offers memberships in its club; rapidly
growing chain of RV parks geared toward retired RVers; toll-free
reservation system; discounts on camping; over 60 company affiliated parks.

Coast to Coast (CCC)
64 Inverness Drive East
Englewood, CO 80112
(303) 790-CAMP

Founded in 1972, this is the largest of the RV resort membership
systems, with over 500 affiliated resorts located throughout the
United States and Canada; members can camp for $1.00 per night at
any resort, or rent other resort accommodations at a nominal charge;
resorts generally have a full range of amenities; other services for
members: central reservations, 24-hour emergency road service, RV
financing, group insurance, trip routing, and deeply discounted
world-wide travel packages.

National American Corporation (NACO)
12301 NE 10th Place
Bellevue, Washington 98005
(206) 455-3155

Founded in 1967, NACO owns and operates 30 private membership
campgrounds in 14 states and 8 resort communities in 7 states. Owns
Resort Parks International (RPI). Full range of family-oriented amenities and social activities. Campgrounds are called "preserves" as they
try to maintain the wildlife and the landscape's natural beauty.
Preserves in: AL, CA, IN, MA, MS, MO, NJ, NC, OR, SC, TN, TX, VA,
WA.

Resort Parks International (RPI)
PO Box 7738
Long Beach, CA 90807
(310) 595-8818
(800) 635-8498

Founded in 1981, the RPI system has over 300 private affiliated RV
and condominium resorts in the United States, Canada and Mexico.
Members pay $2.00 per night for RV sites or can rent other accommo-
dations.

Thousand Trails, Inc.
12301 NE 10th Place
Bellevue, WA 98005
(206) 455-3155

Founded in 1972, Thousand Trails, the nation's largest private network of membership campgrounds, is a publicly traded company operating 39 camping resorts in 15 states and British Columbia. Resorts are called "preserves" as they try to maintain the wildlife and the landscape's natural beauty. Rental trailers and cabins available. Full range of family-oriented amenities and social activities. Preserves in: AZ, BC, CA, FL, IL, IN, MI, NV, NC, OH, OR, PA, TX, VA, WA, WI.

Non-Membership RV Resort Chains

Outdoor Resorts of America, Inc. (ORA)
2400 Crestmoor
Nashville, TN 37215
(615) 244-5237

Outdoor Resorts has 15 resorts in destination locations in FL, CA, TN, TX & SC. Most locations have health spa, pools, recreation hall, golf course, marina, tennis courts, and many other amenities associated with a luxury resort. Sites are for sale or rent.

Camping Industry Associations

National Association of RV Parks & Campgrounds
11307 Sunset Hills Road, Suite B-7
Reston, VA 22090
(703) 471-0143

Trade association geared specifically to the needs of the commercial campground/RV park owner/developer; limited information for the general public.

Go Camping America Committee
PO Box 2669
Reston, VA 22090
(703) 620-6003
(800) 47-SUNNY for camping vacation planner

Promotes camping and is a clearinghouse for information on RVing and camping. Send for free 16-page camping vacation planner that is packed with information and lists of whom to call for camping & RV information. The planner also includes a coupon for a free night of camping at one of hundreds of campgrounds nationwide.

State Campground Associations
For a list of state campground associations, call the Go Camping America Committee's special number: (800) 47-SUNNY and ask for their free 16-page camping vacation planner. Also, each state's travel information center can send you a list of the state's campgrounds.

Camping on Public Lands Information

Bureau of Land Management (BLM)
Office of Public Affairs
1849 C Street, NW, Room 5600
Washington, DC 20240
(202) 208-3435
Write for their "Recreation Guide to Public Lands" and map of Federal Recreation Lands.

USDA Forest Service (USFS)
Office of Information
PO Box 96090
Washington, DC 20090
(202) 447-3957
Write for brochure FS-418 which lists all the National Forests and their phone numbers.

National Park Service (NPS)
Office of Public Inquiries
PO Box 37127
Washington, DC 20013-7127
(202) 208-4747
For the National Park Service's *National Park Camping Guide*, write to:
US Government Printing Office
Superintendent of Documents
Washington, DC 20402-3925
Request stock #024-005-01080-7
Send $4.00.

US Fish and Wildlife Service
Office of Public Affairs
1849 C Street, NW, Room 3447
Washington, DC 20240
(202) 208-5634

US Army Corps of Engineers
Regional Brochures, CEWES-IM-MV-N
3909 Halls Ferry Road
Vicksburg, MS 39180-6199
Send for their 10 regional brochure/maps.

State and Local Parks. Call the state tourist bureau (see Appendix 9)
for information.

Directories, Guides & Publications

Campground Directories

AA Camping and Caravanning in Britain. Is published by the British
Automobile Association, and is available from the British Travel Book-
store, 551 Fifth Avenue, New York, NY 10176 or call (212) 490-6688.
Price is $16.95 plus $5.00 p&h.

AAA CampBooks; (11 regional US/Canada editions). Contact your local
AAA chapter for more information.

American P.C. Campground Directory. Directory has detailed information on over 6,000 free or nearly free public campgrounds in all 50
states; send $12.95 plus $1.80 p&h to: American P.C. Campground
Directory, PO Box 820009, Dallas, TX 75382-0009 or call (214) 987-3440.

Anderson's Campground Directory. Regional directory listing over
1,600 public and private campgrounds from PA to FL; send $7.75
(includes p&h) to: Anderson's Campground Directory, Drawer 467,
Lewisburg, WV 24901 or call (304) 645-1897.

Camping Canada Campground Directory. The directory is published
as one issue of Camping Canada Magazine, and covers over 4,000
campgrounds. For the directory only, send $5.00 (US; includes s&h) to:

Camping Canada Magazine, 2585 Skymark Ave., Unit 306, Mississauga, Ontario L4W 4L5, Canada, (514) 624-8218.

Camping Fuhrer. Put out by the German Automobile Club (ADAC); directory is in German; club has a lot of English speaking members; available in German bookstores or at the club's offices.

Europa Camping + Caravaning International Guide (ECC). Lists more than 5,500 campgrounds in 40 countries in Europe, the Near East and North Africa; detailed list of services; maps; information on ferries, tunnels, traffic regulations, beaches and international telephoning; "help" phrase list in seven languages; campground listings in German, French and English. Order from REI: (800) 426-4840 or through bookstores.

Guide to Free Campgrounds by Don Wright. Lists more than 6,300 free campgrounds in the US. Includes state maps, detailed directions and information on available facilities and activities. Ask for their free RV Travel Adventure Library catalog. Send $14.95 (includes p&h) to: Cottage Publications, Inc., 24396 Pleasant View Drive, Elkhart, IN 46517, (219)-875-8618.

KOA Directory/Road Atlas/Camping Guide. Lists the more than 600 KOA locations nationwide; free at any KOA or send $3.00 to: Kampgrounds of America, Inc., P.O. Box 30162, Billings, MT 59107-0162, (406) 248-7444.

Save-A-Buck Camping by Don Wright. Book lists thousands of campsites with fees under $4 not included in other directories; largest collection of county and city parks ever compiled; includes public fishing lakes, and hunting, fishing and wildlife area camps. Send $16.95 (includes p&h) to: Cottage Publications, Inc., 24396 Pleasant View Drive, Elkhart, IN 46517, (219)-875-8618.

Trailer Life Campground & RV Services Directory. Directory has over 18,000 listings of campgrounds, RV service centers and attractions in the United States, Canada and Mexico; RV troubleshooting charts; information on bridges, ferries and tunnels; military campgrounds; state atlas maps showing towns with RV services; directory discounted when purchased through Good Sam Club; available in bookstores or from TL Enterprises, 29901 Agoura Road, Agoura, CA 91301, (818) 991-4980.

Wheelers RV Resort & Campground Guide. Directory covers United States, Canada and Mexico, listing over 16,000 private and public campgrounds; dealers and suppliers; send $12.95 (plus $2.50 p&h) to Print Media Services, 1310 Jarvis Avenue, Elk Grove Village, IL 60007 (708) 981-0100.

Woodall's Campground Directories. Directories include complete information on thousands of North American campgrounds, RV sales/ service facilities, camping suppliers, attractions, military campgrounds; information on travel to Mexico and Canada; atlas maps showing towns with RV services; tunnel, bridge & ferry information; available in bookstores or from Woodall; for Eastern or Western edition send $13.70, and for North American edition, which lists over 12,000 campgrounds, $20.70 (p&h included) to: Woodall Publishing Co., PO Box 5000, Lake Forest, IL 60045-5000, or call (800) 323-9076.

Yogi Bear's Jellystone Park Campground Directory. Lists the approximately 70 resort-parks in their system. Leisure Systems, Inc., 6201 Kellogg Avenue, Cincinnati, OH 45228, (513) 232-6800.

Cookbooks

Dining With Zock, A Complete Guide to RV/Tailgate Cooking by Zock Clahan. Send $19.95 (plus $3 p&h; CA residents add $1.65 sales tax) to Dining With Zock, PO Box 16157, Encino, CA 91416-6157, (818) 782-1008

The Good Sam RV Cookbook. Send $14.90 to the Good Sam Club, PO Box 500, Agoura, CA 91376, (818) 991-4980. A basic RVers cookbook with over 250 recipes.

The Happy Camper's Gourmet Cookbook by Joyce Ryan; send $11.95 (plus $2 p&h; Texas residents add 96 ¢ sales tax) to Butterfly Books, 4210 Misty Glade, San Antonio, TX 78247.

Woodall's Campsite Cookbook. Send $7.45 to Woodall Publishing Co., PO Box 5000, Lake Forest, IL 60045-5000, (800) 323-9076. A good, basic camping cookbook.

Woodall's Favorite Recipes from America's Campgrounds. Send $13.45 to Woodall's at the above address. More than 350 authentic country meals from around the country.

Travel Guides & Recreation Directories

Parks Directory of the United States. Comprehensive guide to our park system; directory covers more than 3,700 state and national parks, historic sites, forests and recreation areas in all 50 states; listings cover facilities, recreational activities, special features and reference information; extensive section of park-related organizations and all state tourist agencies; send $85 to Omnigraphics, Inc., Penobscot Building, Detroit, MI 48226; (800) 234-1340.

Rest Area Guide to the United States and Canada. Provides information on driving regulations in each state or province, and services and rules of usage for all major rest areas; order from American Travel Publications, 6986 El Camino Real, Suite 104-199, Carlsbad, CA 92009; (619) 438-0514; $9.95 (plus $2 p&h).

The U.S. Outdoor Atlas & Recreation Guide by John Oliver Jones. Published by Houghton Mifflin Company, 1992; $16.95; a comprehensive state-by-state guide to more than 5,000 wildlife and recreation areas, including national and state parks, wildlife agencies, BLM sites, private reserves, and sanctuaries; full-page maps with accompanying charts provide information about the sites in more than 50 categories; location index by state and town; absolutely everything you will need to know about enjoying these recreation areas.

RV Magazines & Newspapers

Camp-orama
Published by Woodall Publishing Company
PO Box 5000, Lake Forest, IL 60045-5000
(800) 323-9076
Subscription: $15/yr; $25/2; monthly
Covers Florida.

Campers Monthly
PO Box 1716, Lansdale, PA 19446
(215) 368-2807
Subscription: $9/yr; monthly
Two editions: Mid-Atlantic and New England.

Camperways
Published by Woodall Publishing Company, Inc.
PO Box 5000, Lake Forest, IL 60045-5000
(800) 323-9076
Subscription: $15/yr; $25/2; monthly
Covers: DE, MD, NJ, NY, PA, VA.

Camping Canada Magazine
2585 Skymark Ave., Unit 306
Mississauga, Ontario L4W 4L5 Canada
(416) 624-8218
Subscription: $16 (CDN), $35 (CDN) for foreign
7 issues/yr, including campground directory and RV buyer's guide
"The RV Lifestyle Magazine"
Covers all aspects of camping in Canada.

Disabled Outdoors Magazine
2052 West 23rd Street
Chicago, IL 60608
(708) 358-4160
Subscription: $10/yr, $18/2; quarterly
Articles and information on all kinds of outdoor activities for the
physically challenged.

Family Motor Coaching
Official Publication of The Family Motor Coach Association
8291 Clough Pike, Cincinnati, OH 45244
(800) 543-3622; (513) 474-3622
Subscription: $24/yr; monthly (free to members)
National magazine for motorhomers.

MotorHome
Published by TL Enterprises
29901 Agoura Road, Agoura Hills, CA 91301
(818) 991-4980
Subscription: $24/yr; foreign, add $10; discount for Good Sam Club
members. National magazine covering all aspects of motorhoming.
For the RV enthusiast.

Northeast Outdoors
PO Box 2180, Waterbury, CT 06722-2180
(203) 755-0158 (800) 325-6745
Subscription: $8/yr, $11/2, $13/3
A monthly targeting the Northeast states (New England, New York and New Jersey).

Out West
10522 Brunswick Road, Grass Valley, CA 95945
(800) 274-9378 (credit card orders)
Subscription $9.95/yr; quarterly
Unique travel paper written on the road.

RV Life
PO Box 55998, Seattle, WA 98155
(206) 745-5665
Subscription: $12/yr US; $19 Canada (US)
Monthly geared toward Northwest United States and British Columbia.

RV Times Magazine
PO Box 6294, Richmond, VA 23230
(804) 288-5653
Subscription: $15/yr; 11 issues
Concentrates on Mid-Atlantic area.

RV Traveletter
Published by Cottage Publications, Inc.
24396 Pleasant View Dr., Elkhart, IN 46517
(800) 272-5518 (credit card subscribers only)
Subscription: $18/yr ($24 by credit card)
"Newsletter for the RV enthusiast." Travel tips, industry consumer information, discounts on goods and services and extensive list of RV & travel related books.

RV West
4133 Mohr Ave, Suite I, Pleasanton, CA 94566
(510) 426-3200
Subscription: $12/yr, $21/2, $29/3; monthly
Covers Western United States.

Slow Lane Journal
PO Box 876, Sacramento, CA 95812-0876
(916) 632-2489
Subscription: $9.50/yr (add 69 ¢ in CA); quarterly
Roving reporter writes about out-of-the-way places, unusual characters, and oddball attractions around the country.

Southern RV
Published by Woodall Publishing Company, Inc.
PO Box 5000, Lake Forest, IL 60045-5000
(800) 323-9076
Subscription: $15/yr; $25/2; monthly
Covers: FL, GA, KY, NC, SC & TN.

Trailer Life
Published by TL Enterprises
29901 Agoura Road, Agoura Hills, CA 91301
(818) 991-4980
Subscription: $22/yr; foreign, add $10; discount for Good Sam Club members.
National magazine covering motorhomes, trailers and truck campers.

Trails-A-Way
Published by Woodall Publishing Company, Inc.
PO Box 5000, Lake Forest, IL 60045-5000
(800) 323-9076
Subscription: $15/yr; $25/2; monthly
Covers: IL, IN, MI, OH, & WI.

Western RV News
1350 SW Upland Drive, Suite B, Portland, OR 97221
(503) 222-1255
Subscription: $8/yr; monthly
Market is primarily Washington & Oregon.

Workamper News
201 Hiram Road, Heber Springs, AR 72543
(501) 362-2637
Subscription: $18/yr $33/2; bimonthly
"America's guide to working-while camping"; lists job opportunities throughout the country that are suited to RVers; also, résumé clearinghouse for subscribers and mail order books featuring titles on

retirement, RV travel and "making money on the road." Send for book list.

RV Caravan and Rally Operators

Alaska-Yukon RV Caravans
3810 Eastwood Loop
Anchorage, AL 99504-4435
(907) 333-3371 Alaska & Canada
(800) 426-9865
Sponsors caravans from British Columbia through the Yukon to Alaska; includes boat trips; many extra side trips available; can also create your own "independent" tour; fishing/flightseeing/rafting; RV rentals available; cruises; complete tour arrangements; caravans limited to 21 rigs; founded 1983.

Aztec Custom RV Tours
PO Box 1478
Aztec, NM 87410
(505) 334-9255
(800) 962-6073
Sponsors over 10 caravan tours to Mexico, Central America, and Four Corners; see Colonial Mexico, Yucatan, Copper Canyon, Belize, Guatemala; complete tour arrangements; will customize tours for groups during October, November and December; founded 1988.

Baja California Tours
PO Box 3239
Sumas, WA 98295
(604) 644-8832
Company sponsors six caravans to Baja, Mexico; complete tour arrangements; tours limited to 20 rigs; book and video on Baja available.

Camping Company, Inc.
251 West Road
Clarksburg, MA 01247
(413) 664-7221
(800) 858-8099
Sponsors caravan tours and rallies in New England and along the East coast; offers custom rallies and tours for organizations.

Campo Caminos RV Caravanas
1131 South A Street
Santa Rosa, CA 95404
(707) 578-0881
(800) 241-4024
Sponsors four tours of Mexico; complete tour arrangements; limited to 20 RVs; send for detailed itinerary.

Caravanas Voyagers
1155 Larry Mahan Street, Suite H
El Paso, TX 79925
(800) 933-9332
Sponsors over 40 tours, rallies and river cruises; complete tour arrangements, including route & event planning and RV park reservations; destinations: Mexico (Copper Canyon, Baja, Yucatan), Central America, Australia & New Zealand, Nova Scotia, Alaska, UK, Europe, RV river barge cruises and rallies to many exciting events. Average tour size: 20-25. Call for descriptive brochures. Founded in 1969.

Carrs RV Tours
11781 Hunter Avenue
Yuma, AZ 85365
(602) 342-6595
(800) 526-6469 (US & Canada)
Sponsors over 29 caravans & rallies; complete tour arrangements; destinations: Mexico (Yucatan, Baja, Copper Canyon), Alaska, Grand Canyon, Calgary, Albuquerque balloon fiesta, Rose Bowl; founded 1981.

Creative World Rallies and Caravans
4005 Toulouse St.
New Orleans, LA 70119
(800) 732-8337
(504) 486-7259
Sponsors over 35 caravans, rallies and river cruises; complete tour arrangements, including route & event planning, RV park reservations, etc.; destinations: Scandinavia, Alaska, Canadian Rockies & Maritimes, Newfoundland, New England (fall foliage), Ozarks, European Alps, British Isles, Australia/New Zealand, river & bayou barge floats, and rallies to major festivals & events, showcased by Mardi Gras and the Calgary Stampede; caravans average 30 rigs; founded in 1976; send for detailed information.

The Good Sam Club
See listing under RV Clubs

International Caravanning Association (ICA)
See listing under RV Clubs

Pathfinder Adventuretours
PO Box 26564
Albuquerque, NM 87125
(210) 630-0341
Company specializes in tours to Mexico and Central America; destinations: Colonial Mexico, Yucatan, Cancun, Belize, Guatemala, Panama; also the Calgary Stampede; Argentina and river cruises in the planning stages; tours limited to 15 rigs; complete tour arrangements.

Point South RV Tours
11313 Edmonson Ave.
Moreno Valley, CA 92555
(909) 247-1222
(800) 421-1394 (US & Canada)
Sponsors over 47 caravans, rallies and river cruises; tours limited to 25 rigs; complete tour arrangements, route planning, RV park reservations & sightseeing tours; destinations: Alaska, Mexico (Baja, Copper Canyon), Canadian Maritimes, New England foliage, Guatemala, New Zealand, Rose Bowl, Branson, MO Music Festival, Nashville County Music Heritage, Oregon Trail and Pendleton, OR Roundup; send for vacation planner.

TourMasters World of Tours
4401 Harlan
Waco, TX 76710
(817) 751-1572
(800) 729-1406 (US & Canada)
Sponsors RV/piggyback and passenger train tours of Mexico's Copper Canyon; also: bus, self-drive and fly-in tours of Texas' Big Bend area and Branson, MO; call or send for brochure.

Tracks to Adventure
2811 Jackson, Suite K
El Paso, TX 79930
(800) 351-6053 (US & Canada)
Sponsors over 30 caravans, rallies and river cruises; complete tour arrangements, including route & event planning, RV park reservations, etc.; destinations: Mexico (Copper Canyon, Yucatan, Baja), Alaska, Albuquerque Balloon Festival, Calgary Stampede, fall color tour to New England, Montreal, Quebec, New York, Pennsylvania, and Washington, DC, Mardi Gras, Australia & New Zealand, Maine & northeastern Canadian provinces, Mississippi river barge cruise, Branson, MO rally (country music); tours limited to 18 rigs (Alaska & Yucatan) and all others except barge cruises are limited to 20 rigs; brochures & videos (Mexico, Alaska & Mardi Gras) available.

Wagons Ho! RV Caravans
Box 268
Kernville, CA 93238
(619) 376-3273
Wagons Ho! specializes in caravan tours to Baja, Mexico; tours limited to 15 rigs; approximately 6 tours per year; sightseeing tours and campsites included.

Woodall's World of Travel
306 Maplewood Drive
PO Box 247
Greenville, MI 48838
(800) 346-7572
(616) 754-2251
Sponsors over 15 caravans, rallies & barge cruises; other non-RV tours; complete tour arrangements, including route & event planning, RV park reservations, etc.; destinations: Alaska, Nova Scotia, Newfoundland, national parks, New York City, fall foliage in New England & Dixie, Australia & New Zealand, and rallies to Walt Disney World, music jamborees and other interesting events. Caravans have from 20 to 50 rigs. In business 20 years and part of the Woodall Publishing Company, publishers of the campground directory and other books and magazines on camping and RVing.

RV/Camping Clubs & Associations

Many manufacturers sponsor national clubs for their brand of RV. Contact a dealer or the Recreation Vehicle Industry Association (RVIA), which will send you a list of the brand name clubs with their RV information packet.

Americamp
64 Inverness Dr. East
Englewood, CO 80112-5101
(303) 792-7273 (800) 932-6797
Club offers 25% camping discount at affiliated public campgrounds on space available basis; over 100 locations in US and Canada; toll-free reservation system; directory; dues: $34.95/yr.

Escapees
100 Rainbow Drive
Livingston, TX 77351
(409) 327-8873
The Escapees Club provides a support network for its 28,000 RVer members; founded 1978; 33 geographical chapters in US, Canada and Mexico; has sponsored 14 non-profit RV parks from Washington State to Florida; bimonthly newsletter; directory; rallies; seminars; mail & message forwarding service; discounts on products & services; many other services; $5 to join and $40 yearly membership fee; for Canada and Mexico, add $10; money returned if not satisfied; write or call for more information.

The Family Motor Coach Association (FMCA)
8291 Clough Pike
Cincinnati, OH 45244
(513) 474-3622
(800) 543-3622
FMCA is an international non-profit association of motor coach owners and industry-related companies; purpose is to promote ownership, use and enjoyment of motorhomes and exchange information; founded 1963; 85,000 members in over 300 chapters; directory; benefits include: monthly magazine, trip routing, youth activities, emergency road service, mail and message forwarding, air ambulance, RV financing, insurance, conventions and rallies; legislative advisory; dues $35 first year, $25/yr. thereafter.

The Good Sam Club
PO Box 500
Agoura, CA 91376
(818) 991-4980
(800) 234-3450 (member services)
Largest RV/camping club in the world; more than 2,000 local chapters; discounts at affiliated campgrounds, service centers, attractions; full service travel agency; worldwide RV rental discounts; trip routing service; emergency road service plan; insurance for all vehicles & health/life; RV/auto financing; mail forwarding; campground directory; *Trailer Life* and *MotorHome* magazines; monthly members magazine; rallies and caravans; many other travel related services; dues $19.

International Caravanning Association (ICA)
c/o Jim Davison (ICA Vice Chairman & Membership for US and Mexico)
13008 Thompson Road
Fairfax, VA 22033
(703) 860-2316
Club established to encourage and promote caravanning in all countries and to organize events; membership is open only to owners of any type of RV; club members organize own rallies, tours and caravans throughout the world; rental RV arrangements available; bimonthly magazine; member handbook; founded 1969; dues $20, plus $5 initiation (checks payable to Mr. Davison).

Loners of America, Inc.
Rt. 2, Box 85E
Ellsinore, MO 63937-9520
(314) 322-5548
Nationwide, not-for-profit, member-owned club for singles only; chapters in 20 states; rallies, caravans, campouts; newsletter; directory. Membership: 1,450; dues $23/yr, plus $5 one-time fee; founded 1987.

Loners on Wheels, Inc.
PO Box 1355
Poplar Bluff, MO 63901
Fax (314) 686-9342 (Secretary)
Camping/travel club for singles only; over 65 chapters in the US and Canada; rallies and campouts; newsletter; directory. Membership:

3,000; dues: $26 (plus $5 initiation), $31 US in Canada; founded 1969.

National Campers and Hikers Association (NCHA)
4804 Transit Road, Building 2
Depew, NY 14043-4906
(716) 668-6242
Canadian office:
51 West 22nd Street
Hamilton, Ontario LC9 4N5
NCHA is a non-profit, international, educational, RV/camping association; chapters throughout the US and Canada; industry spokesman to government; helps promote conservation, environmental and wildlife programs; members receive discount catalog, a KOA discount Kard, monthly magazine; free membership in many European campgrounds & clubs through FICC; RV insurance, travel medical insurance, air ambulance and emergency road service available; sponsors rallies, caravans, river cruises and campouts; teen programs; retiree rallies; specialized chapters: backpackers, young adults, square-dancers, retirees, single parents, etc.; dues: $20/1 year, $38/2, $55/3.

North American Family Campers Association, Inc. (NAFCA)
PO Box 730
21 Superior Avenue
Dracut, MA 01826
(508) 459-2836
NAFCA is an RV/camping club with chapters throughout New England; sponsors state and regional rallies; monthly campouts and social events; campground information service; monthly newsletter; dues: $12/1 year, $20/2; $26/3.

RVing WOMEN
Box 82606 Y
Kenmore, WA 98028
A nationwide informational and support network for and by women RVers. Rallies, caravans, membership directory, trip routing service, and bimonthly newsletter. The phone link (support/information) number is:
(800) 333-9992.
Membership: $39/yr. Includes newsletter.

S*M*A*R*T
Special Military Active Retired Travel Club, Inc.
600 University Office Blvd. #1-A
Pensacola, FL 32504
(904) 478-1986
Club has 27 chapters nationwide with more forming; membership limited to active or retired members of the armed services; seminars & workshops; rallies & caravans throughout the country & Mexico; assists military installations with the improvement of their campgrounds; quarterly newsletter; emergency road service & travel insurance plan.

RV Industry Associations

Recreation Vehicle Dealers Association of Canada
#201-19623-56th Avenue
Langley, British Columbia, Canada V3A 3X7
(604) 533-4200
Trade association for retail sector of RV industry; government lobbying; helps RVers find sales/service facilities; refers consumers to rental firms; assists in accessing camping/RVing information for destinations and facilities.

Recreation Vehicle Industry Association (RVIA)
PO Box 2999
1896 Preston White Drive
Reston, VA 22090-0999
(703) 620-6003
National trade association of RV manufacturers and component parts suppliers; sponsors shows & expositions; information to media & public; market research; maintains an inspection program to monitor compliance with industry safety standards; industry spokesman to government. Send $3.00 (includes postage) for 24-page descriptive guide about RVing "Set Free in an RV." Ask for their catalog of other RV lifestyle publications.

Recreation Vehicle Rental Association (RVRA)
3251 Old Lee Highway, Suite 500
Fairfax, VA 22030
(800) 336-0355
(703) 591-7130

Publishes directory, *Who's Who in RV Rentals*, with over 250 listings of RV dealers in the US, Canada and Europe who rent all types of RVs. Categorized by state & city; describes RV sizes, services offered & rates. Available free with orders for "Rental Ventures," a 32-page guide to renting RVs. Cost: $7.50, first class; $6.50, third class, prepaid.

North American RV Rental Agencies

The firms listed below are RV rental agencies specializing in rentals on a national basis. There are also hundreds of local rental agencies run by RV sales companies, but they may not be able to offer the range of services needed if you are touring.

America on Wheels
768 Walker Road, Suite 223
Great Falls, VA 22066
(800) 682-8262
(703) 757-7515
(703) 759- 4361 (Fax)
Custom trip planning; campground reservation service; provisioning; airport pickup; on-site car parking; one-way rentals available; nine rental sizes: 21' (sleeps 4) up to 34' (sleeps 7); locations: Norfolk, VA, Philadelphia, PA and Washington, DC, with 6 more to open by the end of 1993. All locations are company owned.

American Safari
2675 Johnson Road NE
Atlanta, GA 30345
(800) 327-9668
(404) 321-6211
Oldest national motorhome rental company, founded in 1971; 30 affiliates in 18 states: AK, AZ, CA, CO, CT, DC, FL, GA, MD, MA, MI, NJ, NM, NY, PA, TN, UT, WA; five rental sizes: 21' (sleeps 2 adults & 2 children), 23' (2 & 3), 25' (2 & 3), 27' (2 & 4), 30' (4 & 3); no pets allowed; emergency road service; company provides extra personal touches, including custom trip planning service and arranging RV rentals in other parts of the world.

Cruise America/Cruise Canada
5959 Blue Lagoon Drive, Suite 250
Miami, FL 33126
(800) 327-7799 (US, Alaska & Canada)
Largest motorhome rental & sales company in the world; over 4,000 rental vehicles in fleet; one-way rental for extra fee; no pets allowed; luggage storage at some centers; over 100 locations in North America.
Five models to choose from:
Camperhome - sleeps up to 3
Deluxe Camperhome - sleeps up to 4
Intermediate Motorhome (Class C) 21'-24' - sleeps up to 5
Large Motorhome - (Class C) 25'-27' - sleeps up to 6
Deluxe Motorhome (Class A & Class C) 28'-31'- sleeps up to 7

Go Vacations
129 Carlingview Drive
Etobicoke, Ontario, Canada M9W 5E7
(800) 387-6869
(416) 674-1880
(416) 674-7875 (Fax)
Founded in 1972; over 2,000 vehicles in fleet; manufactures own motorhomes; 10 company owned locations: Vancouver, Calgary, Toronto, Montreal, San Francisco, Los Angeles, Denver, New York, Orlando, Miami; luggage storage; no pets allowed; one-way rental for extra fee.
Vehicles available:
17'-18' van conversions - sleeps 2 adults
21'-27' Class C - sleeps 4-5 adults or 4 adults & 2 children
Travel permitted to Mexico, Alaska, Yukon, and Northwest Territories with extra $200 security deposit & $200 surcharge.

Foreign RV Rental Agencies

Auto Europe
Box 1097 Sharps Wharf
Camden, ME 04843
(207) 236-8235
(800) 223-5555
Rents four sizes of RVs in Germany, and camper vans in France, Britain, Australia and New Zealand; vehicles for the physically challenged and one-way rentals available; insurance included; RVs have fully equipped kitchen.

Britannia RV Rentals, Inc.
2349 Brannen Rd, SE
Atlanta, GA 30316
(404) 241-7511
(800) 872-1140
RV rentals and caravan tours in Great Britain, and ferry connections
to Europe; RV rentals in Europe, Australia & New Zealand; hotel
reservations for renters, if necessary.

Connex International, Ltd.
23 North Division Street
Peekskill, NY 10566
(914) 739-0066
(800) 333-3949 (nationwide)
(800) 843-5416 (Canada)
Rents RVs in Britain, Holland, France and Germany; several models
to choose from; will sleep 4-6; insurance extra; most RVs have
bedding & kitchen equipment; VAT extra.

Europe By Car
One Rockefeller Plaza
New York, NY 10020
(212) 581-3040
(800) 223-1516 (except NY State & CA)
(800) 252-9401 in California
Leases VW diesel campers in Brussels for 3 weeks to 6 months; tax-
free rates include full insurance.

Global Motorhome Travel, Inc. (GMT)
1142 Manhattan Avenue, #300
Manhattan Beach, CA 90266
(310) 318-9995
(800) 468-3876
GMT, based in Frankfurt, Germany, with offices in Amsterdam,
Berlin, Munich, and Paris, leases four categories of RVs from 19'-22'
that will sleep from 4-6 adults. Rentals include unlimited mileage,
full insurance, green insurance card , airport pickup, bedding &
kitchen equipment, and local tax (VAT). All units are fully equipped.
They also sponsor caravan tours.

Holiday Autos
1425 W. Foothill Blvd., Suite 240
Upland, CA 91786
(714) 949-1737 (Administration)
(800) 422-7737 (Reservations)
Rents van conversions and motorhomes in Great Britain, Canada, and the US. British vehicles are supplied with kitchen equipment and bedding; motorhomes have flush toilets and showers; sleep 2-6 adults.

Visit Australia Tours
A Division of Eliza Travel Pty. Ltd.
PO Box 385
Mount Eliza, Victoria 3930 Australia
011-61-3-787-7633
011-61-3-787-7194 (FAX)
A central booking service for RV rentals in Australia and New Zealand, representing all the major and regional operators; arranges escorted RV tours in Australia, UK & Europe; books RV rentals in Europe, UK, South Africa, Turkey and North America; also, special interest, non-RV, group tours of Australia and New Zealand.

Other RV-Related Services

First Aid Kit Suppliers
First aid kits geared to travelers can be purchased from the following supplier. They will send you a catalog on request.

Atwater Carey Ltd.
218 Gold Run Road
Boulder, CO 80302
(303) 444-9326
(800) 359-1646
Full line of medical kits for the outdoors.

Elderhostel
75 Federal Street
Boston, MA 02110-1941
(617) 426-8056
Elderhostel is a non-profit organization offering a wide variety of low cost, short-term courses at colleges and conference centers in the

United States, Canada and 43 other countries. Registrants must be over 60 years of age, but a younger companion can attend. For the RVer, they offer courses in AZ, CO, GA, MI, MT, NM, NC, OR, SC, TX, UT, VA, WA. Write for their most recent catalog for an update on courses and states. You must have an RV, travel trailer or tent. Pets may be permitted at some locations.

Scots-American Travel Advisors
26 Rugen Drive
Harrington Park, NJ 07640
(201) 768-1187
Agents for several ferry companies with service throughout the British Isles and to the continent.

Travel Companion Exchange, Inc. (TCE)
PO Box 833
Amityville, NY 11701
(516) 454-0880
TCE is a unique company that acts as a clearinghouse of information for single, widowed or divorced travelers; major service is to match singles who don't want to travel alone; informative newsletter has travel tips, up-to-date travel information and listings of people looking for travel companions; two membership categories from $36 to $66 for six months (newsletter included); newsletter subscription only $36/yr; sample copy $4 ppd.

Glossary

Back and fill. The process by which a driver has to back in, then pull forward several times in order to get the RV level or straightened out.

Barge trip. RV caravan operators arrange for RVs to be placed aboard a barge for a cruise down a river.

Black water tank. A holding tank in the RV for sewage.

BLM. Bureau of Land Management.

Boondocking. Camping without hookups.

Cabover. A section of the RV's body that extends over the cab and is used for a bedroom or storage.

Convenience kits. A package of items provided by the rental agency at an extra cost that may include kitchen utensils and equipment, bedding, and towels.

Full-timing. RVers who live on the road all year round.

Galley. The kitchen.

Gray water tank. A holding tank in the RV for water from the sinks and shower.

GVWR. This is the Gross Vehicle Weight Rating, the maximum weight allowed for a fully loaded RV, including fluids, cargo and passengers.

Monitor Panel. A panel usually located near the galley that has indicator switches for checking the battery, waste tanks, LP-gas, fresh water tank and water pump.

Pull-thru or **drive-thru**. A campsite that allows the RVer to drive in and pull straight out.

Shoreline. A heavy-duty electrical cable with a 3-prong grounding plug at one end. It is permanently attached to the RV's power center and can be pulled from its outside storage compartment and plugged into an external source of power.

Slide-out. A side or rear section of some RVs that can be extended at a campsite to provide additional living area.

Snowbird. An RVer who goes from colder to warmer climates in the winter.

Index

Order Form

Please send me the following books:

King of the Road @ $12.95 _____

King of the Road Diary and RV Trip Planner @ $10.95 _____

Postage & handling @ $2 _____

Buy both and SAVE! I pay the postage. $21.00 _____

PA residents add 6% sales tax _____

Add $3.00 per book for Canadian orders _____

Total amount for books _____

Please make check payable to **REMINGTON PRESS, LTD.**

Mail book(s) to:

Name: _____

Address: _____

City: _____

State/Zip: _____

Allow four to six weeks for delivery.

Remington Press, Ltd.
Box 8327, Radnor, PA 19087
(215) 293-0202
(610) 293-0202 after January 1, 1994

Thank you for your order!